Circa
(and other life-altering experiences)

MW01107434

R. Scott Morris

Copyright © 2012 R. Scott Morris

To Mark,
I hope you get
well very soon
you're a great guy
Scott

This book is dedicated to my wife Carole who has put up with me for some35 year s (she always doubles that number). She has been a loyal, trusted friend and spouse who by me to living her life to the fullest has inspired me to do the same.

CONTENTS

1   Getting Hooked   Pg #1

2   Drifting away from   Pg #26
     my boating roots

3   Years in the   Pg #35
     wilderness

4   The road back to   Pg #69
     boating

5   Whiskers   Pg #75

6   Buzzards Bay   Pg #106
     Regatta etc.

7   Martha's Vineyard   Pg #115

8   To Marblehead to   Pg #143
     follow Chief Brody's
     advice

9   Meeting Carole   Pg #153

10. The Mattapoisett Inn   Pg #169
     Challenge Cup and
     other races

11. Another   Pg#207
     Circadian Rhythm

12. End of the   Pg#232
     Circadian rhythm
     Saga

Acknowledgements

I would like to acknowledge the contributions to this project made by Peter Richards who kept a meticulous log of our first summer on the C&C 25 *Circadian Rhythm*. Peter lent me his log which proved invaluable by setting the record straight about several of our adventures that summer. I would also like to acknowledge the encouragement I received from my friends and family who reviewed portions of the book and commented about its content. I am particularly indebted to Wendy and Phil as well as Geoff, Ed, Teddy, Randy, Dennis and my sister Deb all of whom took the time to read and comment on the manuscript.

~ *Chapter 1* ~

Getting Hooked

Sailing is a chronic disorder that inflicts an estimated ten to twenty million souls. This insidious condition is global in its sweep and respects neither age nor gender. Youngsters of six or seven have been known to spend hours in square bowed "opti" dinghys doing their best to cope with this condition and women in their sixties along with their equally afflicted spouses have raided their retirement savings to spend lavishly on long, pointy pieces of fiberglass attempting alleviate the symptoms of this illness. Early signs of this disease are easy to spot, an insatiable desire to feel salt air on one's face while holding a beer in one hand and a steering wheel in the other, the burning craving to neatly fold huge triangular pieces of Mylar, the indelible imprint of a cleat on one's buttocks. Yes, sailing truly is a disease for which there is no known cure.

I was infected with this "bug" at an early age as a result of my lineage and the locale of my birth. I was raised in the coastal port of Fairhaven, Massachusetts by a father who was a chief engineer for the Mobil Oil Corporation and two uncles who were commercial fishermen in the local fleet. Like most youths of my day, I was burdened with the traditional obligations of American community life including school, church (Saturday catechism classes with Belgian nuns at St Joseph's school were murder) Cub Scouts, Little League. However, I was more fortunate than most of my contemporaries, because I was afforded the opportunity to disrupt this monotony with occasional maritime diversions. These included visits to my Dad on his tanker when he offloaded in Portland, Maine or Paulsboro, New Jersey and often helping my Uncle Charlie stow the trip's grub on the dragger *Linus S. Eldridge*. These "diversions" made an indelible impression on me and set the stage for my compulsion with things maritime. This common theme would lead me to find and forge lifelong bonds with close friends and would inevitably guide me to my soul mate and the love of my life. I have been incredibly

1

fortunate, my family instilled in me a moral sense of right and wrong which has helped me to make largely correct decisions, but a persistent theme throughout this play has been the sea.

When I was nine years old, my Uncle Charlie was the cook onboard the *Linus S. Eldridge* when she served as a dragger/scalloper in the New Bedford fishing fleet during the 1950s and 60s. During this period New Bedford was the premier fishing port in the world with landings worth hundreds of millions of dollars. All fishing trips began with preparation and as I mentioned, my brother Butch and I would often help our Uncle Charlie to "grub up" the boat prior to her ten days of work on George's Bank. These episodes were particularly poignant for me since they would consume most of the day and were filled with masculinity.

These adventures would begin with the arrival of Uncle Charlie and my cousin Randy at our house around 8 o'clock on a Saturday morning and after a quick breakfast of juice and doughboys, Butch and I would complete the quartet that would head down to Kelley's Shipyard in Uncle Charlie's Cadillac. He always drove a Cadillac, even when he and Aunt Edie could hardly afford one. Charlie was an unassuming, gregarious fellow, everybody liked him. Like most American commercial fishermen of his day, he worked hard and drank hard. Although he was the boat's cook, he also helped on deck with the catch even though he was not required to do so. His Portuguese and Norwegian counterparts also worked hard, but many of them didn't drink as much. As a result, today most of the fish boats in the New Bedford fleet are owned by descendants of those Norwegian and Portuguese fishermen instead of their Scotch/Irish contemporaries.

On boat grubbing Saturdays, we would arrive at Kelley's just about the time the truck from the New Bedford Ship Supply had finished unloading the provisions on deck. Usually, the *Eldridge* was secured right next to the dock, so that we little tykes could easily scamper over the rail and onto the deck. There were instances; however, when she would be abreast another boat that was at the bulkhead. On these occasions, we kids would have to climb over the inboard boat to reach the *Eldridge*. Charlie would always be right there helping us to get onboard the first boat and then across the deck that was littered with our boxes and other gear and then over the side to the *Eldridge*. Once we were aboard, Uncle Charlie would begin to hand boxes of grub over to us and we would then be instructed to slide these boxes down the ladder into the fo'c'sle.

Those readers who have never been aboard an eastern-rigged fish boat of the 1950s will need to know some of the details of this vessel in order to better understand what will unfold.

Eastern rigged dragger

For the most part, wooden-hulled fish boats in New England in the mid-twentieth century evolved from the sailing schooner design of the late nineteenth century whose narrow hull provided a clean entry being fair to 'midships where her beam was carried. I'm not referring to the "Fredonia-style" schooners of the early or mid-nineteenth century, but the "Indian Headers" and "Knockabouts" that originated from the genius of Thomas F. McManus in the late nineteenth and early twentieth centuries. McManus was obsessed with improving the stability and; therefore, the safety of the New England fishing schooner. Although he would not compromise safety for speed, his designs were safe vessels, but his keen eye for a fair hull also made his vessels very fast. McManus spent little time at sea, but had an impeccable eye for vessel design and fully understood that vessel safety required attention to fore and aft buoyancy in a hull design. As a result, his successful schooner hulls had (what was then considered to be) excessive shear. From a high bow they faired to the midline and then faired up again aft of the beam to provide a clean exit which ensured a good turn of speed for a sailing vessel attempting to reach port early to secure a good market price for her catch. In a mechanically powered hull this efficient design resulted in lower fuel costs translating to better share returns for the skipper, owner and crew. Like the quintessential knockabout, the mid-twentieth century eastern-rigged fish boat hull was graceful, exhibiting a good deal of shear from fore to aft. This provided added buoyancy in a seaway and saved many a loaded vessel from foundering in a heavy quartering or following seas.

In keeping with the traditional schooner design, the eastern-rigged vessel's helm was located well aft of the main working deck in the protection of a wheelhouse. The working deck was amidships, because, unlike today's predominantly stern hauling western-rigged boats, the eastern-rigged fish boat used the otter trawl and as such hauled nets amidships, over the rail.

McManus Designs: Helen B Thomas   **Schooner Adventure**

The main engine room with associated mechanical equipment was located well aft under the wheel house and behind the fish hold. As a result, like the fishing schooners of the nineteenth century, the crew (for the most part) was housed in the fo'c'sle forward of the of the fish hold and in some cases, under a whaleback. Since the vessel was quite narrow forward, the fo'c'sle started out fairly wide at the companionway, and gradually became more cramped as one moved forward.

Typical fo'c'sle

Patterned after a schooner, the crew's bunks were stacked in twos along the outboard bulkheads leaving the center portion for seats that contained storage lockers underneath. A double drop-leaf V-shaped table ran the length of the bunks providing a common eating setting for the crew. While fishing, it was customary for the off-watch crew to be in their bunks while the watch crew was eating only inches from their sleeping shipmates. Of course these activities were done in a gyrating, heaving vessel with only two inches of yellow pine separating the crew from the wild ocean. It was a difficult life, especially for the older guys. However, in port, the crew's fo'c'sle was a wondrous place for a nine year old. Any number of imagined adventures and dangers would rear up during our few minutes of waiting for Uncle Charlie to get below and begin his management of us.

After sliding all of the ship's stores down the companionway ladder, Charlie would supervise the examination and uncrating of the boxes.......all was in a major jumble, but Charlie was unruffled and encouraging in his comments and the work went smoothly. Canned goods into the lockers under the table seats, bread into the larder near the stove, (the stove was hot, with a coffee pot held in tangs and percolating away). Stowage of perishables such as eggs was carefully supervised by Uncle

Charlie ensuring that we ham-handed youths didn't break anything. We toiled away under Uncle Charlie's direction for a couple of hours and finally all the grub had been stowed. With that done, we arrived at the moment that we had been waiting for; finally Uncle Charlie offered us our reward, two Hostess chocolate cup cakes and a bottle of coke. This wasn't just an ordinary bottle of Coca Cola, this came from an industrial, 24-bottle rack and there was three or four of these stacked in the fo'c'sle, …I mean, whoa! This was real man stuff. Adding to this, when Uncle Charlie was up on deck, Randy (who was well aware of the proclivities of the boat's crew) would lead Butch and me to one of the crew berths and unearth a girlie magazine. Once again….Whoa! What amazing macho, man stuff; Butch and I ate it up. Of course, when Charlie started down the companionway ladder, we'd scramble to replant the girlie mag and get back to the table munching contently on our cup cakes to dispel any suspicions on Charlie's part. No need to worry, as he would say later if challenged about our exposure to what passed for pornography in the 1950's…"What's the problem?…. its just a girl's tittie". It was pretty tame stuff in comparison to the smorgasbord of sexual perversion served up daily on the Internet today.

For a nine or ten year old American male (whose father was at sea for ten months a year) thirsting for manliness in their world, all of this was quite intoxicating. There was never any reluctance by Butch or me to help Uncle Charlie grub up the boat. We loved those Saturdays with our cousin and Uncle Charlie and I always will.

My other uncle, Eddie, was the Ying to Uncle Charlie's Yang. Eddie was the baby of my mother's family, he had entered the Navy in WW II at the tender age of 17. The family story was that Eddie had come under the unseemly influence of an abundance of older men (I guess, like 22 and 23 year olds) who had corrupted him while serving in the Navy and he had become a changed man. While that may have been the case, his brother Charlie was only three years older than Eddie and he had survived the Battle of the Bulge. Interestingly, Charlie never mentioned that experience in all the years I knew him. Charlie was as fond of the drink as

Eddie (as were most Irishmen) but he didn't sling the line of bullshit that Eddie did. Now, I must admit that although I took most of what my Uncle Eddie said with a LARGE grain of salt, I loved the guy, because he was always upbeat and pretty positive in the brief dealings that I had with him.

My life went on in Fairhaven in a typical fashion for an adolescent of that time. In 1959, my parents chose to buy a house on Cherry Street and this event proved pivotal in my association with boats and the water. Following the move, I became far more interested in events on the waterfront because our house on Cherry St was a mere two blocks removed from Fairhaven harbor. As I learned more about my immediate environs, the history of the neighborhood came to the fore. Cherry St. was one of the original colonial regions of the town, known locally as "Poverty Point" and had been a shipbuilding and ship provision settlement supporting the New Bedford whaling fleet in the eighteenth and nineteenth centuries. As part of this history, there was a monument that commemorated the founding of the settlement by Pilgrim John Cooke in a park at the bottom of the street adjacent to the water. After we had lived in the neighborhood for a year or so, a second memorial was erected in this park. Unlike the Pilgrim's commemorative, this second monument was dedicated to the first solo circumnavigator of the world, Joshua Slocum. I dug a bit into the history of this exploit and discovered that Capt'n Slocum (who was a "bluenose" from Nova Scotia) had purchased his vessel "Spray" from a local farmer and refitted her at the bottom of Cherry St. He actually set sail on this world-renowned trip from the bottom of my street. Needless to say, heroic images of an old salt like Slocum starting out from Fairhaven and circling the globe alone further kindled my imagination and interest in the sea. I then read his book "Alone Around the World" and became even more inspired. To top it off, the neighborhood was filled with boys of my age and several owned small powerboats.

That was all of the impetus I needed to begin pestering my mother (Mary) at every chance I could to persuade my parents to buy Butch and me a boat.

Mary (at extreme right) with my wife Carole (left), her sister Wendy and Donald Bernard, circa 1976 (*the uniform is too long a story*)

Butch took up the case as well and when my father (Benny) returned home for his one month "vacation", the two of us began to work on him. We pleaded our case on every available occasion as Benny began to adopt his legendary stoic indifference about the issue. There were times when our pleading would border on embarrassment, but he would not budge. He would discourage us as much as possible to test our resolve and dampen our spirits. Each time we'd raise the issue, he would appear to listen intently (just to throw us off) and then quickly change the subject; ......how discouraging; exactly his intention. Finally, with less than a week left in his vacation, just when we thought all hope was lost, he took us on a ride in the family's 1958 Chevrolet station wagon to the north end of New Bedford.

Mary, Benny, Butch, Debby and me with the family "limo"

To set the stage for what unfolded in this drama, the north end (or nordend as it's called) of New Bedford is a veritable rabbit run of streets that run perpendicular to the main thoroughfares, the "boulevahd" and the "avenah"; these being the provincial, colloquial sobriquets favored by the natives for Ashley Boulevard and Acushnet Avenue.

On one of the seemingly innumerable quiet streets we stopped in front of a red and white open boat that was sitting on a home-built trailer parked on the street. Initially I was shocked, I couldn't believe that the "old man" was actually going to buy a boat! Benny casually opened his door and got out, while Butch and I stumbled, pushed and bumped one another trying to be the first out of the door and ran over to inspect this seemingly magnificent craft.

In retrospect, what appeared at the time to be the paramount motor yacht in the eyes of a nine year-old, was actually more like many of the second generation Portuguese girls in my junior high classes; sturdy and wholesome, but rather dowdy. It was a plain, home-built fourteen footer, sturdily constructed of marine plywood with fiber glass on the outside, containing three thwarts (seats) and a small forward deck. There were substantial 1 x 4" wood floor boards connecting the wooden ribs and a three-foot-long deck on the bow provided a modicum of shelter for stowage. The inside was painted grey with red and white speckles, the hull was white and the gunwales, seat and deck were red. The boat was named; unfortunately, "Mary Jo" (gets back to the Portuguese girl thing). Presumably, this was the name of one of the owner's daughters, wife (wives?) sisters, or mistresses. I hated the name and two years into owning "the boat", as I called it, much to my mother's distress, I painted over "Mary Jo". Even so, undaunted, my mother persisted in referring to it as the "Mary Jo". The trailer was a really clunky single axle job, no fenders and fitted with snow tires. As a result, "the boat" always looked awful sitting on this home-made monstrosity. It was functional; however, and was visible only when launching and hauling "the boat" or when it was stored in our next door neighbor's driveway.

Apparently, Benny and the boat owner (Mr. Pacheco, if memory serves me correctly) had haggled about the price beforehand as they discussed delivery arrangements that afternoon. This being early August, I couldn't believe my luck that I would actually have some time to be in my own boat before school began.

Not only did Mr. Pacheco deliver the boat to Fairhaven, he helped us launch it and provided instruction on the proper use of the vessel's 18 horsepower *Evinrude* outboard motor. Benny had persuaded me to enlist the assistance of my new neighborhood friends in securing and deploying the necessary hardware for an appropriate mooring for our new boat. An old engine block with 40 feet of 3/8" chain, shackles and a float were acquired and placed on the beach at the bottom of the street. Once we launched the boat at the Bridge St boat ramp, Mr. Pacheco towed the empty trailer back to our house on Cherry St and Benny, Butch and I proudly powered under the Fairhaven, New Bedford bridge covering the ½ mile distance to the beach at Cherry St in about 5 minutes. During this initial "shake down" we became somewhat familiar with the speed and handling of "the boat". It seemed to be well powered, but the narrow beam made her somewhat tender in a tight turn; if you didn't hold on tight you could be jettisoned to the uphill side by the centrifugal force of the turn. Made a mental note of that one!

 We arrived at the beach where my new friends were waiting with the mooring gear situated on a small raft. We connected to the raft and towed it out about fifty yards off the beach where the water was about five feet deep at low tide. At the appropriate time, over the mooring went and our new boat now had a new home. We spent the rest of the afternoon cruising around the upper harbor (north of the bridge) getting used to the boat and its performance. Of course, impromptu "races" ensued between us and our friends and "the boat" held her own despite carting a five-passenger load. Although the hull was technically a modified "V", she would plane if the passengers move forward of 'midships, this would improve the speed dramatically.

 I was twelve years old that summer and following this initial introduction to power boating I would then enjoy many a summer of fun with my neighborhood friends on the harbor in that silly boat. Benny laid down two rules that required strict adherence. The first was that Butch and I were required to be back at the mooring by 5 PM for dinner and the second was that, under no circumstances, were we allowed beyond Fort Phoenix which, together with Palmers Island formed the south entrance of the harbor in 1959. Seven years later, the completion of the New Bedford hurricane dike would change all this. New Bedford's inner harbor is approximately 1.5 miles long and ½ mile wide, is still heavily industrialized with a fleet of some 200 commercial fish boats. In addition, large ships regularly visit the harbor, discharging and loading cargoes ranging from oil and road salt to fish and fresh fruit. Today, the harbor also shelters some 500 pleasure boats on moorings and in slips around the periphery of the port.

 Looking back on the boating experiences of my youth with respect to today's parental paranoia, it strikes me as amazing that my parents allowed me to use this potentially lethal marine vehicle in a very busy, crowded industrial harbor with a minimum of instruction and oversight. I didn't even wear a life jacket in that harbor (or elsewhere) until I was 56 years old, due to either to my becoming wiser with age, or more cautious.

What is commendable here is that my parents and my friend's parents had sufficient confidence in us juveniles to expect that we would do the right thing and not endanger ourselves or others; and woe be unto us if we did. Much of this had to do with the reporting network at the time. My parents knew when I misbehaved even if they were nowhere in sight. What's even more amazing is that their bet paid off! I used that boat for four summers along with my eight or so friends with their boats and there was never an accident, serious injury or legal problem. Perhaps this was in some ways due to the proximity of these events to the end of WW II when young people of that age put their lives on the line in the military on a daily basis. Our parents were those people and knew, full well, that our activities were literally "child's play" in comparison to what they had experienced and witnessed. Whatever the reason, it worked and we had a blast and memories to last a lifetime.

To some extent I pity today's children with their overly protective parents. The twenty-four hour news cycle has certainly contributed to today's parental paranoia. No wonder that drug addiction amongst teens today is at epidemic levels, many of these kids are well aware that they don't have their parents' confidence. What's more, they may not fear their parent's wrath as we did, with the advent of the nanny state and government oversight of parental discipline, but enough of political commentary.

I should, at this point, describe the major body of water to the south of New Bedford harbor that will be a centerpiece of much of this subsequent narrative. Buzzards Bay is the name of this watercourse and it encompasses approximately 233 square miles of area. The bay is about 28 miles long and from 9 to 10 miles wide with an average depth of 36 feet. There are numerous harbors, coves, inlets and many rivers and streams that form incubating estuaries for migratory fish and birds. The mouth of the bay faces southwest and is about eight miles wide. At the head of the bay is the Cape Cod Canal a major transit for coastal shipping seeking to avoid the hazards of Nantucket Shoals. The bay has a wide mouth and a slightly triangular shape which combine to funnel and accelerate developing sea breezes from southwest to northeast. This makes the local prevailing wind a sou'wester. This prevailing sou'westerly sea breeze usually develops after noon caused by the thermal gradient between the bay and ocean to the south and the warmer air over land to the north. As the air onshore heats up, it rises causing a vacuum to develop which is quickly filled by the cooler bay air. On most summer days, the sou'wester (or sou'westah in the local vernacular) is quite predictable and is affectionately referred to as the "afternoon hurricane" as velocities of 25 to 30 knots are not uncommon. In the late summer it is also called the "smoky sou'wester" as the very humid air has a smoky appearance with limited visibility. This stiff afternoon breeze and the rather shallow depth of the bay will quickly generate seas and builds them to impressive heights. The shallow bay also makes these seas very steep and causes them to break with regularity. In the summer, with consistent sun exposure, the shallow bay water warms into the 70's, but conversely as winter approaches, the water cools quickly and ice formation in the harbors and bays can be a regular occurrence.

The bay together with Cape Cod and the islands were formed at the end of the last great glaciation some 10,000 years ago. The mainland on the north side of the bay is composed of granite bedrock with a thin soil overburden. By contrast, Cape Cod and the islands are composed of glacial moraine which is essentially the outwashing of rock, sand and debris from the mile thick glaciers as they melted and receded. Interspersed within this outwash were innumerable giant granite boulders that were worn round as a result of their scraping over the granite bedrock of the mainland as the glaciers advanced. These boulders and thousands of their smaller cousins are scattered all over Buzzards Bay and Vineyard Sound and they make navigation very challenging. Most of these rocks are well marked with cans or nuns and have acquired colorful names such as "Hussey Rock", "Brooklyn Rock", "Inez Rock" and "Old Bartlemy". Others are not as well known such as the one that poked a hole in the QE 2 as she steamed along toward Newport from the Vineyard in 1992. Taken together, these factors make Buzzards Bay a potentially nasty place when weather the conditions are unfavorable. In fact, many exams for initial captain's licensing use the chart of Buzzards Bay (NOAA Chart #13230) as means to test the skill of students employing a difficult navigation example. Each year there are several drownings in the bay as a result of boating accidents and it's not uncommon for a commercial fishermen to lose his life working on or transiting the bay. As a result, it was not surprising that my parents and those of my friends wanted us to stay in the harbor during our nascent boating years.

My brother Butch was active with the boat the next summer, but as he approached the driving age at sixteen, his interest in boating waned significantly. I was nearly two years younger than he, as were most of my boating friends; boats became the center of our social world whereas cars and girls were Butch's focus. That was fine with me since, by default, that made me the master of the vessel.

In the summers of 1960, '61 and '62 as I finished my Jr. High experience and entered High School, my daily boating excursion would begin at 7 AM when I would jump out of bed, and into my blue jeans, T-shirt and *PF Flyer* sneakers. I would then dash down Cherry St. to my pram (dinghy) that was chain locked to a granite block on the beach at the foot of the street. Five gallon gasoline can in hand, four bucks in my pocket, a sandwich and a coke, I'd row out to the boat, get aboard, hook up the gas tank, start her up and be underway by 07:27. The harbor was usually glass calm at that time of the day and I'd fly along at full throttle headed out toward the imaginary boundary line between Fort Phoenix and Palmers Island. As I approached, Benny's voice would begin to boom in the back of my head,......**DONT GO BEYOND THE FORT!** Just as I approached that invisible line, I'd look over my shoulder to be sure the coast was clear then turn hard a'stahbahd and head back up the harbor.

My daily boating routine encompassed powering around the docks looking at the fish boats (I knew them all by name and could easily identify each by silhouette years later) until around 11:30 when neighborhood friends would start showing up in their boats. We would meet in a quiet part of that busy harbor, exchange insults and braggings and then power around the harbor in line or tandem killing time, soaking up the sun and wasting time and gas. Around 12:30 I'd beach the boat behind the Skipper restaurant on the Fairhaven side of the harbor, grab the empty gas tank and walk up to Joe's Texaco station about two blocks away from the beach on Water Street to gas up. Back then, gasoline was 25 cents a gallon, so I could fill up for around $2 including oil which had to be mixed with the gas in that old two–cycle engine. Back to the beach I'd go where I'd eat lunch and then off again for more gas burning. I could repeat this routine for a few days until my allowance and odd job money would run out then I'd be forced to hitch a ride with a friend or sit on the sea wall at the end of the street and watch the boats go by. It didn't take long for me to realize that I would need to work in the summer if I was going to afford my boating passion. So, like my contemporaries, at age 14½ I began my working career. I took a summer job with a neighbor (Bob Tetrault as mentioned later in this narrative) helping to construct a large boat storage shed in Acushnet. Bob worked for Leo Murach at the small boatyard on Elm Ave. in a cove close by to us. The shed we built was for Mr. Murach to store boats during the winter little did I know at the time that "Leo" would become yet another constant in my boating life. Working on the shed helped me with the gas money and other expenses, but seriously crimped my boating time.

Butch would use the boat from time to time, mostly to transit out to a raft across from our little cove where he and his friends would water ski from Walt Parshall's 18 ft Penn Yan runabout. Man, what a boat! It was a dark green lapstreak model with a forty HP Johnson OB and could easily pull two skiers at 20 knots. The inside was immaculate with a split forward seat for the driver and passengers, and an aft facing seat for the

15

safety observer. To top it off, there were girls involved. Parshall was a cool dude and rich, so the girls flocked to him. That was the major attraction for Butch and his buddies, not the skiing, the two-piece bathing suits. Butch and his "homeboys" were two years older than me and their hormones were raging. The raft became quite the "hot spot" as the summer wore on. Butch was quite a social guy and he was well liked. He got in pretty tight with the Parshall crowd and after a while, he became embarrassed to be seen in "the boat" which had lost its luster in comparison to Parshall's Penn Yan, his fast friends and the associated accoutrements. When I would show up at the raft in "the boat", Butch would squirm a bit to have his little brother at the raft in that clunky boat. He would rather not be associated with that thing and his dorky brother. Of course, his attitude just ran off my back even when Parshall's friends would poke fun at me and "the boat". I didn't care, I loved that little boat.

There was a whole host of other characters that emerged in these early boating days, Wayne Gifford, Bobby Anderson, Richie, and Charlie Mitchell, among others. Wayne lived next door to us and was athletic, funny and personable. Bobby Anderson was something of an entrepreneur even at his early age. He worked part-time at the Bridge gas station and he always seemed to have money. Richie, on the other hand, was known as the sponge, always borrowing money. We had a flotilla some six or seven small outboard boats that would regularly cruise the harbor in company during those sultry summer days in the early 60s. One of our favorite haunts was Palmers Island, a six acre spit of land at the entrance of the harbor. It was uninhabited at that time and featured a small lighthouse that faced the channel which in the 60s had been abandoned by the Coast Guard and had become largely dilapidated. The island itself was very historical having served as refuge in 1675 when a garrison and fort was located on the island to protect the settlers from the Wampanoag Indian raids during King Phillips War. In the 1860s an old whaleship was beached on the island which served as a brothel entertaining whalers and local miscreants until it was burned to the ground by some sanctimonious citizens. The lighthouse was established in 1849 and was made famous in

the 1938 hurricane when the keeper Arthur Small was saved by tending
the light while his poor wife, their house and all its belongings were
washed into the harbor by a 30 foot tidal surge.

Today, as in the 1960s, the south end of the island has a 60 ft high
stone hill, the west side a 100 yard long sandy beach and the east side has
a 20 foot high granite cliff that faces the harbor channel. These features
provided plenty of diversions for teenagers including swimming off the
deeply inclined sandy beach even though the harbor water was considered
to be polluted. We didn't mind, it was cool, relatively clear and inviting
on a hot August afternoon. Palmers became a regular stop for most of us
during our harbor excursions. On one memorable day, we were joined on
the island by some of the "older" neighborhood youths (they were in their
late teens) who stopped by to harass the younger "punks" and presumably
assert their authority over Palmers.

At first it was a bit tense, but after a bit of false bravado on both
sides, we all decided to peacefully coexist and enjoy the beautiful summer
day on the island. As I mentioned, the beach was narrow and had a steep
drop off so that swimming was possible at either low or high tide. The
older group didn't use the island as much as we did, so we were well
versed in the subtleties of securing one's vessel to account for the tidal rise
along the beach; the older crowd was not. The assemblage spent an hour
or so swimming at the beach ignoring or clearing the industrial debris that
the tide regularly deposited on the island's shore from the fishing boats,
repair yards, fish houses and manufacturers along the harbor's rim. The
intense industrialization of New Bedford harbor was in stark contrast to
this little haven of tranquility on an uninhabited island in the middle of
that harbor. The older group had arrived at Palmers in two boats, one was
a 14 ft outboard skiff and the other was a 14 ft lapstreaked Lyman
runabout with a full mahogany windshield owned by Reverend Baldwin
and operated on this day by his youngest son Randy; it was quite new and
quite expensive. Randy was joined by two or three of his friends and they
chose to pull the boat up on the beach and simply drop the anchor right in
front of the boat. At the time the tide was out and his boat looked quite

secure. We younger Palmers Island cognizanté knew better than to rely on a short anchor lead. All of us pulled our lighter boats further up the beach and then secured our anchors a full thirty feet from the bow sunk into the sand. Randy's boat was quite heavy and he and his friends were a bit too lazy to pull it very far up the beach.

As the day wore on, small groups set out to explore the island leaving no one at the beach to watch the vessels. After a couple of hours, my friends and I were standing on the stone hill admiring the view of the harbor and watching a 250 ft bulk freighter back away from the State Pier located about1/2 mile north of Palmers. With the assistance of a couple of tug boats, she turned her bow and began heading down the harbor in the channel toward the harbor entrance, a 6 minute steam at best. Palmers Island sits adjacent to the harbor channel, so we would have a ring side seat when she passed by. As we stood there jabbering inanities at each other, as teenager boys will do, something appeared in my peripheral vision off to the left of the island. I turned and saw a lovely white lapstreaked Lyman runabout slowly drifting toward the channel propelled by the building sou'wes wind. The boat was unmanned and as we stood there, we could see a group of figures running wildly toward the beach from the lighthouse yelling as they ran. Witnessing his spectacle, we all quickly realized that Randy Baldwin's boat had drifted free of the beach with the rising tide and was headed directly toward the channel and the oncoming freighter. The unmanned boat and unloaded ship were on a collision course to meet in the channel in about five minutes. My friends and I stood there transfixed and watched as this play as it unfolded:

The freighter continued on her course down the channel and began to increase her speed.

Two members of the "older crowd" reached the beach and quickly launched their skiff beginning a wild dash toward Randy's boat; I remember that Randy was left standing on the beach wringing his hands and sweating it out.

The Lyman continued to drift toward the channel with her anchor rode hanging vertically from the bow which kept her head to the wind.

The skiff and its rescuers continued toward the "casualty" undaunted by the continuous blasting of the freighter's horn warning them of the impending disaster.

The Lyman had now drifted to the west side of the channel as the freighter began closing in at 10 kts.

As we watched incredulously, the rescue skiff suddenly darted across directly in front of the freighter with a mere twenty feet to spare and all the while the freighter continued blasting her horn.

At this point, the rescuers, their skiff and the Lyman disappeared from our view behind the freighter and amidst the almost unendurable tension of the moment, one of my more cerebral friends, Reggie, attempted to engage me in a conversation about which books I had completed as part of my school-required summer reading list. He continued to yammer at me about this until I lost all patience and screamed at him **SHUT UP!**

Then, we all stood there quietly, holding our breath, not knowing what had happened.

After about thirty seconds of anxiety, the freighter finally passed by down the channel and revealed the skiff, its occupants and the Lyman all safe and in one piece bobbling in the ship's wake.

We all gave a rousing cheer and then ran down the hill to the beach to welcome the rescue party. When they arrived, with Randy's boat in tow behind the skiff, Randy was practically in tears thanking them. The rescuers then described how they just managed to get to the other side of the ship and grab the Lyman as the ship passed by a mere ten feet from them. To make matters worse, the unloaded ship was high in the water so her wheel (propeller) was partially exposed and churning menacingly not ten feet away from the rescuers. Years later the legend was that the older of the two rescuers was smoking a cigar which had become extinguished during their mad dash toward Randy's boat. He needed to cut the "stogie's"end to relight the thing so as the whirring propeller came by he was so close that he leaned forward and allowed one of the propeller blades to cut off the end of his cigar. Had they been any closer, the wheel would have turned both boats into match sticks and the occupants into ....well, you can figure that one out. I thought to myself....WHAT IDIOTS! No way would I have done that, let the damned thing get wrecked, Randy should have known better. Well, it was a dramatic lesson for him and his friends and a warning to us all; **Be Careful in that harbor!** Especially if you smoke cigars.

Another singular personality from those early boating days that deserves special mention is Charlie Mitchell. I have known Charlie since childhood as my parents were good friends with his parents. The Mitchells lived on Main St in the Fairhaven Center and my mother became friendly with Louise Mitchell who lived across the street from the apartment building that we occupied for the first few years of Mary and Benny's marriage. Charlie and Butch were the same age, so while I was still a "wee tyke" before we moved our new house on Adams St. in 1951, the two families spent a great deal of time together.

Butch, me and Charlie, note that he was a Capt'n early on

Mary and Louise were members of the Fairhaven Mother's Club and expanded their relationship through that venue as well. Butch and I had a common joke about Mary that whenever she needed to project authority she would invoke her "Mother's Club voice". This would often occur at PTA meetings or when speaking with her Mother's Club friends about club business. Our jest wasn't meant as a pejorative, but it was just odd to us (as juveniles) how she could radically change her persona, so completely. Once we became adults we could better appreciate the role politics can play in warping personalities. This trait would remain with her throughout her life. One particularly funny aspect of her habit was evident when I was in college (I was living at home at the time) when a college chum would stop by. I was in my late teens by then and we had moved to a house on Cherry St in Fairhaven. Mary had developed the habit of watching old movies on TV (until 2 AM) while sipping white wine. My chum and I would sit in the "sunroom" with her and as we discussed some technical subject and invariably Mary would chime in with her "Mother's Club" voice of authority, albeit a bit slurred, and pose what she considered to be a particularly poignant question about the subject that was being discussed. Depending upon the time of evening and the volume of wine that had been consumed, the question could be quite insightful or completely irrelevant. Either way, it was always delivered with the "Mother Club voice" of authority. As she became more involved in addressing her subject, she would become more serious and her words would become more slurred and pointless....but would still be delivered with authority. My chum would begin to get uncomfortable and eventually I would find it necessary to disarm her with some off-the-wall remark that would bring her back around to her senses. At that point she would usually retreat gracefully to her glass of wine and bid us "Good Evening" and get back to her movie.

Getting back to Charlie Mitchell, Charlie was an amicable fellow who enjoyed teasing his contemporaries to get a rise out them. He tended to be a bit edgy at times, one could claim pugnacious, but he was generally an affable soul. Charlie's dad, Bob Mitchell, (a sterling character of a man by anyone's measure) ran a small diesel repair shop in a one-story, building on Middle St., in Fairhaven close to the harbor. Bob had just taken on a line of small air-cooled diesel generators from a British company. The outfit was called Lister and this proved to be a very fortuitous decision for Bob and his son Bobby who would inherit the business. When Bobby came aboard, the company became known as R.A. Mitchell & Son a diesel generator company. Today, a third generation of Mitchell's (Bobby's daughters) is running the business which has expanded further and now sells domestically and internationally.

Like many of male Fairhavenites in the 1960's Charlie wanted a boat so Bob gave in and bought Charlie a locally built 16 ft runabout. It was powered by a 25 hp mercury outboard that Bob had purchased used. What was clear from the outset was that (at this time in their lives) Bobby had inherited most of his father's mechanical ability and Charlie got the short-shrift as his outboard proved cantankerous, requiring lots of care and feeding. During my second boating summer, more than once, I saw Charlie in the blue runabout (no name as far as I recall) being towed over to the beach behind the Skipper as his Dad (Bob) was coming down to the beach to fix the outboard. On at least one of these occasions, I towed Charlie and I witnessed his volcanic, but funny temper. He had a short fuse (still does) and when the outboard died, he'd walk aft to fiddle with it and you could see his anger building by the minute. He'd start to tinker with the fuel line which would do nothing, then to the throttle connections;….nothing… he would start to mutter curse words and then fiddle a bit more. Then back to the ignition switch, ….turn it over…nothing…louder curse mutterings, then finally he'd explode and start hitting the engine with his shoe yelling…"GOD DAMNED MACHINE!…..GOD DAMNED MACHINE!". He'd do this a few times to vent his anger at the object of his frustration and then settle back as I towed him to the beach behind the Skipper restaurant.

On the occasion of note, I waited for him to fetch Bob who, although he was trying to run a business single handed, would walk down to the beach and patiently address the engine trouble, calmly explaining to Charlie what was wrong and how to deal with it should it happen again. Charlie would sort of listen, but he was not happy and I don't think it all sunk in, because like clockwork a few days later, there he'd be at the end of a towline headed for the beach behind the Skipper. Charlie would be banging on that Mercury outboard with his shoe yelling "GOD DAMNED MACHINE!"

Charlie went on to college at U Mass in Amherst then entered Georgetown Law School. As he explained later, he thought he wanted to be a lawyer so that he could make enough money to afford a big boat. After a year, he found that he didn't like law school so after a hitch as an officer in the Navy, he returned to Fairhaven and worked for Eddy Sanchez of Sanchez Marine. After "learning the ropes" of the tugboat biz, Charlie bought an old 63 ft harbor tug from Sanchez and renovated it to start his own business. He called the tug *Fort Phoenix* and his business became known as Mitchell Towing and Salvage Co. He was quite successful and as a result, in 1978 he traded up to a steel tug named *Jaguar* (Charlie was always a sucker for cats). She was 65 feet, he laid out the basic design and she was built to his specifications by Gladding-

Hearn shipyard in Somerset Mass. This outfit has been in business since 1955 and has completed more than 350 steel and aluminum vessels. Tugs, pilot boats, fast catamaran ferries and patrol craft are among the products built by this fine shipyard.

Charlie has had many adventures with the *Jaguar* over the years and being a neighbor and friend I have had the pleasure of participating in some of these. More on all this later....

Charlie's brother Bobby became his Dad's partner in the diesel generator business. Bobby expanded the business dramatically from the early days at the "shop" when his dad was splitting his time between rebuilding gen sets and helping Charlie with that "God damned machine".

One story about Bobby will aptly portray his character. After attending the Lister training program in the UK and working for his dad for a year or so, Bobby became the "field" technician, responsible for attending to generator equipment issues on the fleet's fish boats. By this time there were a fair number of boats that had Lister generators installed and, although they were quite reliable, there were occasional equipment problems. Bobby was dispatched to deal with these and on one particular occasion (as the story goes) he was inspecting a unit on an older scalloper and there were three or four crewmen in the engine room with him observing his progress. Commercial waterfronts are generally rough and tumble places and New Bedford was no exception. The characters on the waterfront from fish buyers to fish boat crews have a macho attitude and will test the mettle of anyone that they feel is not worthy to work there.

Such was the circumstance that Bobby found himself that day in the engine room of the scalloper. The crew was jerking him around, asking stupid questions, dropping his tools in the bilge when he wasn't looking and generally trying to tweak the nose of the new guy. I'm sure Bobby's dad had been through the same "right of passage" when he first began working on the waterfront, but he had earned his reputation and was generally respected by those that worked there. Now it was Bobby's turn to be tested and he rose to the occasion. After about ten minutes of being the butt of the crew's jokes, Bobby had had enough, he turned from his work, looked at the four jerks who were tormenting him and yelled out "okay…that's it, all of you up on the dock….NOW! This took the crew by surprise and with their guard down, they complied with Bobby's demand and scurried out of the cramped engine room and up onto the dock. I believe one or two of these jerks were doing this just to see what would happen next. As Bobby emerged from the boat and stood facing his adversaries on the dock, they glared at him as he rolled up his sleeves and exclaimed "Okay, let's go, who's first? I'm going to kick the shit out of each one of you, who wants it first?"

The crew was dumbfounded, standing before them was a 5'6" guy in khaki pants and he's threatening to take them all on! They stood there looking at one another, nobody moving forward to take Bobby up on his offer. After a few tense moments, the "leader" of the group looked at Bobby and said "well, that's enough, let's get the generator fixed". Bobby had made a statement and the tale of that exploit spread around the waterfront. He was now one of the guys, no one would mess with him again, …..."he'll kick the shit outaya".

~ *Chapter 2* ~

Drifting away from my boating roots

After my sophomore year in high school, I found that like my brother before me, I too was beginning to succumb to the attractions of life beyond the waterfront. I had always liked girls, but now they were becoming far more interesting as was high school sports and cars. By the start of my junior year, I had accumulated quite a few school friends and I was the oldest of the group. I turned sixteen in March of 1963 and all my friends were looking forward to riding with me after I obtained my driver's license. This turn of events, as with my brother before me, caused me to outgrow "the boat". As my interest waned, so did the attention that all marine craft require. The last summer that we had "the boat", it developed a small leak that was later found to be attributable to a hull strake that had pulled away from the bottom. These strakes were two ½" boards on either side of the bottom at the chine edge which were used to help the board turn, since it had very little keel on the semi-V bottom. These boards were secured to the boat bottom with two-inch bronze wood screws and with age and abuse, on some unknown occasion, half of one of these boards had broken off and left a quarter inch hole in the bottom. This formed a seemingly undetectable leak that caused water accumulation over a period of days.

Since my interest in boating was fading, I would occasionally row out to bail the boat, but with my many distractions, these visits became more infrequent. One day it happened, I walked to the bottom of the street and there she was, sitting upside down at the mooring. On this occasion, Benny happened to be home and he went into action yelling commands and invoking demands that provoked me to row out and retrieve the casualty. This may well have been my introduction to marine salvage. We managed to the get boat righted and bailed. We removed the outboard and Benny took it to Bob Mitchell's shop to be rehabilitated. Needless to say this was the end of the boat. Benny sold it before the summer ended

26

claiming that if I couldn't be responsible for the damned thing, it was
gone. He was right….as usual in those days.

    I passed the driver's test in the summer of 1963 having survived
Tillie Torman's driving school. The Torman driving school was a creation
of the omnipresent political culture of Massachusetts. Claiming to being
responsive to the escalation of teenage driving accidents, (this was
probably the result of demographics, since the baby boomers were coming
of driving age) the "Great and General Court" (Massachusetts Legislature)
enacted a law that provided an auto insurance discount to those
adolescents who successful completed a state-sanctioned driver's
education program. Consequently, a myriad of driver's schools sprung up
overnight to meet the newly created demand. I'm sure that many a
politicians palm was greased in the process of sanctioning these "schools".
The approved program lasted ten weeks to extract the maximum amount
of cash from the "students" and after passing the DMV driver's test, the
insurance discount was granted. The classes were a joke and actual on the
road experience was crammed into a week or so before the DMV test. I
survived, and obtained my license so from that time on I was far more
interested in acquiring gas money for use in the family car than I was in
boating. To fund the gas money addiction, I took a full-time summer job
working as a hamburger flipper in the kitchen of the Beverly Yacht Club
in Marion. It was there that I got my first taste of sailing, from shore
rather than on a boat. I found the concept of sailing appealing, especially
the part about the wind being free; no need to buy gas.

    About this time, my mother found an old carvel planked yacht
dinghy for sale in an antique dealer's shop in Freetown. My mother loved
to poke about in old shops looking for "deals" on furniture, dry goods and
miscellany in the myriad of antique shops in Southeastern Mass. She
engaged in these sojourns when Benny was away "on a trip" working on

offshore tankers for Mobil Oil. The cat was away, so she and her friends would spend much of their leisure time "antiquing" as they called it. The Morris family usually worked on a tight budget, or so we were told, but Butch and I found it curious that Benny had no problem paying for my younger sister (five years my junior) Deb's private school tuition at Sacred Hearts Academy. Butch always claimed that he and I had been reared when the family was poor and Debby was raised after we got rich. At any rate, Mary was always under the gun from Benny to hold down her spending, but she resisted and was never very good with finances. The old story was that she often would walk into the National Bank of Fairhaven and, in a huff of total frustration, throw her check book at the teller exclaiming,

"I can't balance this damn thing….you do it!"

The bank manager was a very patient fellow and he would lead her over to his desk and walk her through the process of check book balancing. She never did quite get it (she was never good with numbers) and this same scene was repeated several times a year.

After Benny returned from four months at sea, my mother's poor book keeping skills would force him to wrestle with the family's finances for the first week of his "vacation". Once we were back on an even financial keel, he would leave strict orders for Mary regarding what she could spend and how she could spend it. Needless to say, antiques were not on the acquisition list. This state of affairs lasted about a week or so after Benny had shipped out. My mother could not pass up a good deal, so she would buy an item and then juggle the check book to pay for it. Hence the aforementioned constant confusion with her check book. Following this maneuver, she would then conspire with her "partners in crime" (antiquing buddies) to store the item at their house until she could convince Benny (when he returned from his trip) that she had bought the thing because we "really needed it". This drama was enacted countless

28

times during my adolescence, but I remember one item in particular that stands out as unique. She bought a twelve foot "deacons' bench" expecting to have a carpenter friend eventually cut the thing in half so that it would fit in our kitchen. She arranged with one of her friends to "hide" the bench at her friend's house until she could make the carpentry arrangements and explain the concept to Benny.

Well, the bench resided very happily at her friend's house for more than a year until one night when Benny and Mary were visiting and after a few drinks her friend spilled the beans about the bench. As you might imagine, this surprise didn't "sit" (pun intended) well with my father who retained his composure until he and Mary were in the car headed home. During the ride, he made his displeasure abundantly clear, but fortunately, Mary's friend had become attached to the bench, so she reimbursed Benny for it. This immediate crisis was resolved, but despite the embarrassment and sting of being chastised for her errant merchandizing behavior, Mary continued to "soldier on" with her antiquing when Benny was at sea. The previous scenario would play out many times during their marriage.

On another occasion in the Fall, while searching for crystal glassware in an old barn shop in Freetown, she came across the aforementioned ten-foot long yacht dinghy. It was dusty with bare wood, but otherwise in reasonably good shape with no dry rot in the ribs and all the thwarts were solid. The dealer talked her into buying it for Benny (it didn't take much convincing) as a personal sailing dinghy. The problem was that this boat was not set up for sailing there was no centerboard box, no rudder, no sails. It did; however, have a mast that was in two sections with a scarf joint in the middle. I knew nothing about sailboats, but even my novice eye could easily discern that a 25-foot mast was too large for a ten-foot sailing dinghy. Although it was abundantly clear to all that the mast was not intended for this boat, it came along with the purchase, further sweetening "a really good deal!"

Having bought this thing, and we transported it in the back of our 1958 Chevrolet *Bel Air* station wagon to Fairhaven to Bobby Tetrault's house on Oxford St, a block from our house. Bob worked for the previously introduced Leo Murach who owned a small boatyard in the neighborhood. Bob (at nineteen) was something of a shipwright, a good carpenter and a very nice person. He realized my mother's plight (Mary had many friends being very popular in the neighborhood and throughout Fairhaven) and agreed to "hide" the boat in his garage and work on it over the winter. He promised to help surprise Benny with a classic sailing dinghy by the following summer. Bob was good for his word and by early June the boat was finished and looked reasonably good. Bob cut one section of the huge mast down to seven feet for use with the dinghy and obtained a large wooden dowel for a gaff. He designed a sail and had a local loft (E.W. Smith) build it for the lug rigged dinghy. The boat was painted white with a light blue interior and when Benny arrived home that July, Mary proudly led him up to Bob's and showed him his new boat. In light of Mary's previous commercial indiscretions, Benny was at first very apprehensive and his demeanor was a classic example of extremely mixed emotions. On one hand he was very pleased with his new toy and touched by Mary's thoughtfulness, but, as I watched his facial expressions, I could see that the wheels of his mental calculator were turning as he struggled to forecast the cost of this new bauble. As it turned out, Mary couldn't keep this fact a secret, because this project had gone way over budget. What began as a "great deal" at $25 had now ratcheted up to around $800 - $1000 with the labor, materials and new parts. So, rather than enjoying his new trinket with no strings attached, Benny was now saddled with about 80% of the expense. He was pretty PO'd at first, but then he got into it and forgave Mary.

Buying and repairing boats was one thing, but when it came to naming them, my family seemed to be hamstrung. Consequently, as with "the boat", I was mortified by the name choice for this new vessel. Benny and Mary had visited Pennsylvania "Dutch Country" the summer before and had bought a few souvenirs, one of which was a "hex sign", a placard containing a delicate Amish design. The one the settled on was Distelfink which was a stylized goldfinch. This became the name of this dinghy......"Oh Gawd" was my only response.

Benny spent a few weeks trying out his new toy and then began his program of sailing instruction for my sister Debby (who was about 11 at the time) and me. In retrospect, I think his instructional program may have gone smoother if Benny had taken a few lessons himself before becoming the instructor as he was often times flustered about the proper techniques and lexicon of a sailing. What made matters worse was that the centerboard box leaked and the mast was too heavy, so the boat was always down by the bow. In addition, the lug rig had too little sail area to power the boat and she wouldn't point (tack upwind) for beans. The final insult was that the lug rig and small sail area made the boat very difficult to tack, she was constantly "in irons" head to wind and moving backwards. Debby was younger and more tolerant than me, so she persisted much longer with Benny's sailing instruction program than I did.

For me, the culmination occurred one afternoon when Benny sent me out solo while he stood on the beach yelling instructions. The sou'wester was puffing at its usual 12 to 15 knots and "Distlefink" was bravely trying to respond to my clumsy, inept helmsmanship (it was quite evident that I was a product of the Benny Morris school of sailing). Several times, I nearly flipped her as she was a very tender vessel in these weather conditions. Finally, I'd had enough so put the helm down and headed for the beach to end this frustrating exercise. I began with a broad reach, (not that I knew what this point of sail was at the time) and then went to a dead run, headed right for Benny who was standing on the beach. Fortunately, the tide was in, so there was sufficient water depth to keep me from grounding out until I reached "terra firma". While I was executing my "flawless" plan, (in reality, the situation was forcing my hand) I occasionally caught a glimpse of Benny gesticulating like a mad man and hopping up and down while yelling at the top of his lungs at me. I couldn't make out what he was trying to communicate as I was far too busy trying to keep the boat upright while pursued my course for the beach. What's more, he was downwind so his voice was plucked away as he yelled.

I finally ran her up hard on the sandy spit, and Benny ran over to me

31

screaming that I hadn't raised the centerboard; I guessed that was what he was trying to convey to me during my wild ride. As it turned out, because I was running her dead downwind, the centerboard just collapsed into the box as she ran up the beach thereby inflicting no damage. He was not happy about all about this and continued to chew me out until finally I had enough and told to keep his bloody sailboat and walked on up to the house. That was the last time I sailed the thing whenever he was home. From then on, he took a page from Joshua Slocum's book and he singlehanded Distlefink. This was by chance rather than choice, because no one (not even my mother) would sail with "Captain Blyh" again. It seemed that he could not leave his professional demeanor of a ship's officer ashore even when on a ten-foot sailing dinghy.

There was one other notable sailing occasion on the old "Distlefink" that should be recounted. In advance of this, I should state that I have long suffered from otosclerosis which is a hereditary condition that causes hardening of the bones in the inner ear making them less likely to vibrate, hence causing a form of deafness. I shared this condition with my paternal grandparents and Benny, but Benny developed it at a much later time in life than me. I became "hard of hearing" in high school and by my senior year needed a hearing aid to assist in class. Both grandparents (Pop and Flo, described later) wore hearing aids and had a respectable backlog of older devices that had been sidelined as the technology crawled toward improvement. Having survived the "Great Depression" Pop, Flo and Benny tended to err on the side of fiscal frugality rather than being spend thrifts and as such they seldom discarded anything considered to be of value. Consequently, when Pop learned that I needed a hearing aid his immediate response to Benny was:

"Eeeerr, not to worry, we've got a lovely bunch of good 'ole earnin' aids that we dowint use no more….. Scotty kin 'ave one a tese,….. 'ill be jost fowine"

Like many Brits who immigrated to the US for work in the textile industry (my grandparents had been in Fairhaven since 1922) although they'd been in America for decades, they couldn't shed their accent, so you'd think that they had just stepped off the boat from England. The worst part about all this was that Benny (that cheap skate) went along with the plan so that he wouldn't be required to buy me a proper aid. And me, like a dope, went along with it as well.

So, I ended up with what looked like a 1960s transistor radio (probably did have discrete transistors in it) with a wire running from the "aid" to my ear that housed the "speaker" (earpiece). I guess I was lucky that Gramps didn't have an aide that contained vacuum tubes, otherwise that would have been mine. Can you imagine what that would have looked like…..probably the size of a 1930s Zenith console radio. I wore the "transistor radio" aide around my neck, clipped onto a rawhide necklace so the speaker (which was in the middle of the "box") was aimed directly at whoever was talking to me. I used that damned thing throughout four years of college until I could finally afford to buy a small, behind the ear aide.

With the scene set, on one sultry July evening, when I was in college, a friend (John Hatfield Jr.) and I ambled down to the waterfront with the Distlefink, bound to do some sailing after dinner. The breeze was up as was the tide and we launched the vessel and clambered aboard. Benny was "at sea" so he wasn't around to harass us. We left the beach with no problem and sailed out about 50 yards off the beach toward the bridge. We beam reached back and forth in the anchorage and the boat was handling fairly well despite the blustery conditions. My buddy John was at the helm and I was tending the mainsheet and hiking out to provide ballast and keep the boat on her feet when she healed.

All went well while we tacked, but once out in the anchorage, we chose to jibe the boat to head back toward the beach…………MISTAKE!

The damned thing was so tender and the boom so heavy that the two of us couldn't adjust our weight in time to prevent a broach. And broach she did, as she quickly filled with water I began to climb the mast thinking that I had to protect my 'eerin aid" from getting soaked. As the boat settled, I realized that my efforts were fruitless and let fate play out as I sat down in the seat. With the boat filling with water, I sank up to my chin, drenching me and my aide. Fortunately, the vessel didn't sink and we were able to get her to shore and bail her out; so much for that evening of sailing. My brother Butch was on hand at the beach and when I told him that the hearing aide got doused, he took me up to the house to remedy the problem. He was very positive as we washed the device out with tap water and then preheated the oven to "warm". Butch then placed the washed out hearing aide on a cookie sheet and from there into the oven to dry it. I had my doubts that any of this would work, but after ten minutes, the device was pronounced "done" as Butch removed it from the oven. I placed a new battery into it and.....viola!, the damned thing worked perfectly. What's more, it worked faithfully for another two years until I finally retired it and bought a new "modern" device.

Yes,........ as you might surmise, Gramps asked for the old one back....."never know,....... might jost need it agin ya 'new"

~ Chapter 3 ~

Years in the wilderness

Stung from this early uncomfortable experience with sailing, I put the sport on the back burner and lived out my life of High School and then college at a local university. Although I had always been an above average student in High School, I was one of those who didn't "test" well. I hated aptitude tests and although my grades were okay, my College Board scores were at best average, which severely limited my college choices. In fact, my choices were so limited, that I ended up enrolling at Southeastern Massachusetts Technological Institute. How's that for a mouth full? This was actually the local technology school founded to provide technical training for the workers in the multitude of textile mills in New Bedford in the late 19th and early 20th centuries. Many of those mills had, by 1965, folded, but the school had expanded and besides textile technology, now offered liberal arts programs as well chemistry and engineering. For the uninitiated, New Bedford is one of the larger cities in Massachusetts, while Fairhaven is, by comparison, a small town. The history of New Bedford is very rich and the population very heterogeneous. The late nineteenth century was the setting for a boom in the textile industry in New Bedford (and other Massachusetts cities) and immigrants from all over Europe (including my paternal grandparents) flocked to the place because of the availability of work. New Bedford was a boom town in those days, but when I was ready to attend the college, in 1965, the city had fallen on hard times with the attendant shabbiness.

Textile School, New Bedford, Mass.

NBIT circa 1930

In 1964, the "textile" school on Purchase St. was still called New Bedford Institute of Technology, but the name was changed in 1965 when NBIT merged with a similar institution in Fall River called Durfee Institute of Technology. This merger was the beginning of an institution that is now the University of Massachusetts at North Dartmouth. I was accepted in the chemistry program which was modest, but was accredited by the American Chemical Society. I distinctly remember many of my High School chums claiming that I would never make it through the chemistry program. I had confidence though, because I love a challenge.

Following the school merger in 1964, the new institution SMTI had two campuses, one in New Bedford and one in Fall River. The New Bedford campus of SMTI was located in two buildings on Purchase St. The old building was the original NBIT school and was constructed around 1880. The second building was directly across the street and was been built around 1955. There were no athletic fields, but the school's basketball team did have a gymnasium that occupied a portion of the newer building. The population of the New Bedford campus was predominantly male and they expressed only a passing interest in the school's basketball team. Some comedian did compose an unofficial team cheer; however, that circulated around campus (small campus, not hard for anything to get around). It went like this:

"A rooty toot toot,
A rooty toot toot,
We are the boys of
Southeastern Massachusetts Technological Institute"

It really lent itself to large numbers of cheering fans…..NOT! As one might imagine, this tongue in cheek cheer was a clear indication of low esprit de corps and attendance at the basketball games was anemic. Yet another aspect that dampened school spirit but reinforced a resignation in some of us was the common claim in greater New Bedford about "tech". The old adage was "if you can't go to college, go to tech". Well, for me, I was at "tech" and I was determined to "make a go of it".

Contrary to basketball, I observed that the most popular team sport on campus was card playing (poker mostly) at the snack room in the basement of the "new" building. There were always one or two card games in progress no matter what the time of day, the weather or time of year.

For my first two years of college I referred to it as NBIT. I was able to secure an old NBIT decal of a whale holding a harpoon (the school's previous mascot) and proudly displayed this in the window of my car. My attitude was that I was essentially attending NBIT, no matter what the Massachusetts Legislature had chosen to call this school.

There was, of course, another reason for my insistence on this. My grandfather, Benson Morris Sr. had also attended "tech" while working as a loom fixer in many of the mills in New Bedford. Gramps and Gramma (Florence) had immigrated to American from England in 1922 having grown up in Lancashire County where the textile industry was the main source of employment. They married before leaving England and harbored no illusions about their adopted country. America was "terra incognita" for both of them since they were the first of either family to venture west. As I mentioned earlier, they never lost their Lancashire accent, I believe they cultivated it over the years. I remember when I was in my twenties introducing new friends to my grandparents and later the friends would remark how cute my grandparents were and wondered how long they had been in this country. My standard answer, "thirty years", would invariably evoke disbelief.

Benson had served honorably in WW I as an infantryman with the East Lancashire Regiment which took part in the invasion force at Gallipoli, that glorious, heroic, misguided mistake that cost so many lives in a botched attempt to break the trench stalemate on the western front in Europe. Benson was always proud of his service in the "Great War", but he never dwelled on nor would he detail any specifics of his activities. It wasn't until years later that I learned that he was stranded in a Turk trench when on advance patrol with a handful of his mates. As luck would have it, this patrol was ambushed by "Jonny Turk" and at the outset three of his mates were killed by the enemy.

As he and the last of the survivors retreated down the trench line, the Turks kept coming and shooting. Benson soon found himself alone, all his mates had been killed. He was in survival mode and continually fired on the enemy to save his own life. As he retreated back to his own lines, he picked up rifles as he went and fired at the oncoming Turkish soldiers. He was singularly responsible for killing four or five Turks and was himself shot in the hand as he fell back to the British lines. He lived to tell the tale, but lost a finger to gangrene from this combat action. I always wondered about his lost middle finger and asked about it many times. When questioned, Gramps provided many different answers ranging from "lost it in a weaving machine" to "an engine fan took it off when I was changing the oil". He never did tell reveal the true story of how he lost that finger. I discovered this from an old newspaper article that appeared in a Lancashire periodical. Old warriors are often reticent about their exploits in war. I think it brings back bad memories that they would just as soon forget. He was that kind of guy solid as a rock, he liked the ladies and the drink, but he was a loyal as an old sheep dog and just as lovable. He lived to be 93 and he drove his old Rambler until he flunked the eye test at the Registry when he was 91. The day that occurred I asked him how he managed to get home after flunking his driver's test and he answered "Well,…..I drove".

So, with this personal history and a general desire to succeed in the study of chemistry, I entered SMTI and began four years of intensive study. I won't bore the reader with the details, but I will describe a few extracurricular activities to my scholarly pursuits at SMTI.

Besides card playing, at which I'm still very bad, the other diversions at SMTI were Friday night frat parties and the "Dipper". Of the three fraternities "on campus" Delta Kappa Phi (DK) was the wildest. I was befriended by several DK brothers and attended a few of their parties. My last party at the "house" involved a female, a close friend and beer. My friend was serving as sergeant-at-arms on this particular occasion and we conversed as the "party" commenced then drifted to different parts of the crowded basement. I became acquainted with a young female (probably not a local coed as we had few at NBIT) and bought her several beers while chatting and dancing with her over the period of an hour or so. Now, affording beer for me was a dicey proposition considering the fact that my only income was from whatever part time work I could find when not attending class or studying. I was able to swing a gig as night manager at *Howdy Beefburgers* conveniently located right next to my school on Purchase St. This wasn't a complete coincidence, since the "store", as it was called, was owned by my parents' neighbor, John Adams. No,…. not THE John Adams, this was John Adams from Burlington, Vermont. Through a bit of lobbying by my mother, John agreed to hire me to work when I could and this eventually evolved into my working as the Saturday night manager of the store. I worked for John as Saturday night manager for three years while attending SMTI. Although *Howdy's* served the community at large, many of its patrons were students from SMTI. In fact, many of these same students also worked at the store. John was really good at allowing split schedules which served the students, but also served him. He was a real great boss, always positive and fun. He liked practical jokes and he was a great neighbor to the university. During hell week, John would let pledges conduct skits as part of their initiation on the roof of *Howdy's* . John was also involved in the community and an excellent neighbor.

Revisiting the DK frat house......... on this particular night after spending my hard earned money on a "femme fatale" I expected that she would pay some attention to me and I was hoping to, perhaps, "score". As I came back from the bar with another round of beers, I found my new "flame" cozying up to some other fellow in a blue blazer. I was somewhat drunk at this point and quite incensed, so I acted incredibly discourteous and tossed my beer at her. She screamed as I walked away and then next thing I knew I was on the floor wrestling with the guy in the blue blazer. At this point, the call of SERGEANT AT ARMS, SERGEANT AT ARMS rang though the house. Suddenly I was physically lifted off the floor and as I stared momentarily at a fist headed right for my face, I suddenly heard the familiar voice of my buddy Geoff (the Sergeant at arms) exclaim....."Oh no...not you!" I was caught (luckily he held his punch) and about to be ejected, but at that point, my adversary ("Boog Powell") stood up and claimed that he jumped me because I splashed beer on his jacket. I immediately apologized (so much for chivalry, right?) and offered to pay the cleaning bill. He demurred and claimed a beer would suffice. All three of us repaired to the bar where I bought a round and all was forgiven, but when the beer was gone, so was I. I was not invited back to the DK house.

There were two other DK brothers who were absent from the party that night, but they would later be involved with me in sailing experiences.

These two were Ed Ilsley and Peter Richards, more on these two later.

The Dipper was the other social diversion available to "tech" students. Officially known as the Dipper Café, but affectionately called "the dirty "D", this tavern was located in the basement of an old building and had been a local watering hole for "tech" men for generations.

I believe this to be the building that predated the original Dipper Café, the building changed, but the "D" was installed in the basement

Since it was in a basement, there was an old saying that when you entered the Dipper you took two steps down, physically, intellectually and morally. Two Lebanese brothers named Bhutt and Shah Thomas owned the Dipper. The old "D" was located at the intersection of Mill St and North Second. Today, the successor or the "new" Dipper is located on Purchase St.

Bhutt was a very large fellow, standing about 6'2" and weighing about 250 lbs., but he was a little slow witted, he reminded me of Lenny in Steinbeck's "Of Mice and Men". Shah, on the other hand, was diminutive and suffered from gout, but he was the brains of the outfit, not that it took much brains to run the "D". I was initiated into the Dipper fraternity by Bob Rustle who, as I understood it, been a regular patron, beginning with his senior year at New Bedford High School. I had known Bob for a number of years as his mother Jane was good friends with my mom. Bob was an Art major at SMTI and the rumor was that he put his talents to good use in a side business making fake IDs for friends and acquaintances. An ID wasn't needed at the "D"; however, if you were introduced to Bhutt by someone who he knew. Bhutt would ask you if you went to "tech" and if you responded in the positive you were in. If you were in you were in, if not, Butt would employ his enormous hands to escort you to the door.

The Dipper was not far from campus, so many a Dipper lad would stop by for lunch between classes. If you played it right you could have lunch and enjoy recreational pursuits for about one dollar. Here's how it worked: steamed hot dogs were two for a quarter and a Bud was thirty cents. The shuffleboard bowling game was a dime. So if you were thirsty you could have two dogs and two beers and a game of shuffle bowling and still have a nickel left over. For those who preferred better nutrition and exercise you could have four hot dogs, one beer and two games of shuffle bowl. Either way, it was the best deal in town.

Another salient characteristic of the Dipper was the three-gallon jar of pickled eggs sitting at the end of the bar. Most taverns in New England in the 1960s had a jar of pickled eggs at the bar. In the Dipper, this particular jar had been sitting on the bar for some time with what appeared to be the same quantity of eggs in it. As the alum and vinegar in the pickling solution aged, the protein in the eggs continued to crosslink. And the solution became increasingly turbid. It is my guess that the eggs probably had the consistency of tennis balls and undoubtedly tasted about the same. My buddy Ed Ilsley who was a regular, regular at the Dipper claimed that he never saw anyone buy or eat one of those eggs during the four years of his "hitch" at "tech". I would think that one would need to be incredibly inebriated and half-starving to even have a notion about eating one. Eventually, with the passage of the Clean Air and Clean Water Acts of 1972, I understand that this jar was declared to be hazardous waste and subsequently removed by men in full hazmat suits with respirators when the old "D" was demolished in the 1970's during

42

"urban renewal". From there it was undoubtedly taken to an appropriate disposal site (Yucca Mountain leaps to mind) where the offending jar and its contents was vitrified in glass to protect the human race from exposure for the next 10,000 years.

My fondest memory of the "D" was on Friday nights when the Dipper fraternity would gather for a few beers before heading out for greener pastures where we could find women. There were never any women in the Dipper on Friday night it was strictly a male enclave heavy with testosterone, lewd jokes and remarks, lots of whooping and hollering.

The Friday night scenario would play out more or less like this: You'd walk down the two steps to the front door and pause briefly listening to the yelling and raucous activities going on inside. As you opened the door and started to walk into the smoke-filled room, the place would become deathly silent as all at the bar swung around to identify who was entering. When you were recognized by someone at the bar they'd yell your name at the top of their lungs and all would join in chanting your name. This would last until you had walked the short distance to the bar and then all would return to their previous activities and the din in the place was deafening. You'd find your friends and Bhutt would give you a nod and a Bud and you'd begin plotting the night's activities based on the latest rumors of parties and such. This ritual would be repeated as each new person walked through the door until around eight thirty. Inevitably, around this time, the door would open, the place would momentarily go still as everyone (all were quite drunk by now) would wheel around in anticipation of emitting yet another round of uproarious cacophony to greet a new comer when who should walk in...but a "Salvation Sally" (Salvation Army member, usually a female) on her rounds of the city's bars soliciting donations. Immediately as if prescribed, all of the bar patrons would turn their backs to the solicitor and pretend to be in deep, quiet, extremely important conversation with their bar mates. The Salvation Army lady would quietly walk through the place and politely ask for donations (she'd get a few, but no one would talk to

43

her) and then leave. Upon her exit, probably before she reached the top step, the place would immediately return to bedlam. The Dipper was a fun place and helped us to deal with the poor of social opportunities on an urban campus in an otherwise rundown city.

My freshman chemistry class was filled with fun-loving guys who were serious about academics, but also saw and appreciated the humor in life. I have fond memories of Rustle Mellor, Stanley Baczek, Paul Falcon, David Brown and Bob Mackenzie. Most of the instructors were eccentric characters who couldn't make the tenure cut at large universities or didn't want the pressure of a large school so they settled for this academic backwater. Of these, the one who was the most conspicuous was Professor Louis Feneau. "Louie" as we students referred to him (but never to his face) was from the old school he was in his early sixties and had been an instructor at tech for many years. He had a moderate to severe speech impediment and appeared to have disequilibrium or poor balance. I suspected that he may have been a stroke victim, but the lab stock room technician disagreed and claimed that Louie was injured in a lab experiment gone bad many years before. Several in the class claimed that he'd been damaged by breathing bromine fumes; who knew? That was the rumor in the Department, but in any event, he was a very nice person, even if he was difficult to comprehend. With his advancing age and disabilities, Louie's class load was reduced to two chemistry courses and one textile chemistry course.

He was my class's Analytical Chemistry instructor in our second year. Fortunately, for us, he adhered closely to the textbook which resulted in fairly easy, predictable exams. Had this not been the case, we would have been in deep trouble. One particular incident illustrates my point. Most of his lectures, took place in a small classroom with a wall mounted blackboard and a large wooden table directly in front of the

board. Louie liked this room, because it was small and he could lean against the table while lecturing; he enjoyed the informality of this venue. While he spoke, there were many times when we wondered what he was saying and quizzed one another attempting to decode his garbled dialect. At one point he was trying desperately to make himself understood, but no one could make out the word he was uttering and finally in a fit of frustration, he stood up from the table faced us and announced "I'll write it". With that he turned around to walk to the board and ran smack dab into the solid maple table leg whacking his knee with an audible thud. Wincing in pain and holding his knee he hobbled to the board, but as he reached it, he was far too close to it so that when he began to write, he banged the chalk onto the surface of the board, lost his balance and fell backwards over and onto the table. Wincing again, he pulled himself up and once again wacked the board with the chalk and commenced to scrawl several strange markings. This was the first time we had actually observed Louie writing anything on the blackboard and now we knew why. His penmanship was as bad as his diction, his scrawl was totally illegible. Unflustered by this seemingly tortured, herculean ordeal of writing on the board, Louie turned around and proudly pronounced his scrawl repeating the word ….."dumerator…dumerator", each time he stated the word, he underlined his blackboard scrawlings. We all looked at one another, dumfounded, muttering,
"dumerator, what the hell is a dumerator?"
until one or two of the guys exclaimed "Oh numerator!" Louie then chimed back "yes, dumerator" He had invented a new word by combining numerator with denominator to get dumerator! No wonder he was only teaching two classes!

Besides picking up a little Analytical Chemistry once in a while in Louie's classes, we were also learning to be linguists and detectives. And there was no extra tuition for mastering the latter two skills.

Louie was a good man though and cared deeply about his students and the school's athletics which was his passion.

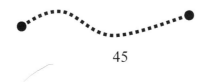

In my freshman year I bought a red 1959 Triumph TR3 sports car for transportation and fun. Old British sports cars were very popular with the college crowd and there were quite a few of them around. Benny loaned me the $600 needed for the purchase and I spent the rest of that winter pouring whatever money I could earn at odd jobs into that car. It was pretty to look at, but what a piece of junk. With the arrival of spring, I still hadn't made a dent in the original $600 loan so I agreed to get my seaman's papers to ship out on one of Mobil's tankers during the upcoming summer, should a job became available. When classes ended, there was no sign of a job from Mobil, so I accepted an offer from one of my Howdy's buddies, Mark Treadup, to paint water towers at Otis Air Force base on Cape Cod. I showed up on a clear early June Monday morning and Mark introduced me to the project foreman who proceeded to escort me the ladder leading to the top of the 150 foot tower. His first order was to climb on up and find the supervisor who would show me what to do, the ladder that had a protective cage all around so the climb up wasn't too unsettling. When I reached the summit, the "Super" greeted me, tied a safety line around my waist and said "right about now you feel as though you got a little shit in your blood, don't you?" Boy was he ever right, the roof sloped down at about 15 degree angle and it was slippery. He handed me a scraper and set me to work. I didn't need to move the scraper much as my hand was shaking so violently that the scraper was working away almost involuntarily.

After an hour or so, I was assigned to scrape the ladder and felt more comfortable with the safety cage surrounding me. As I contently scraped paint on the ladder, I suddenly heard a loud thump from within the tank and assumed that a member of crew working inside had dropped a tool. A few minutes following this event two fellows came running up the ladder shouting for me to get out of the way. One was a paramedic dressed in whites. I climbed on down and discovered that one of the other kids on the job had fallen inside the tank when a support rod on which he was

46

sitting had failed. The poor kid had fallen fifty feet to the bottom of the tank and the medic and his fellow workers were trying to stabilize him and extract him from the tank. After about an hour, they finally managed to get the poor bastard out through an access door at the bottom of the water column that is used to pump water into the tank. They had him strapped to an emergency litter; his back was broken. He was heavily sedated and murmuring as he came out, covered with mud and sediment from the tank. He was medivac'd him to Boston in a chopper and I immediately tended my resignation to the boss shortly after he left. The pay was good, but this was long before OHSA and it was obvious that safety was not the uppermost priority for this company. I felt that there was no need for me to risk my life for a summer job. Mark (whose nickname was Nummy) stayed on and later helped paint the Bourne Bridge…AAAGGGHHHH! Not me!. I went home and to my great relief I was informed that a job had opened for me on a Mobil tanker.

A word or two here about *Howdy Beefburgers*, John Adams and Nummy: John Adams who owned *Howdy's* was a very good businessman. In 1962, he realized that the fast food business was in its infancy so he chose to get in early and, to his credit, he made a small fortune. John bought into a new franchise called *Howdy Beefburgers* originally founded by a fellow from Boston named William Rosenberg. Mr. Rosenberg was the genius behind *Dunkin Donuts* which was and still is wildly successful. He began *Howdy Beefbugers* to compete with *McDonalds*, but by 1980, the dye was cast, *McDonalds* won the hamburger fast food race and *Howdy's* folded. There were two *Howdy Beefburgers* stores in New Bedford, one on Cove Road in the south end and one on Purchase St directly next to SMTI.

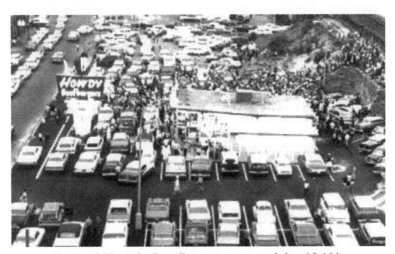

Typical Howdy Beefburger store of the 1960's

John Adams owned the Purchase St store and benefitted from the heavy influx of students at lunch and dinnertime. I started working for him in the summer of 1966 working the fryolator on Friday afternoon. At rush time I was going 500 mph trying to keep up with the orders for fish and chips. I guess I worked out, because John kept me on and after learning to work the order window (where I learned how to make change) I was moved over to the grill. As the weeks wore on I became more experienced with the various aspects of the operation. By December, John offered me the Saturday night manager's position, which I gratefully accepted. John had a few full time employees, but most were "tech"students who worked when they could on weekends and between classes. He must have had 200 guys on the payroll and he was always juggling schedules to cover the floor with workers. I had a more or less regular Saturday night crew, but after working a few weeks as night manager, John introduced me to a new guy that would be starting on Saturdays. The "new guy" was John Mark Treadup, aka Nummy. Nummy was about six feet tall, with a ruddy complexion and was the classic "low talker". He was articulate, but spoke very softly. I liked Nummy as did most of the crew and I think John liked him, because Nummy was so weird. Unlike the rest of us, Nummy attended U Mass

48

Amherst and made it a point to be at *Howdy's* every Saturday night regardless of the weather. To accomplish this, he rode his full-fairing BMW motorcycle from Amherst to New Bedford usually arriving at 4:45 Saturday afternoon to start a 5:00 PM shift. He was a little late during snowstorms, but he would invariably arrive clad in full riding leathers over which he sported an expedition parka and pants with a balaclava hood under his full facemask helmet.

Nummy was a bright fellow and when the store was slow, he would usually become bored leading him to play practical jokes. One of his favorites was stacking all of the empty 4 ft x 4 ft hamburger bun boxes in front of my closed office door without me knowing. I would be absorbed inside the office balancing the night's receipts against the register drawers (had to do this each hour) so I wouldn't notice Nummy's antics. After completing his labors, Nummy would feign that some disaster had occurred in the restaurant and I'd fling open the door and run right into the stacked boxes, throwing them all over the place. My action was then met with hilarious laughter from all of my crew and Nummy. Such was life at Howdy's on Saturday night. Nummy went on to obtain a law degree from the University of Georgia then he came back to New Bedford (he was a true blue New Bedford boy) and hung out his shingle. It was difficult breaking into the law trade in New Bedford (far too many lawyers) so Nummy drove a cab for a number of years until he had to quit, because he kept picking up his clients. He later became successful in politics and eventually was elected as the Bristol County Registrar of Deeds. He and his family still live in New Bedford with their golden retriever named "spot".

After 10:30 on most Saturday nights at *Howdy's* we would have many a wild occurrence when the drunks and partiers would get the munchies and would seek out the famous 15¢ hamburger. The front of the store was about 20 feet high with two service windows and a large glassed-in vestibule to protect the customers from the weather. There were two infrared heaters above each service window, swinging doors at either end of the vestibule and a double sliding glass door in the center.

Before the advent of OSHA, NIOSH and all the other alphabet soup agencies convened to presumable protect Americans from themselves, there generally were no warning stickers on large plate glass panels as there are today. On a chilly December night at about 11:00 PM it was quiet in the store as a car drew up in front of the building. A man exited the car and began walking toward the vestibule slider that was closed due to the cold. He walked briskly up to and then directly through the glass slider which shattered, spilling glass (it wasn't a tempered product in those days) everywhere. A shard came down and inflicted a very nasty cut just above his eye, but thankfully glanced off him and broke on the concrete floor. The man paused and appeared to be stunned for a moment and then completely undeterred he continued walking up to the service window. To the astonishment of the *Howdy's* employee manning the window, the wounded patron calmly ordered two cheeseburgers and a regular coffee. The kid at the window froze, stared at the man, whose face was quite bloody by this point, and after a few moments haltingly called for me to help. I came out of my office, saw the man who, by this time was baffled by the delay, was becoming insistent and demanded his cheeseburgers. I calmly offered him a towel for his face, told the kid to fill the customer's order and then called for an ambulance. The ambulance arrived and treated the man who blithely munched away on his cheeseburgers as the med tech administered first aid. Strangely enough, it appeared that this fellow was sober at the time of this incident. Luckily, he was not badly injured and he didn't sue, but John headed off future problems the very next day by placing *Howdy's* stickers all over the replacement glass sliding door.

Returning to my Mobil Oil Co. adventure,........my trip to New York to join my ship began with suitcase packing which was conducted with Benny hovering over me peppering me with instructions. I was to

2544424

join the *Mobile Fuel* at the dock in Staten Island NY and, as such, I had to take the train the next day from Providence to Penn Station. As with sailing instruction, Benny's method of tutoring me in the mysteries of the 'Big Apple" was much the same as that previously employed to teach me to sail the Distelfink. In his manner of coaching, every move was crucial and a potential life or death situation. I was solemnly instructed that upon my departing the train at Penn Station, I was to walk briskly up the ramp without making eye contact with anyone, especially the vagrants. If they could see that I was new to the city I'd immediately become a potential mark and ultimately a victim (of what?). I'd never been to Manhattan before, and now I was going alone. I was 20 years old, but I'd only been to Boston one or twice, I had walked through South Station once. The most important part of Benny's instructions was that I should act like a local when I dealt with the cab driver. If he detected any weakness or confusion I would be taken for an expensive ride all over the city chewing up whatever cash I possessed. This was well before the days of credit cards and cash was king. I was to hail a cab, briskly open the back door, toss in my bag, climb in and robustly proclaim to the cabbie "SOUTH FERRY!"

All the way to New York I kept going over the instructions in my mind and more than once I murmured the command "South Ferry!" Upon arrival at Penn Station, I detrained, and anxiously walked up the platform, keeping to myself as I walked out to the cabstand. I noticed several vagrants on the way who inspected the newby, but eventually averted their gaze as I walked by. Upon reaching the cabstand, I spotted a vacant cab and held up my right hand in a brisk fashion (as instructed). The cab pulled up, I opened the back door, tossed in my bag, jumped in after it and heartily exclaimed:

"SOUTH STATION!".

As I did this, I suddenly noticed that the cabbie, who had turned around to look at me when I got in, had a very perplexed look on his face as he responded:

"South Station, ..."where the hell is that?"

"Oh God!" I thought,......"NOW I'm dead, I've really screwed up!" He'll take me to Brooklyn or Queens, wherever the hell they were, he'll drive me all over tarnation, and then drop me off at some vacant lot. He'll demand all of my money as cab fare for this abomination. I'll be facing mother stabbers and father rapers, I'll become an instant pauper. I'll be forced to beg on the street for days to scrape together the ferry fare, How will I eat? Where will I sleep? I'll be shamed for the rest of my life,...I'll miss the ship...I'll........."

As I slowly exited this fog of self-pity and recrimination I glanced over at the cabbie who was staring at me, obviously wondering what the hell I was doing, so I gathered myself and meekly proclaimed:
- "Oh, sorry, I meant south ferry"
- "Oh, okay,... no problem" he responded.

We were there in about ten minutes and he charged me five bucks, so much for my father's paranoia.

My experiences onboard the *Mobil Fuel* that summer were very memorable. I met another whole cast of characters like the Bos'n Wally Harmon and the Pumpman Jerry O'Leary. It was a new world and as it unfolded, I became more understanding of my Father's sacrifices for his family. I had more respect for Benny by the end of that summer.

The *SS Mobil Fuel* was a replacement for an older ship of the same name, but of a decidedly different design.

SS Mobil Oil, same class as the Mobil Fuel

Back when the Mobil Oil Co. was called the Sacony Vacuum Co., it established the T2 tanker design prior to WW II and this design became the standard tanker model for many years thereafter. A new design was initiated with the construction of the *SS Mobil Gas* and with it Mobil's new class of tanker ships began. This first ship was followed by others such as the "Fuel", "Oil", "Light", etc. By today's standards these ships would be considered small, even at 210,000 BBLs carrying capacity. All system valves were manual, but the new constant-tension mooring winches were a welcome feature, despite the fact that the inland fleet had them for years. The self-adjusting winches maintained the ship on station during loading and unloading when the ship would rise or fall by twenty or more feet. This was a decided advantage over the old system, where spring lines would need to be constantly attended to and altered manually to adjust for the ships vertical movement. In addition, these same winches made it possible to move the entire ship several feet fore or aft simplifying the job for the Pumpman and Mate when connecting the ship's discharge manifold to its shore side counterpart. There were twenty-four men onboard my ship, but unless you were in or around the crew's mess room, you could prowl the ship all day and seldom see another soul. I could better understand the loneliness of a merchant seaman after that experience. It was even worse for the officers, of which Benny was one, because they could not fraternize with the average crewmen and there were far fewer officers than "ratings" onboard. For reasons of choice rather than rules, off-duty seclusion was common for officers, because they had to maintain discipline and get the job done. Often they were compelled to demand hard sometimes dangerous work from the crew. Consequently, they couldn't compromise their authority by becoming friends with a crewman. I only served on the *Mobil Fuel*, for six weeks, but I garnered quite a few memories from that job. Because of the 1967 Mideast war, we were carrying crude oil from Texas to the refineries in the northeast that year. The Saudis had turned off the crude oil spigot to the US so that the major oil companies were compelled to redirect their ships and carry West Texas crude up north to keep the northern refineries running. Normally the coastal tankers would carry refined product from port to port along the east coast, consequently, they seldom ran "in ballast" with seawater in their tanks. Since we were carrying crude north and no product south, we steamed 'in ballast" with sea water in many of the tanks on the return trip to Texas. This situation offered an opportunity for the captain to order tank cleaning of the empty tanks on each of the southerly trips. The ship held ballast in about half of her tanks and so that she rode high out of the water as we steamed slowly south. The unfilled tanks were then cleaned. Tank cleaning was an onerous job, but paid well for the off watch crew. I was assigned to the 4 to 8 watch, so I was off-watch during the day and as such I qualified for "time and a-half" pay (1.5x my hourly rate) when working on ship's maintenance. This maintenance was always conducted during the daytime and the ship was constantly in need of repair. This is quite normal for any ship, as they all take a beating in the incredibly hostile environment of the sea. As the old saying goes "The only thing a ship does on its own is rust" (Skip Bowen and Twain Braden "In Peril, A Daring Decision, A Captain's Resolve and a Salvage that Made History" Lyons Press, 2003).

Tank cleaning took several days to accomplish and entailed the use of heavy, brass cleaning devices known as "Butterworth machines". At least two or three Butterworth machines were employed on each tank and ran for four or five hours to complete their task. The process consisted of opening inspection ports on decks above the tank and replacing the port cover (a one inch thick steel plate about five inches in diameter) with the Butterworth machine which was invented by Arthur Butterworth in 1923. Each tank had at least six inspection ports at various locations around the tank so that a cleaning machine could be placed at the middle and edges to properly do the job. After placing the machine on the port, one then "dogged down" the

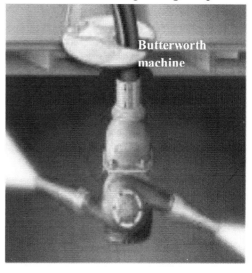

Butterworth machine

machine by bolting it onto the threaded studs permanently welded and protruding from the deck. Next, a high pressure, hot sea water hose was attached to the appropriate port on the Butterworth machine and the water valve was opened. Once activated, the Butterworth machine sprayed high pressure seawater all over the tank from a set of nozzles that spun in rotating circles. After four hours of washing, the machines were removed and the inspection port covers were replaced, then the "fun" began.

Besides inspection ports, each tank had a raised bunker with a six-foot diameter hemispheric steel cap. This bunker was similar to a raised manhole and that was its purpose, i.e. to provide manual access to the tank. Just below the opened hatch was a small platform and from there a ladder (with handles) that led down to the bottom of the tank about forty five feet below deck. This was the very bowels of the ship and it was quite dark, save the light emanating from the open tank hatch above. The work crew consisted of about a dozen men with the Bos'n and the third mate supervising. The Bos'n (Wally) was always in the thick of it working with the guys, while the mate stood on deck peering down into the black void offering encouragement. He was always referred to as "Mr. Mate" or Mr. _____; whatever his last name happened to be.

The work itself was very dirty and hard. The Butterworth machine had washed all of the remaining crude into the tank bilge along with rust, scale, dirt and whatever else happened to be in the tank. Our job was to use brooms and shovels to clean up the remnants, shovel it into buckets which were hoisted up to the deck and thrown overboard. This was long before the existence of the EPA and I'm sure this type of activity is performed very differently today. We'd spend about four hours working at this until the tank was pretty clean and then we'd all retreat to the surface for fresh air. After my first experience with tank cleaning, my clothes were filthy, but I was advised to change my clothes and shower, but to hold onto the "tank cleaning" clothes until the end of the trip as they would be needed for more tank cleaning over the next few days. I followed this advice and held on to the clothes washing them at the end of the trip south. I guess I performed well during the tank cleaning, because the older guys were beginning to treat me more like a human being rather than an insect. I was beginning to become part of the crew by sharing in the hard and dirty work without shirking or complaining; it was a nice feeling.

There were two time-honored methods for ridding your tank clothes of oil. One was to soak your jeans in gasoline on the well deck (a sheltered area under the fore deck, would have been called the f'oc'sle on old ships) then air dry and launder them. The other was to tie the jeans onto a ½" manila line, attach the line to the radiator in your stateroom and throw the jeans overboard from your porthole. Dragging the pants at 15 knots through the Gulf of Mexico and Atlantic Ocean for five days usually did the job of removing the oil. On one particular occasion, I chose to try this alternative method as the former had failed to meet my standards of cleanliness. After we left the Sabine River in Texas, I attached my soiled jeans to a sturdy line acquired from "ships stores" and then over the side they went. I checked on them for first few days to be sure that they hadn't become shark bait, but by the end of the fourth day, I'd forgotten about them. All was going well on the trip back north and we had entered the Delaware River moving up toward Philadelphia and a terminal to discharge our cargo. I was sitting aft with "the guys" around 15:30 enjoying a cup of coffee when the "old man's" voice crackled over the PA system announcing that we would be meeting our tugs at 16:20 and expected to begin docking at 17:00. There was a pause and then he said "Tell Morris to get those *%^%* blue jeans onboard!" I just about fell over backwards in my chair as I became the butt of this apparent joke which lasted for about two or three days. To make matters worse, my watch was just beginning and I had to be present on the bridge with the Captain to raise flags. I was red faced throughout the ordeal, but was finally ordered forward to help with securing the tugboats towing lines. I worked that summer and managed to pay Benny back, I sold the TR3 before I had left for the ship and I'd replaced it with a Volvo 544 sedan. It wasn't as sexy as the TR3 but it was a damn site more reliable and warmer.

During my junior year at SMTI I survived Physical Chemistry and looked forward to working on Cape Cod. I had some high school friends (Dennis and Roger) who were attending Cape Cod Community College (four C's as it was called). I had spent a weekend or two with them at their rented house in Yarmouth. I did this to be with old chums, but also to feel better about the poor socializing options in New Bedford during the winter. Cape Cod in the 1960s was a VERY dismal place in the winter. During the summer, the situation reversed as the population more than doubled with summer vacationers and daytrippers coming over the bridges for some fun in the sun. In addition, there is a huge influx of college students seeking summer employment. In the 1960's most businesses were closed during the winter, there were few department stores and only one movie house in Hyannis. Since all my friends were under the legal drinking age of 21, none could enter the few bars that were open in winter. As a result, on most weekends 4C's students usually went home which made for an even more dismal experience for those few who, with no transportation, were compelled to stay behind. Roger was one of those. Roger had been nicknamed "Goose", because he was a bit flighty and, on one occasion, he remarked to a mutual friend that he had noticed that he was getting a bit forgetful of late, "just like a goose". The friend's retort to Roger was that it appeared he'd confused the goose with the elephant, which is commonly known as the animal that never forgets. To this "Goose" answered, "yeah whatever"; and so, the nickname stuck.

Goose was the ultimate "fall guy", meaning that on many occasions, fate and his unpredictability conspired against him As an example, Goose had been working all winter at the local Stop & Shop to pay for his schooling at 4 C's. Since he worked part time, he never had much money and lived almost exclusively on rice and beans. When school ended, summer jobs were beginning to appear which offered better remuneration than the restocking job at the supermarket. So, with high spirits, Goose quit the supermarket, but after a couple of weeks of job searching, he hadn't landed suitable employment. Finally, he found the right job and worked all week, without pay since it was a common practice in the 1960's to work the first week of a new job without pay to catch up with the pay cycle. It was early spring and like clockwork, all of his roommates who owned vehicles went home for the weekend, leaving Goose alone in the cottage. On Sunday, he was out of money and out of food. He had a dime left to his name and a friend who lived in the next town. As he walked around the deserted streets of Hyannis on a cold, clammy afternoon he had to decide whether to spend the dime on a candy bar or use it to call his friend to borrow some additional money until payday on Monday. He chose the latter and walked over to a payphone, deposited the dime and then he proceeded to dial. Unfortunately, he dialed the Wrong Number! That was Goose.

When school ended that year I moved in with Dennis and his crowd for a week or so to find work for the summer. I bumped around in a few jobs until I ended up with two other SMTI students that I knew from *Howdy's*. John (JT) was a business major and in the winter was a *Howdy's* manager. Geoff (aka Rog, Gator) was a psych major and was part of the crew at *Howdy's*. Both JT and Geoff were no strangers to the Dipper. Geoff and JT rented a two room cottage and invited me to share the place, I got the couch.

Another Goose story is needed here. In the 1960's the rental cottages on the Cape were usually furnished, but nearly all lacked a television. Goose had spent the entire winter without a television and on weekends, as previously detailed, he was often alone with no entertainment. During the week, he and his five roommates would drink beer and play cards, but he dreaded weekends, with its loneliness and boredom. As it transpired, in the early summer, Goose was between rentals and so he moved in with JT, Rog and me in our two and one-half room cottage; Goose got to sleep on the floor. The first Friday after Goose moved in, Geoff was headed home to pick up some personal items and upon hearing Goose's stories about not having viewed TV all winter, Geoff announced to Goose's delight that he would be bringing a 20 inch TV back with him for all of us to enjoy; WHAT A TREAT!

On Saturday, late morning, it was as if nature was joining in Goose's reverie about the TV, the weather was gorgeous! Around 11:00, Geoff pulled up in front of our cottage in his black TR 3 and seated there in the passenger's seat was the TV. Goose was lying on the couch and could clearly see Geoff through the side window, as he proudly announced to Goose that "HIS" TV was on its way! Goose was quivering with anticipation and could scarcely contain himself. The excitement was electric, one could almost hear heart rending violins playing in the background. At last, the long-suffering Goose was about to be reunited with a TV. I can still see the scene as it unfolded in slow motion, Geoff was a big boy (he is about 6'4" tall and weighs around 220 lbs.) and easily hoisted the TV onto his shoulder and as he held several articles of clothing under his opposite arm. He took three steps to the porch, stepped up onto it then briefly fumbled with the clothing as he reached for the screen door to enter the front room. While this was happening, Goose was singing, "I'm going to watch TV, I'm going to watch TV" in an impromptu song of joy. However, as Geoff jostled with the clothing, he lost his grip on the TV which suddenly slipped off his shoulder and fell slowly backwards onto the granite step leading up to the porch. As this transpired, the expression of excitement and anticipation on Goose's face faded and his expression turned at first to shock as the TV slipped and then to horror as he watched it hit the step and finally to unmitigated grief as he realized that once again television entertainment had been denied to him. He rolled over on the couch banging his fists and kicking his feet moaning "No...no....no". After Goose collected himself, we all stood on the porch in shock until Geoff finally dropped his other possessions and scrambled down to the broken TV. The end of the cathode ray tube had borne the brunt of the impact and was broken completely off, now attached to the box by a few wires. Geoff, who was also dumbfounded, repeatedly mumbled something about how "it can be fixed....it can be fixed...right?". We tried to offer some comfort to him and I tried to console Goose, but we were all well aware the TV was way beyond any salvation. After a few minutes of tepid consolation, Geoff realized that the fate of the TV was sealed and brought it inside, propping it up in the corner on a table with artificial flowers on top. The three of us then climbed into Geoff's TR 3 and headed for a package store to locate our "dealer" who was old enough to buy beer for us to use to drown our sorrows.

Through the grapevine Geoff and I found work at a seafood restaurant up the street from our house called "Lobster in the Rough. It was a "fast food" seafood restaurant relying on volume rather than price to make a profit.

The food was good, but simple and there was no shortage of customers. Angie was the no nonsense manager of the place and although she liked a good time, she took no guff from anyone. She was strict, but fair and I think she enjoyed the antics of the teenage and twenty something staff. The kitchen crew was mostly male and always rambunctious. The layout of the kitchen was such that there was a long wall between the kitchen and the front counter right in the middle of this partition was a raised stand. This six-foot square platform held a 100 gallon boiler pot with a hinged lid and was employed to boil lobsters, several dozen at a time. One of the kitchen staff's assignment each evening was to tend this device by adding live lobsters to the pot and then retrieving the cooked ones. Like all jobs in the kitchen, this was a revolving duty. The lobster cook had to wear a white jacket and hat and in the summer with the boiler going, it could be 120 degrees up on that stand. A jar of salt tabs was present on a shelf next to the entrance to the boiler platform to maintain the boiler cook's electrolyte balance since gallons of water were consumed by this person during the course of an evening's work.

The front counter wait staff was composed entirely of college coeds (thank you Lord!) and they were mostly cute for obvious reasons. Weekend warrior husbands could usually be convinced to purchase more food than their family needed by these cute coquettes which, in turn, was very good for business. The coeds waited on the customers from the front order counter and were usually tipped very well for their service. On the kitchen side was a second counter with a three-foot vertical slot between the two where the waitresses placed their orders and the kitchen "waiters" assembled the cooked order for the waitresses. The kitchen was a cacophony of noise and appeared to be bedlam, but, in fact was well organized and the system worked very well. All menu items were assigned a number and upon receiving a dinner order form a waitress, the kitchen waiters would yell out the order number and quantity to each cook station where the order was repeated back to the wait staff. We served about 2000 people on an average night. It was crazy, but a lot of fun.

Here's a couple of fond memories: The guy that was working the lobster boiler had a panoramic view of the dining room whereas the rest of us had to peer through the vertical counter slot to catch a view of any of the customers. When the boiler man saw a cute babe, he'd yell out "HOGUY" to the whole kitchen and all the guys in the kitchen would run to the slot at the kitchen wait counter to get a view. The "Rough" had been in business for about twenty years and this had become one of the "traditions" of the place. This "HOGUY" was an interesting outburst considering that the person doing the yelling was informing the rest of us about a girl; one would logically think that the outburst should have been Ho Girl! I guess it was meant to be Ho Guys, but after our initiation to the "Rough" culture, anytime we saw a cute girl, at the beach or on the street, we "Rough" veterans refer to them as HOGUYS. Angie would tolerate these interruptions so long as they didn't occur too often and didn't greatly disrupt the work flow in the kitchen. On occasion, she would simply clap her hands and the guys would get the message and immediately get back to their stations.

Another memory of the Rough was the antics of Jack Klim washing dishes by the back door at the far south end of the kitchen. The kitchen was about 75 feet long with the walk in cooler at the north end and the pot washing station down south. All of the ovens, fryolators and other "hot" equipment were clustered in the center with a huge metal hood over the area connected to large exhaust fans on the roof. This center work area had passageways on four sides. Everyone in the crew had to "pull" pot washing duty at least once a week. Jack was one of the boiler men and loved the action up front. He hated pot washing and his lack of enthusiasm was always evident as piles of stainless steel pots built up on the floor surrounding him. On this particular night the climate in the kitchen was hot and humid causing Jack to sweat profusely. He became more and more depressed as he labored away over the huge institutional kitchen sinks. I was working the "gopher" (go for) station which meant that I was charged with the responsibility of supplying all of the kitchen work stations with prepared food from the walk in and "putting out fires" as they occurred. It was a stimulating job, because you had to be everywhere at once throughout the evening; I loved being the gopher.

At one point, I was required to retrieve a stainless steel insert (about 1 gallon cylinder) of chopped celery for a new batch of lobster salad that was being prepared. I delivered the full container, took the empty one and I headed back towards the walk in. I stopped at the north end of the passageway and briefly glanced at Klim at the south end hunched over a huge wash sink, elbow deep in wash water, totally depressed and lost in his thoughts. I then bowled the container down at Jack who was waist deep in surrounding, stacked metal kitchen hardware. As I let her go I yelled out "Comin' Down!" and the container flew down the aisle, but Jack didn't hear my warning and the container hit the base of that pile of hardware which sent pots and pans flying all over hell and tarnation. It literally scared the hell out of Jack who jumped about three feet. He broke out of his stupor and proceeded to yell a string of four-letter expletives at me, but he remained alert for the rest of the night not knowing when the next one would be comin' down.

The great thing about working at the "Rough" was that, as

employees, we were eligible for two meals a day….anything on the menu, with the exception of whole lobster. This meant that after rent and gasoline, we could spend the rest of our income on beer! We also liked the girls at the "Rough", but fraternization was greatly discouraged. Angie did not want any love triangles to develop that could complicate or mess up kitchen production. Generally, Angie's rule was closely adhered to and in rare instances when love blossomed, the affair was kept as clandestine as possible.

Geoff and I became very friendly with most of crew, but of these, one group was particularly remarkable. They were part of a house populated with guys from Stoughton, Mass. and we had some great times with them that summer. The most conspicuous members of this group were Jack Klim, John Clarke and Bill Cougart. They were of the same age were enrolled in colleges in the Boston area. Jack was anointed with the sobriquet "clam", because of his uncanny resemblance to the clam characters in the BC cartoon strip. Jack had an overhanging brow and small eyes, these beady eyes were set back behind his brow which was similar to the clam characters who looked out with their beady eyes from between two partially opened shells. "Clarkey" and "Cougart" were a couple of fun-loving cut ups and all together it was a house full of "wild and crazy guys". They were all Catholic (as was I) and no matter the degree of debauchery that occurred on Saturday night, without fail, they were all at Mass on Sunday morning. This remarkably religious behavior came from a group of guys who, when the first awoke, greeted each morning with two words….Fuck Off! I think that this had to do with their hangover, lack of sleep and the work imperative. At the time, Clarkie worked for a construction company and had to be on the job by 07:30. But his attitude was work be damned and he'd party hardy with the rest of us till one AM (we didn't start work till noon or four). Without fail when quizzed about work the next day he would invariably respond with "it's okay, …I don't have to get up till early". We all adopted this phrase and used it unsparingly when the hour got late at wild parties that summer.

It was with a heavy heart that we ended that summer and headed back to school after Labor Day. The fun was over, now it was back to the daily grind of college and studying.

In my senior year I applied to several graduate schools to major in Biochemistry. I gained acceptance to two and of these and chose to attend the University of Vermont. After graduation from SMTI in June, I headed back to Cape Cod for another summer of fun before knuckling down to work at graduate school. In the summer of 1969, I chose to room with Goose and one of his friends named Mo. We rented an outbuilding located at the end of a driveway in Hyannis on the property of a nice, but rather stern fellow. Our new landlord laid down the law concerning parties and female friends. Women were prohibited from staying overnight and that was final. He informed us that he had teenagers in his family (living about 50 feet away) and he would not tolerate any hanky panky or unacceptable behavior. We agreed and promised that we would behave. What kind of promise was that from three wild animals from New Bedford?

We minded our manners for the first couple of weeks, but Goose had a long-term girlfriend who lived in town, I met a girl who became an amorous acquaintance and Mo had a long string of women arriving on a regular basis. We did abide by the "party' prohibition rule and the only loud music we generated was from the three of us having a few beers on Friday before heading out (ala Dipper) for other diversions. We were all working long hours which didn't allow much time for hosting parties. Surprisingly, halfway through the summer the landlord approached us one afternoon as we stood in the driveway and he complimented us for being so quiet up to that point and with a wink and a nod mentioned (in passing) the ladies that he'd noticed leaving in the morning. I guess he had been a "kid" once as well and was now living vicariously.

The summer of 1969, I graduated from college and an American stepped foot on the moon. I distinctly remember that event as I was riding a bicycle on Rte 28 toward the pizza joint where Goose worked to speak with him about our impending summer's end. Neil Armstrong had walked on the moon, probably the defining event of the decade, but it had very little bearing on me at this stage in my life. Another equally noteworthy event that summer occurred on Max Yasgur's farm in White Lake, New York. It was called Woodstock "An Aquarian Exposition: 3 Days of Peace & Music" and it siphoned off the youth population of Cape Cod. It seemed that all of the college students on the Cape had heard about this rock & roll concert and wanted to be part of it, so they left en masse. There were jobs available all over the Cape in restaurants and bars and the wages were high, supply and demand was working. I took a job at the Howard Johnson's restaurant in Hyannis washing dishes for the unheard salary of $5 per hour! I needed cash on that final weekend before heading off to Vermont to begin my graduate school.

With the end of summer I packed up and headed for Burlington, Vermont. I settled in an apartment that my girlfriend had helped me find on a scouting expedition several weeks before. My mom provided me with some furniture and other goods to make the apartment a home; I very much appreciated her efforts. After a few weeks in school, the novelty of graduate school wore off finding me once again submersed in the dry, monotonous world of academics. My situation caused me to reconsider the advice provided me by an old friend of my mother's. Miss Hastings had been an educator for more than fifty years and was a frequent holiday guest at my parent's house. At Thanksgiving dinner in 1968 as I prepared for graduate school, Miss Hastings had recommended that I take a year or so off to get away from the pedagogic discipline of the university. At the time the Viet Nam war was raging, but I had no problems with the draft because of my significant hearing loss (I was 4-F). Over time, it appeared that she knew me better than I knew myself. This was true because, by January of 1970, I discovered that I didn't like Burlington or the University or Biochemistry or the Biochemistry Department. So, in May of 1970, I quit the program, loaded up my stuff in my Volvo and headed back to Fairhaven.

This was a personal defeat, but when I arrived home, my mother was welcoming, but Benny acted as though I had personally insulted him. While I had been at UVM, he was bragging to all who would listen that his son was going to be a PhD and now he apparently felt as though I had let him down. It seemed to be lost on him that he hadn't offered me any financial, moral or spiritual assistance while I was at grad school. I had made my decision to apply for acceptance, I had paid for the application as well as my apartment and moving expenses and I was supported by a university stipend. He had no part in any of this, but he was angry, because I had decided to drop out. Well…..EXCUSE ME! Where did he figure into all of this? In the end, I'll give him this, he at least allowed me to live at home for three months until I could get back on my feet and move back to the Cape. This is what I did at the earliest possible moment.

In early May and I managed to secure a job in a restaurant called "The Forge and Sea" which was owned by the same group that owned the "Rough". The Forge (as it was called) was a far more upscale venue than the "Rough", but offered a similar menu. I lost my Volvo 544 on Route 6 in Wareham to a rear end collision while traveling to my new cottage, so I spent the summer without a car. Jack Klim joined me at the Forge, but Geoff moved onto to teaching tennis at the Bass River Tennis Club. Geoff was a very good tennis player (and still is) and had been nationally ranked as a small college player while SMTI. Although he took his tennis seriously, he took partying more seriously, so his stories about tournament play were nothing short of hilarious.

He once recounted how his coach would push the team relentlessly during the regular season to ensure that they would be eligible for the post-season small college tournament in Kansas City, Missouri. His coach was also a party animal, but he had an overbearing wife who cramped his style. As a result, once the team was safely in KC, the coach (freed of his wife) would begin partying with his tennis buddies, leaving the team to fend for themselves in the tournament. On one occasion, Geoff and his doubles partner were the envy of two other more promising doubles partners, because they were knew where the great parties were. Geoff had been up late raising hell the night before his match and because he and his partner were not seeded very high, this match would normally be overlooked by most of the spectators. However, the aforementioned promising doubles team was in attendance at Geoff's match (hoping to witness a screwup) and this attracted many spectators who wrongly concluded that Geoff and his partner might be a dark horse. Geoff was suffering in the heat with a terrific hangover and pleaded with his partner to keep the ball in the front court. Well, as luck would have it, one serve got past the front court and Geoff moved into position to return it. At this point in the story he always precluded the climax by stating that in national tournament play, one never misses the ball. So, as he stepped forward under the crushing weight of his hangover, the heat and humidity he swung his racket to return the serve and, of course,.......he missed the ball. There was a hush in the crowd, with the exception of one person who was applauding and cheering like a madman in celebration of Geoff's incredibly embarrassing moment. That person was his coach! He was still in party mode from the previous night.

On the Cape in the summer of 1970, Geoff, several other New Bedfordites and I shared a rented house in Yarmouth and had quite a time. Another summer on the Cape, but it was getting time to buckle down. In the fall of 1970, I managed to secure a job as a clinical lab technician at Cape Cod hospital in Hyannis. I worked at this for about a year and I was able to afford to buy a 1962 Ford Econoline van for transportation. It was not in very good shape, but it was cheap. A high school chum, Bob Jones, outfitted the inside with an elevated bed, cabinets and two louvered windows. I paneled the inside and it became a camper or passion pit....your choice.

I worked diligently at Cape Cod Hospital, but I wanted to do chemistry research, so I left the Cape in the winter of 1971 for Boston where I managed to secure employment as a research assistant at Children's Hospital.

Over the course of two years and several jobs, I finally landed a job that appeared to have a future.

~ *Chapter 4* ~

The road back to boating

As my life in Boston unfolded, I bumped around from job to job for six months and then ended up as a field/lab technician at a new engineering company in Winchester, MA, a suburb of Boston. The company was called Geotechnical Engineers Inc. or GEI for short. Unbeknownst to me at the time, this proved to be the beginning of my reentry to the sailing life.

GEI was an interesting company with remarkable people and a fascinating origin. Like many of the technical and engineering firms in greater Boston, university academics often founded new companies. By contrast; however, GEI was composed of an entire engineering department from Harvard University. My understanding of how this came to be was that Harvard University made a decision in the late 1960s that the Soil Mechanics Department was superfluous and thereby scheduled it to be closed. In response, the faculty of the department (who were also consulting engineers) raised some capital, bought all of the department's equipment at a discount and started GEI. There were five principals in the company, four of whom were PhDs and one with a Masters Degree. The partner with the MS was not nearly as talented as the others, and it was rumored that his wealthy spouse supplied most of the capital to get the business started and he came along with the deal.

The company was founded in 1970 and did quite well as its opening coincided with the rise of the nuclear power plant industry. Upon my hiring in 1971, GEI was in the process of a rapid expansion with many projects underway simultaneously. Nuclear plants were under construction around the country and all of them required stable foundations that could withstand severe earthquakes. The utility companies did not wish to jeopardize the integrity of the nuclear containment vessel in the event of an earthquake at a plant's location. Geologic faults were better understood as begin the focal point of earthquakes following the establishment of modern plate tectonic theory by 1971. Acceptance of this concept led to field researchers discovering new geologic faults throughout the country raising the possibility of earthquakes in locales hitherto considered immune from such events. Nukes were under consideration for construction throughout the country, so utilities and the federal government became very concerned about the stability of the ground on which these plants were to be sited. This proved to be a boon to GEI, because their specialty was soil mechanics and foundation design which were closely connected. One could not build a stable foundation without first understanding the characteristics of the soil and rock beneath and around that foundation.

The principals of GEI had been close associates of the chairman of the Harvard Soil Mechanics Department; Arthur Casagrande. Casagrande was an Austrian civil engineer and a disciple of Karl Terzaghi, (another Austrian) the father of soil mechanics. Terzaghi had a major impact on the emerging field of soil mechanics around 1924 while working at Bogazici University in Istanbul. While there, he invented the necessary instruments and devised the basic concepts that led to his ultimate publication *Magnum Opus*, *Erdbaumechanik* which revolutionized the field of Soil Mechanics to great acclaim. This book and its basic concepts became the founding principles of Soil Mechanics. Terzaghi accepted a teaching post at MIT in 1925 where he met Casagrande who became Terzaghi's personal assistant. During his time with Terzaghi, Casagrande also invented and improved the equipment used for testing soils and perfected theories that helped further advance the science of soil mechanics. Casagrande eventually was also offered a post at Harvard University in 1932 where he was promoted to the newly formed chair of soil mechanics and foundation engineering in 1946. This was the pedigree of the Principals at GEI.

Of the five Principals at the firm, my favorite was Gonzalo Castro. Gonzalo was from Chile and he was very quick witted and bright. He somewhat reminded me of Ricky Ricardo to the extent that he had jet black hair and spoke quickly with a moderate Spanish accent. He was an expert at the one lab tests that set GEI apart from all of the other foundation engineering firms. This test was the cyclic load traixial test which simulated the effects of an earthquake on a column of soil. GEI had originally developed the test apparatus, but now the basic device has been adopted by a number of engineering firms and an ASTM procedure has been developed for this test. A modern cyclic load test apparatus is shown below.

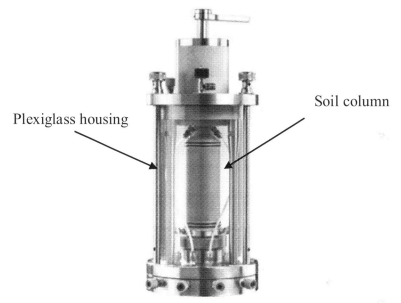

Plexiglass housing

Soil column

Cycle load traixial test apparatus

In our lab at GEI, the test soil column was first obtained in the field at the construction site using a drilling rig to drive a 4 foot long four-inch diameter steel tube into the soil to a specified depth. This "undisturbed" soil sample tube was then transported back to our lab and a six-inch section of the tube was cut for testing using a tube cutter. We then employed an extruder to push the select soil column out of the tube and into a cylindrical rubber membrane. While this procedure was executed, the soil sample itself was held under vacuum to maintain the soil structure. The rubber enclosed soil column was then transferred to the test apparatus and backfilled with water. The test housing itself was then filled with water and subsequently pressurized with compressed air to simulate the pressure of the surrounding soil (same hydrostatic pressure that would be experienced at the depth of the soil sample). Inside the apparatus, the soil sample had two porous metal discs at each end and these were connected to the outside world through the top and bottom of the test housing with stainless steel rods. The rods floated within rubber O-rings that allowed the rods to move, while preventing leakage of water from the test housing. The top rod was attached to a pneumatic solenoid valve that alternatively compressed and then tensed (stretched) the soil sample. The bottom rod was connected to a load cell that recorded the load (or lack thereof) on the sample. Distance transducers were also connected to the top rod and these measured the horizontal travel of the sample as it was loaded in a cyclic manner. The transducers and load cell produced voltages during the course of the test which were recorded versus time on a four channel strip chart recorder that employed electro-sensitive paper. The test cell was fitted atop a large green cyclic load machine powered with compressed air containing electronic solenoid valves that alternatively compressed and then stretched the sample. Opening of closing of the solenoid produced a very audible click, this occurred every second during the course of a test. The sample chamber was held in place in a threaded rod cross bar with a large steel cross beam at the top. The whole thing was quite impressive and when it was running it looked like something from a Buck Rogers serial.

We ran these tests on a daily basis sometimes two or three a day. They were very expensive tests to perform and the Principals loved to see the old green machine banging away. I was one of select few who was adequately trained to conduct this test and when thus engaged, without fail, Gonzalo would come from his office down the hall to observe. He would always say to me "Scutt", (he always called me that) "Please tell me when you're going to start the cyclic load test." So when the time came, I'd call him on the house phone and he would hustle (Gonzalo never walked) down to the lab and off we would go. The test was quite interesting watch. At the beginning, the sample would usually sit quite still as the valves clicked on and off loading and then stretching the column. The strip chart would be spewing out paper and all of the indicator needles on the recorder would move only slightly as the test first began. Finally, depending on the relative strength of the soil column, the recorder indicator needles would begin to increase their movement across the recorder paper as the soil pores in the test sample began to fail.

Once this phenomenon began, the soil column failure would escalate quite rapidly and with loud clicking in the background, we'd usually speed up the paper flow so that small changes in the sensor readings could be more easily detected during later analysis. As the needles would begin flying back and forth across the chart paper, it would be rapidly spilling out of the recorder and building up in a pile on the lab floor. If the sample failed catastrophically a severe sample necking would begin to occur at some region of particular weakness in the column. All through the test Gonzalo was watching the sample intently and when the necking occurred, without fail he would always exclaim "FÃNTÃSTIC!" He must have witnessed hundreds of these tests while I was at GEI and he always expressed amazement with the outcome; he was one who was really in love with his work.

Besides lab work, I also worked in the field and on occasion I would supervise drill rig crews in the process of obtaining undisturbed soil samples that we needed for our work in the lab. This fieldwork would allow me to charge expenses and overtime which could be as much as twice my hourly rate. Since I was single, I was always ready to work overtime whereas the married fellas at GEI were less interested in spending time away from home. As a result, I made a fair amount of money in my first year at GEI, which was burning a hole in my pocket, so I concluded that I was interested in using that cash to buy a sailboat. I was making enough money to afford to buy one on installments, but I did not have sufficient cash on hand to buy one outright.

I considered obtaining a boat loan from a bank, but then decided to approach my brother Butch who, at the time, was working in the maintenance department at Massachusetts Maritime Academy in Bourne.

After High School, Butch worked for a time at a local bank thanks to the efforts of our Grandfather Ben who was employed as a bank security guard. Although the teller job had a future, Butch was restless so he joined the US Air Force. He was stationed in California for a year before he volunteered for a tour of duty in Da Nang, RVN. Before leaving, he married Gwen who was from San Bernadino, CA. During his Vietnam tour, Butch worked as an emergency room medic at the Da Nang base hospital and survived the 1968 Tet Offensive. Upon returning to the states, Butch was mustered out and gathered his wife and one-year old baby girl Gale and headed back to Massachusetts in a VW beetle. He managed to land a job through a family friend who was head of maintenance at MMA. Butch and Gwen had a few bucks in the bank so I proffered that I would rather pay interest to them than to the bank. They agreed to a $1500 loan for nine months at the prevailing interest rate and we drew up a promissory note.

Butch was a wonderful brother and we had many good times together. He was a loyal, attentive, good-natured fellow and he was a better man than me. He volunteered to serve in Vietnam and although he was not in combat, he treated those who had been in the first hour or so after they had been medevac'd from the fighting. He served in the trauma unit at the huge US hospital in Da Nang and this had a lasting effect on him. He saw many a young man of his age or younger die from wounds, sometimes in his arms as he tried to comfort them when they breathed their last breath in this world. Although he didn't actually fire a weapon in anger, he did live through the Tet Offensive which was a major action in and around Da Nang. His hooch was rocketed more than once during that fighting and he was lucky to have survived.

Butch and I had our differences over the politics of the war, but we remained close over the years. Tragically, my brother developed pancreatic cancer in 1998 and passed away eight months later; he was only 52 years old. He was greatly loved and is deeply missed.

~ *Chapter 5* ~

Whiskers

I found the boat I wanted in Swampscot, Mass. offered for sale at $1500. I haggled a bit with the owner over the price and managed to convince him to deliver the boat to Fairhaven as part of the deal. It was a 19-foot Rhodes daysailer of which I had read about and seemed like the perfect starter boat. Being a Philip Rhodes design it was sturdy and sea kindly which were qualities that would be greatly appreciated in the near future. At the time Rhodes 19s were being built by the O'Day Boat Co. in Fall River MA. Here's the specifications and the boat's profile.

"Whiskers
Overall length 19'2" Waterline length 17'9" Beam 7' Draft 3'3" Sail Area
175 Weight 1325

As shown in these pictures, the boat had a fixed iron keel with a lead bulb at the bottom. The boat I bought that had been built in the mid-

1960s, but she was in reasonably good shape despite the fact that the previous owner had raced her. She had a mainsail and jib, but no spinnaker. Since she was an older boat, she had a sealed flotation bulkhead far up in the bow. As a result, there was quite a bit of room in the cuddy cabin for shelter from the weather which would play to my advantage later in the season. My high school chum Dennis, who was rooming with me at the time, agreed to help me escort the boat down to Fairhaven to Murach's boatyard on delivery day in February. We linked up with the boat and the old owner at the junction of Rte 128 and Rte 24 and led him south to Fairhaven. Upon arrival, the boat, sitting on its cradle, was unloaded from the trailer after which I paid the old owner and took possession. Since it was a cold, grey day, Dennis and I didn't hang around long after the delivery, but instead repaired to a local "watering hole" to toast the new boat.

I spent the next few weekends buying and assembling new equipment and settling in with my new toy. I purchased a bilge pump, anchor and rode, boat horn, and a British Seagull 3 HP outboard motor.

The classic 2-cycle 3 HP British Seagull Outboard Motor

I did some research before buying this machine and found that these outboards are simple, (DUH! look at the picture) rugged outboard motors and, as such, are reliable and trustworthy……*Remember those words*. In addition, they're quite light and easy to carry. As I was to discover, these claims assume that one has an intimate knowledge of the product, because as I discovered later, the Seagull was a somewhat temperamental beast. But, until the winter ice broke up in the harbor, this "egg beater" would have to sit in storage.

Spring finally arrived in early April and the harbor ice had melted sufficiently to allow Leo Murach to launch my Rhodes which I chose to call *"Whiskers",* because I was now sporting a full beard. Mine was the first boat in and I believe that Leo was happy to be rid of me as I bugged him every Saturday with a phone call to see if he was ready to launch me. Once again, Dennis came through and agreed to help me get the boat to a mooring just south of the Fairhaven, New Bedford bridge. The plan was to motor over to a granite pier that jutted out about 300 yards into the harbor so that the water depth would allow us to tie up alongside to step the mast. In theory, the operative concept was to lift the mast to helping hands up on the pier, from whence the participants would next step the mast through the opening in the cuddy cabin and subsequently secure the standing rigging. I had also contacted Geoff who agreed to be the helping hands up on the pier. Mind you, I and "my crew" had never stepped a mast on a Rhodes 19 or any other boat of comparable size to that juncture.

Dennis and I got the Seagull started (first time) and off we went motoring under the bridge with the mast laid down on deck to the appointed pier that stood about 50 yards south of the bridge. We rendezvoused with Geoff, tied up, passed the mast up onto the pier and managed to get it seated in the boat with standing gear attached; ……so far so good. Fortunately, the weather to this point on this morning was cooperating with little wind and moderate temperatures (in the low fifties). The mooring that I had chosen was about 300 yards south of the pier and I was ready with a bow line to attach when we arrived at the mooring. I chose not to bend on the main'sal as we had a short distance to cover and I was planning only to moor the boat on this day, not sail her, as yet. I did;

however, bend on the jib, which amounted to a handkerchief on this ¾ fractionally rigged sloop.

Once the mast was stepped and the boat was ready to move, the sou'westerly began to fill in at about 4-5 knots. No problem, we had our outboard and we would soon be underway. To transport us from the boat to shore after we moored her I had borrowed a one and a half man dinghy from Leo, it was very lightly built. It must be mentioned that the Seagull had no neutral gear once she was started off you went, so at the appropriate time, I signaled Geoff to let us go and throw the bow line to Dennis. I then coiled the starter cord around the head of the Seagull and gave a pull.

One other aspect of this outboard that should be known is that to choke it, one must engage a very simple plastic plate that pivoted back and forth on a single mounting point. To choke the engine, one flips the plate into a slot on the external carburetor which limits air flow and makes the fuel mixture rich. After starting, one **MUST** disengage the choke or the engine will flood and there will be the devil to pay to get it going again. I was blissfully unaware of all these details as we began our initial sojourn in *Whiskers* to the mooring. Before I stated it, I had choked the engine and then disengaged the choke, but in haste, I inadvertently flipped the damned thing back into the slot and didn't notice. Another salient characteristic of this engine was that it vibrated violently when running and as such the choke would often self-engage as a result of the vibration....one needed to be vigilant about the damned choke. The vibration was part of yet another charming attribute of the Seagull, it is extremely noisy.

We commenced toward the mooring lampooning waving gestures at Geoff as though we were leaving on a transatlantic voyage. All of this foolishness transpired amid the comforting racket emanating from the Seagull as we chugged along on our way to the mooring. Then, without warning, it happened......SILENCE! As continued gliding forward at an alarming decelerating pace, I suddenly noticed the sound of the wind as it whistled through the standing rigging, "I shouldn't be hearing this", I thought. Dennis looked at me in bewilderment as I exclaimed "OH SHIT!" and quickly attended to the Seagull. As I did, I discovered the engaged choke and once again exclaimed "OH SHIT!"...but all too late, she was flooded. I disengaged the choke, circled the starter cord around the flywheel head and pulled...nothing, so I did again....and again... and again....nothing. This would seem to be an appropriate time and at the same general location for Charlie Mitchell's mantra "GOD DAMNED MACHINE!

While these events proceed, the developing sou'westerly began to blow us relentlessly back toward the bridge. An additional complication involved the tide, which, at the time, was in, and as a result, the clearance at our portion of the bridge was about 11 feet. With the mast stepped, we required some 27 feet of clearance. As they say, "baseball is a game of inches", but this sure as hell wasn't baseball. While I was completely engrossed in trying to get the engine restarted, Dennis suddenly shouted "THE BRIDGE!" During my efforts we had drifted back past the granite pier (and Geoff, who was staring at us in disbelief) and we were now a mere 30 yards from the bridge. As predicament became clear, I dropped the starter cord on the floorboards and rushed forward to raise the jib, hoping to save the day and move us away from imminent danger. With the jib set, I attempted to tack away from the impending calamity, but she was sluggish and wouldn't answer her helm; we made some headway and then began drifting backwards once again toward certain doom. Dennis looked at me again as if to say, "Now what?" I realized that our only hope was to tow the boat back to the pier and once docked, we could get a plan together. You may ask why I did not anchor? Well, I was a neophyte in panic mode and this just didn't occur to me at the time.

I now realized that I had to get into the dinghy and tow the boat back to the pier, so I very quickly apprised Dennis of this plan and then pulled the dinghy up from astern and got in. I let go the dinghy painter and rowed to the bow of the sailboat. We were now about 5 yards from the bridge and rapidly closing. Dennis was at the bow and he passed the bowline to me which I grasped and then looked frantically for something to attach it to; no luck. We continued to drift and I couldn't tie the line to the dinghy because there were no cleats, I couldn't hold it and simultaneously row and there was no time to tie the line around my waist, so I did the only thing that I could, I put the line BETWEEN MY TEETH! Now, firmly attached to the sailboat, I "laid into it" and began pulling us away from the bridge and shear catastrophe. I rowed like a madman and eventually made headway toward the granite pier. While this drama unfolded, Geoff was in stitches on the pier, he couldn't believe that my teeth were holding. Dennis just sat there on the fore deck staring at me in disbelief. When we arrived at the pier Geoff muttered something about the obligation I now owed my dentist.

We managed to secure the Rhodes to the pier after which I bent on the main'sal and Dennis and I sailed her to the mooring with me cursing the Seagull all the way. Safely attached to the mooring, I removed the sails and the outboard and ferried the stuff ashore, then retrieved Dennis and we headed back to my parents house on Cherry St. I was cursing the damned Seagull all the way. Once we arrived, I lugged the "beast" down to the basement, placed it in one of the soapstone laundry sinks and then filled the sink with water. It just so happened on

> **"The infamous Cultivator Shoal, local tales of it persist as a haven for drunkards, whores, brawlers, reprobates, smack dealers, knife wielders, thieves, con men and riff-raff"** (*and my Uncle Eddie!*)
> -*Rose Alley Ale House Website.*
>
> Most of the fish boats in New Bedford in the 1950s-80s paid off their crew at the Cultivator and other waterfront bars.

this particular evening that my Uncle Eddie had stopped by to "see his sistah" as he called his visits. Eddy had just finished a fishing trip and after leaving the boat and was a bit tipsy following his visit to the "Cultivator" where he had been paid off for the trip. Recall that Eddie was a "marine engineer" or at least he served as one on fish boats, so I, of course, sought his counsel in dealing with this recalcitrant piece of marine propulsion. Uncle Eddie made a valiant effort at resolving my problems, but after 15 minutes he slurred a condemnation of British engineering common to many Anglophobe American mechanics "God damned limey outboards" (my sentiments about the thing hadn't included that one…thanks Uncle Eddie!) and stormed off upstairs for another beer. Closely consulting the manual, Dennis and I played with the thing, for an hour or so and finally got it going. I had learned my lesson….DON'T FLOOD IT!

Following my initial introduction to the peculiarities of the Rhodes 19 and the British Seagull outboard motor, and having "cheated death" I was a bit gun-shy about getting back onboard and sailing. In much the same manner as one being thrown from a horse, I felt I had evaded a disaster, the boat was safe on the mooring and I was safe onshore, so why tempt fate yet again. However, I screwed up my courage and set out once again the next weekend to sail her single-handed. This adventure ended almost in the same manner as the last one when I fetched up on the north side of Pope's Island in a building afternoon breeze with no concept of what the hell I was doing. Luckily the water was deep and I didn't ground out, but who was there to welcome me, none other than Geoff who just happened to be driving across the Fairhaven New Bedford bridge and saw a small sailboat in apparent trouble headed for the backside of Pope's Island. As I was fending *Whiskers* off the bulkhead suddenly Geoff appeared and his first words to me were "Now what?" I tried to explain what had occurred and his only response was "ANTICIPATE MORRIS!" Now, Geoff was not a sailor, he was a Psychologist, but I guess his training offered up a universal observation, to wit, in any endeavor, one must anticipate problems before they occur if one is to avoid disaster; I took this to heart.

Having "wet my feet" with my first real sailing experiences, I rented a mooring from "The Outdoorsman" on the south side of the bridge for the month of April and secured *Whiskers* to it before I headed off for a business road trip to North Carolina. GEI had been hired to obtain soil core samples from a potential nuke site near Wilmington, NC and I was assigned to help with acquiring the samples and transporting them back to the lab at GEI. The client planned to build a nuke at the site and although Wilmington and its environs are part of the Piedmont coastal plane where earthquakes were as rare as hen's teeth, an entire assortment of lab tests were on order to ensure the safety of this site. My job was to oversee the site drilling to ensure that the samples were representative of the overburden (soil) and that these undisturbed samples were properly stored and transported.

In mid April, I flew into Wilmington, rented a station wagon and found a motel room in town. The proposed construction site was located about 30 miles outside of Wilmington which, in North Carolina in 1974, amounted to "the boonies". I linked up with the field people of the utility company (I think it was Southern Power) on day two. I met them at a general store on a dirt road near the site, so they could escort me to the drill rig. There were no cell phones in 1974, so the pay phone at the general store would be the field com-link to my colleagues at GEI. The general store was a quintessential rural southern general store, one pay phone, mounted on the back wall, no air conditioning, double winging screen doors at the entrance and the store was crammed with goods, with a large refrigerated soda cooler next to the main counter. You know the type of which I write, it was the size of today's "smart cart automobile" and mounted on four stout legs with a huge refrigerator unit situated underneath.

There was a levered top and the thing was filled with water that was chilled by the "gigawatt"-consuming refrigeration unit underneath that was used to keep the bottles of soda ice cold.

As with most rural general stores in the south during this era, the "menu de choix" was a "whoopee pie" and an RC cola. And, on sultry mid-April days, both sold like hot cakes. Consequently, at most times of the day, there was, invariably, a host of local teenagers hanging around the RC cooler shooting the breeze regarding local gossip; the store was the social center of this rural community. During my two weeks in North Carolina, I made many trips to the store to call the office for advice, so I became well acquainted with locals and them with me.

So here I was, the sole representative of GEI at this muti-million dollar work site and I had no formal training in geology. Despite this, my boss entrusted me with the responsibility of ensuring that we obtained representative soil samples for appropriate testing to determine if this site was acceptable for a nuke plant. This was typical of the pressure of the times, to get sites approved and nuke plants built. Even so, in my case, there was a great deal of leeway in deciding which samples to procure, since many cores needed to be obtained and much data needed to be generated for each site. This would yield a broad cross-section of the site, highly desirable for the foundation design engineers. Consequently, in the end, so long as I followed instructions and packed the samples correctly, I would execute my job as intended. All through this two-week period, I couldn't get my thoughts away from my new "girlfriend" *Whiskers*. I day dreamed about imaginary sailing trips across Buzzards Bay (I had, as yet, never been across the bay) and made mental notes of which gear to take, how to handle emergencies, etc. The end of this job couldn't come soon enough for me.

During this project, I was first exposed to the laid-back work ethic of the southerner and could not comprehend how anything of substance could be accomplished with this attitude. By contrast, my southern professional counterparts were constantly amazed at the level of my achievements during a work shift and considered me to be too much of an "eager beaver". One particular incident stands out clearly. The drill rig got hung up as we were attempting to retrieve an undisturbed sample for triaxial testing and a decision was needed about clearing the rig in order to obtain the sample. The concern was that in the process of freeing the rig we would damage the sample and it would not be considered "undisturbed". I needed to contact Gonzalo to obtain some advice, so we shut down the rig and I trundled off up the road, five mile or so to the store to make the call. At this juncture I should reiterate that I'm legally deaf, but, my handicap is somewhat remedied by a behind-the-ear hearing aid.

In 1974, my aid was not very sophisticated and did not include an inductive microphone that can connect one's aid directly to a telephone earpiece virtually eliminating any background noise. Consequently, when using this older device, I was required to place the telephone receiver next to the hearing aid microphone to listen to my conversant, during which time the aid would also pick up all the background noise in the store. As a result, I was at a definite disadvantage when talking in a crowded venue, which, as previously mentioned, was usually the case with the local general store.

When I arrived at the store I exchanged paper money for nearly all of the change in the cash register, waited my turn to use the phone and then placed the call to my office. This being 1974, I had to interact with an operator and she (after many questions) placed the call to my office. As it turned out, I discovered that my operator would allow me to make a collect call, so I was spared the chore of loading the pay phone with coins. The operator, a pleasant, but business-like lady, had a very thick southern drawl, and to overcome my New England accent I carefully pronounced (over emphasized, really) Gonzalo's name....

- "I'd like to speak to D-O-C-T-O-R   G-O-N-Z-A-L-O
- C-A-S-T-R-O"

I was hoping that I had overcome my New England tendency to mispronounce my "Rs" and made myself clearly understood. The background noise in the store made it difficult to hear, but I made out that the phone in my big boss Gonzalo's office was ringing and he answered with:

"Hallo"

To which the operator responded in a clear, but syrupy North Carolina drawl:

"I have a collect call for Miss Dorothy Castro"..........

> *As is well known, in New England "Rs" are never pronounced when they appear at the end of a word, they are saved and pronounced after "As" when this vowel appears in a word. So, "Doctor" becomes "Doctah" etc.*

"Grimmineee!" I thought, ...I'll be canned after this one. I was somewhat speechless and remained silent hoping that Gonzalo would not be offended and hang up.

After a moment, Gonzalo calmly accepted the call and the operator hung up her end and left us alone. I was mortified, my first statement was

"Gawd, I'm sorry Gonzalo"......
"No Problem Scutt, what's happening?"

I explained the problem and he resolved it and we moved on. What an embarrassment, but that's the way one had to do business in rural America in 1974.

That job finally ended, so I carefully packed up the cushioned samples in crates, loaded the station wagon and headed north. It was the beginning of May and the weather in Fairhaven was becoming increasingly sanguine.

Upon arrival, my first stop was at the Outdoorsman on Popes Island to be sure that *Whiskers* was still intact. It was early afternoon when I arrived on a Sunday and I stopped in the parking lot to see her tugging at her mooring line in the stiff afternoon sou'westerly. She looked great!

I spent the night at Cherry St. and then headed up to Winchester the next morning to start the workweek, but now I was back and nothing would stand between me and my weekends of sailing.

I expected that this first summer of real sailing would be crammed with unknown developments. I had a general plan about what I wanted to do, but as the season unfolded, most of these plans fell by the wayside. The evolving events dictated that I would learn to run a sailboat the hard way, …by making many, many mistakes. Since I lived in Concord and worked in Winchester, I did most of my sailing on the weekends. Looking back on it that may have been a blessing, because it meant that I was restricted to only two days in a week in which I could wreak havoc on the unsuspecting boating public of greater New Bedford. My early power boat experience helped to some extent, but, unlike a power boat, a sailboat is multidimensional and requires far more forethought and, yup you guessed it, ….ANTICIPATION!

When I bought *Whiskers*, I gave her a once over, but I didn't have her surveyed, I mean, what the hell did I know of surveys? Fortunately, the boat was sound, but what I didn't appreciate was that an outboard mounted rudder takes a beating if not attended to. Unbeknownst to me, the previous owner apparently had collided with some obstruction and fractured the rudder at the upper pintle.

Upper Pintle

The rudder is connected to the transom by two pintles that slide into corresponding gudgeons that are mounted on the transom. The pintles are the "male' fittings to the gudgeons "female" anatomy. This is a universal rudder fitting arrangement that is quite strong and allows for nearly 180 degrees of rudder movement.

The upper pintle endures the greatest stress when the boat is underway, because in a Rhodes 19, the mains'al generates considerable weather helm or a tendency for the boat to turn upwind. This weather helm can be counteracted by proper sail trim using the jib to counter the main, but a novice like me (at the time) will usually rely on the rudder to keep the boat on course placing a great deal of strain on the rudder pintles. The rudder on the Rhodes was solid mahogany, but the pintle mounting was only as good as the condition of the rudder's wood and in the case of *Whiskers*, this condition poor. I would soon discover that the rudder had suffered previously damage that was repaired with epoxy. Overtime, water had weakened the wood- epoxy bond and during one Saturday afternoon sail in late May in gusty winds, I unfortunately experienced to this weakness.

I was sailing along with a friend in the middle of New Bedford harbor amidst arriving and departing fishing boats and I was leaning heavily on the tiller to keep the boat on course as we tacked upwind toward the hurricane dike. Suddenly, the tiller became very mushy and as I pulled harder to keep the boat off the wind, she kept rounding up. I finally gave significant a tug on the tiller to assert my authority and the entire rudder parted from the transom as I held onto it before it washed away. My first response was "Oh my God, no freekin' rudder!" It was blowing about 20 knots and my friend looked at me in panic as I shouted "drop the main!" He quickly complied with my order (we had only the mainsail up as the wind was high) and I then proceeded to deal with the Segull. I managed to get it started being very cognizant of the choke and quickly disengaging the damned thing and we then motored back to the mooring about 600 yards downwind,.........another disaster averted. After laying her up for the weekend, I inspected the rudder and found that the area where the upper pintle was mounted had disintegrated; I had to get a new rudder. Fortunately, I was able to buy one from O'Day in Fall River that week and I was ready for another bout of sailing the following weekend.

I do not use the phrase "bout of sailing" idly. At this early stage in my sailing career, the metaphor is appropriate. As the reader will discover, each weekend in my early years was like a prizefight. One did one's best to prepare mentally and physically for a sailing weekend, but the conditions were the final arbiter. You were up against the weather, the state of the boat and your meager comprehension of sailing and seamanship. In the spring of that first year, it was a slug fest and I was usually on the losing end. The weather was usually windy and cold as was the water, because in early May the sun hadn't been able to surmount the heat lost to winter temperatures. One of my favorite quotes about sailing on Buzzards Bay came from Peter Richard's father Thornton Richards who, in his later years, also "commanded" a Rhodes 19 in and around Padanaram harbor and its approaches. At the end of an afternoon of sailing, having picked up his mooring and when safely ashore, his comment was always "Well, once again, I cheated death"; ......how true. When I was a juvenile, my mother had become friendly with several people from the south end of New Bedford (Bob Rustle's mother Jane was one of her buddies) which was an enclave of third generation Anglophiles that really enjoyed a good time. In the process, they had established a blue-collar yacht club called the Low Tide Yacht Club. Founded during the Depression in 1930s, the principals possessed champagne tastes on a beer budget. Quite a few of them liked to sail, but during the 1930s and 40s they could hardly afford the small sailboats that they possessed and having acquired these, could not subsequently afford a dinghy to transit from shore to their moored vessels. Their solution to this dilemma was to moor the boats close enough to shore so that the owners could wade out to them at low tide; hence the name Low Tide Yacht Club, or so the legend goes. The club burgee (flag) featured the common Atlantic horseshoe crab (Limulus *Polyphemus*), an ancient arthropod that has been on the planet for 300 million years, making it a living fossil. This creature is common to the Gulf of Mexico and the Atlantic coast. They migrate to the northeast in the summer often seen in the shallows at low tide. The natural behavior of this creature, as well as its salient visibility at low tide made it the perfect icon for the club.

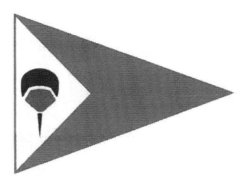

In 1974, the LTYC occupied a vacant house on the grounds of the Fort Rodman reservation located on the tip of Clark's Point in New Bedford. The clubhouse was one of several that originally had been used by the US Army as officer's quarters when Fort Rodman was a military compound (complete with five-inch shore batteries) during WW II. The Federal government had long since ceded the property to the city and the club petitioned the city in the 1960's to use one of the houses as their clubhouse. The city agreed and the club established itself at this locale. I joined, on my mother's suggestion, so that I could race *Whiskers* during the club's Sunday race series in the summer of 1974. It was around this time that I learned that Bob Rustle had also purchased a sailboat and would be keeping it moored off the beach adjacent to the LTYC. He had also joined the club along with his roommates from New York; Peter Richards and Ed Ilsley. "Oh, these three again", I thought to myself, "This should be an interesting summer".

In late May, I was preparing my boat (and myself) for the first LTYC Sunday series in mid June and to be competitive, I needed to equip the boat with a spinnaker. I had one built by Manchester sails in Padanaram and purchased a spinnaker pole and associated lines and rigging to fly this sail. I had never sailed a boat with a spinnaker and had absolutely no idea how to rig and trim this sail. What I did have (and still do) was a healthy-respect for this thing, even though on a Rhodes 19 it is relatively a small because of the fractional rig of the mast. I had the sail and the equipment, but I needed someone to train me in how to use it. Enter the bar of the same name.....The Spinnaker! This was a converted restaurant in Mattapoisett, the first town east of Fairhaven on Route 6. Of course, we New Englanders all called it the "The Spinnakah". This building had seen several businesses come and go over the years, but when some enterprising local businessmen bought it and opened it as a nightclub, it became very popular. It was THE place to be on weekends in southeastern Massachusetts with live entertainment, lots of beer and liquor and many, many twenty-somethings. It was a natural meeting place and many a reunion of old fiends occurred on weekends.

My summer weekends would unfold when I arrived from Concord on Friday to meet friends at The Spinnaker. It was here that I met Ray Andrews, a Mattapoisett native, who loved boats and was way up the learning curve in the art and execution of sailing. Ray was a hell of a nice guy and we clicked immediately. I explained my spinnaker problem to him and he quickly agreed to help. We made the necessary plans and the following Friday afternoon (I took some time off from work) Ray accompanied two of my Boston female friends (Thresea and Gail) and me on Whiskers to "set the chute".

We sailed outside the hurricane dike into the outer harbor and on Ray's command I helped him hoist the chute and we began to sail *Whiskers* dead downwind. Unfortunately, we had jury rigged a downhaul line for the spinnaker pole which and it was not really adequate for the wind conditions (what did I know,......pesky sou'westerly!). As we turned upwind slightly on a broad reach, the chute lifted, (as is their want) the boat healed and the girls screamed. Ray was doing his best to pull the pole down as the jury-rigged downhaul was insufficient and he screamed to me to turn downwind so he could get the sail under control. I finally managed to fall off downwind and Ray signaled that it was time to doff the sail. I agreed and my first spinnaker set came to an end. We hadn't sunk the boat, so after the sail was put away, the beer flowed like wine. When we reached the mooring, Ray and I discovered that one of the jumper struts on the mast had been bent during our spinnaker adventure. Apparently the pole had risen so high that it hit the jumper strut and had bent it. As a result, the next day, with assistance, I journeyed back to the granite pier where we had originally stepped the mast five weeks earlier, unstepped the damned thing again and pulled the jumper strut which we repaired. My mother's gas stove served as the "forge" to heat the strut aluminum tube that we then bent back into a straight position. Following this experience, I obtained the proper hardware to rig a secure downhaul line for the pole.

Now, fully armed with a spinnaker and associated equipment, I was ready to race my boat. The only other problem I faced was finding a crew. As it turned out, I had at least one crewman I could, sort of, count on. I had moved into Cambridge that summer from Concord, left my neurotic roommate Bob Graham in my wake and I was now sharing an apartment with Dennis Mello and Chris Renfree. The nice thing about this arrangement was that Dennis was engaged to a local girl and spent most of not all of his time at his finance's apartment in Boston, but still contributed to the rent. Chris and I had the place to ourselves with the exceptional times when Dennis's finance's parents were in town and he had to bunk with us for a couple of days. The apartment had two bedrooms, a living room, kitchen and one bathroom. The only natural light to enter our "cave" came from a window slot at the outboard wall of the living room. The place was functional, but hardly what one would consider homey or comfortable. The building that housed our apartment was located on Western Ave. about one block from the Cambridge Police Headquarters, so one would think that we enjoyed reasonable police security, but then again, this was Cambridge. Shootings in the neighborhood were common and my car was rifled more than once. This was okay with me, because I owned a 1959 Nash Rambler that I had purchased for $150 in Concord just before I moved.

It was a straight six, three speed on the column, owned by the proverbial "little old lady" and only used on Sunday. I dubbed the car "Ramblin' Rose" after the Nat King Cole song of the same name. I never locked it and I had a habit of tossing my bills up on the dashboard to collect dust for a few weeks before I broke down and paid them. As I weaved my way through the countless one way cow paths that pass for streets in Cambridge, these bills would wash back and forth across the dash and then fall on the floor or get blown into the back seat. By the third week of the month these bills were strewn throughout the car. One morning, when I opened the door and sat in the driver's seat I was amazed to find all of my bills stacked neatly in a pile on the dash in front of the steering wheel. I knew then that my car had been rifled, I had an encounter with what was probably a very disappointed, but neat car thief. The car itself was definitely not worth stealing, by the end of my first year of ownership, the starter was shot and most of the time I needed a push to pop the clutch in second gear to get the damned thing started.

My weekends that summer would begin on Friday afternoon when my buddies at GEI would get behind Ramblin' Rose and give me a send off as I popped the clutch in second gear to get her going. The starter was acting up and I didn't have the time to attend to it. I'd fight the legendary Friday afternoon traffic on the southeast expressway (referred to locally as the southeast distressway) and finally break free onto Route 24 headed south for Fairhaven. After a dinner of fast food at a Burger Chef, it would off to the Spinnaker where I'd meet Renfree and we'd commence the weekend party marathon.

A word or two here about Renfree; Chris Renfree has been a good friend for many, many years. Although he is my sister's age (five younger than me) I consider him to be a contemporary. Chris lived with his parents (Howard and Dottie) and his brother Peter on Oxford St in Fairhaven about a block from my parent's house on Cherry St. Chris was born with the physical affliction of Achondroplasia or dwarfism, but he and his parents never surrendered to the limitations of his condition. As a youngster he was treated the same as his brother and any of the other neighborhood kids. His father, Howard, who Chris referred to as "Big H", did his best to keep Chris "in the game" competing academically and socially with his peers. This prevented Chris from becoming a psychological victim to his infirmity and Howard and Dottie's encouragement pushed Chris on to become a talented and successful architect who today is well respected and well admired by many in his community. When Chris and I were roommates in Cambridge, he worked for a large architectural glass company in Boston (Karas and Karas) and he drove a British Racing Green MGB-GT. Howard was an engineer at the Acushnet Co. in Acushnet MA.(manufacturer of the Titleist golf ball) and, as such, he had invented and built a set of extender pedals (one each) that were connected to the accelerator, clutch and brake of Chris's MGB compensating for Chris's short legs. Chris could drive the car without problem using this modification and did exceptionally well even when he was "half-in-the-bag".

On one particularly raucous Friday night in January of 1975, Chris and I dove to the Spinnaker from Boston and upon our arrival began drinking "rusty nails". This odious-sounding drink was a 50:50 mixture of

Cutty Sark scotch and Drambuie. To lessen the sting, it was served on the rocks helping to keep one's mouth from puckering as a result of the desiccating effects of the alcohol as one consumed the drink. As the evening wore on, I had ingested three of these monstrous concoctions and I was wavering heavily. Around 22:30, I announced to Chris that I needed to go sleep it off, but he was still raring to go as he kept yelling at me over the noise of the place "rally Morris, come on, rally!" I had had enough. He handed me his keys and I stumbled out to his car that was parked directly next to the front entrance and I collapsed in the passenger's seat with my expedition, goose down parka draped over me. I instantaneously fell into a deep sleep (after turning off my hearing aid). I awoke after what seemed like thirty minutes and flung back my parka to find an empty parking lot and a darkened building.

I checked my watch and found that it was 2 AM! I was freezing, where was Chris, what happened? I was still a little woozy, but not nearly as drunk as I had been. So,…. what now? I was a good 15 miles from my parent's house on Cherry St in Fairhaven, it was two in the morning and it was 15 degrees. I did have the keys to the car, so I exited the passenger side and without thinking climbed into the driver's seat and abruptly found my knees up under my chin. Those extender pedals! What the hell! I can't drive this thing, what now? For about ten seconds I did consider removing the pedal extenders, but fortunately, I was still too drunk to focus. At this point, a Mattapoisett Police patrol car drove into the lot doing his late night rounds and pulled up next to me. I got out of the MG and walked over to the passenger side of the patrol car….he rolled down the window and asked what was up.

I then launched in to an explanation about how I had arrived at the Spinnaker at 8 o'clock with my friend who is a dwarf and after drinking rusty nails all evening he gave me the key to his car to sleep it off in the lot. Chris's car has extender pedals, because he's a dwarf and he disappeared - (dwarfs do that, don't they……oh no, leprechauns disappear…well, Chris isn't a leprechaun, how did he disappear?) - and I don't know where he got to and I can't drive the car and……………

After a minute or so, the officer looked at me and said "where do you live?"

I responded, "Cherry St. in Fairhaven"

He paused for a moment and said, "Get in, I'll drive you home"

I literally jumped into his car and he had me home in ten minutes.

I thanked him profusely as he cautioned not to retrieve the car until later that day, how in the hell was I going to do that with the extender pedals in place?

I went to bed and the next day I had an anxious call from Chris asking where his keys were. As it turned out he had consumed one or two more of those nasty drinks (I still believe that he has a hollow leg, he can drink anybody under the table) and a friend took him home. In the morning, he was searching for his keys when he suddenly remembered that I had them. We reunited and he got his car back without his mother being anymore the wiser. He had a phobia about not revealing his wilder side to Dottie who was from the Rodman family; proper, severe Yankee stock.

Chris was a wild man, but he agreed to "crew" for me one Sunday in my first LTYC race. Considering my recent problems with the spinnaker I promised that it wouldn't be used in this race as we headed out to the start off "Davy's Locker" restaurant which is located on a pier on the outer harbor of New Bedford. I had the race circular and instructions, but I wasn't familiar with the procedures. Neither was Renfree who was far more concerned with the relative temperature of the beer in the cooler than with our impending competition.

We managed to get a decent start and followed the boats around the course. Fortunately, the weather was a relatively warm on this late May afternoon, and the winds were moderate. I was becoming very absorbed in the race as Chris steered the boat and I was determined to get more speed out of her, so I told Chris I would hike out to keep her level as I had read in a recent "Sail" magazine article.

This Rhodes had two cam cleats on either side of the cockpit coaming mounted on adjoining pieces of mahogany to raise the cam cleat above the wooden cockpit coaming. Normally, these cam cleats were used for trimming the spinnaker sheets. In this particular instance I surmised that they could be employed as modified hiking straps, so I jammed a piece of manila line into one cam cleat, passed the line over my legs and then tied it off on the stern deck cleat, aft. With this line in place, I enthusiastically began leaning out over the water (hiking) to place weight beyond the rail and help keep the boat level as we headed up wind.

Chris was doing a great job of helming and we were beginning to gain on the leaders. All was going well until without warning, the blocks containing the cam cleat on my left separated and I fell backwards over the side. Fortunately, I had stowed my hearing aid in a safe dry place before I began my hiking activity (ANTICIPATE!). As it turned out, I had the presence of mind to hold onto the manila line as I was dragged behind the boat. Renfree didn't know anything about sailing, but he did say in passing as I was dragged along, "Hey Morris, this is no time to go swimming, get back in here, we're racing!" I told Chris to head up wind to stall the sails as I pulled myself back aboard. I dried off and we had a good chuckle….and a beer and headed for home. We had "withdrawn" from the racecourse, but never mentioned this to the committee boat (what did I know?).

The LTYC sponsored three series of Sunday races that summer. I had entered the first series of four races, but after the first one, my "crew" Renfs, declined to continue participating.

"Oh no Scomo (my nickname) I can't keep fishing you out of the drink in the middle of a race every Sunday, you'll have to find someone else"; was his reply to my crewing request. I couldn't find any replacements.

My first race had been a dismal failure, so, I concluded that day sailing might be a better method for learning this sport. I had better luck locating people to participate in day sails and so for the next few weekends, this venue became my pastime. Sailing around the outer harbor, I would occasionally find myself surrounded by two Hobie 14s, owned by Ed and Peter. They had recently quit their jobs in "The Big Apple" and took employment as insurance adjusters moving to Taunton MA, twenty miles or so north of New Bedford; Rustle stayed in New York. Pete and Ed had each purchased the Hobies and would travel to New Bedford from Taunton on weekends to sail. The Hobie 14 was a small, agile single-sailed catamaran with no comfort accommodations. They were very fast, like most catamarans, so they would sail these around from Padanaram and spend the afternoon buzzing by *Whiskers* and Bob Rustle who would also be out sailing his Cal 25. Toward the end of the afternoon, Bob would repair back to his mooring near the LTYC, the Hobie cats would raft up and the party would begin. After a while, I would sail *Whiskers* over and join in as well.

Peter provided the music entertainment at these impromptu parties. Besides being a "neat-freak" Peter was also a music aficionado and he had hundreds of hours of taped music. He played these on a portable Sony cassette player (a forerunner of the "boom box") and all of his tapes were organized neatly in two or three carrying cases. All of the tapes had labels on the spine of each cassette case and a corresponding label on the cassette itself. Included in the cassette case was a complete, neatly written, folded list of every song recorded on that particular tape, together with the name of the artist and the playing time. I was amazed when I saw this, it was clear to me that Peter had entirely too much free time. Peter also wore only khaki pants and Bermuda shorts, he did not own one pair of blue jeans. He was always neatly dressed and personal hygiene was very important to him. Ed on the other hand was the complete opposite of Peter. Where Peter could be compulsive, Ed was impulsive, Peter's neat, orderly manner was met with Ed's spontaneous, seemingly casual approach to personal matters. When they roomed together, Peter would

handle all of the combined finances and provide Ed with a bill for his
share each month. Ed wouldn't question the amount and would pay Peter
with one check made out to Peter who would deposit Ed's check and pay
each individual bill with his own checks. If Ed didn't have sufficient cash
in his account to cover the check he'd promise to pick up the tab for
dinner that night; and he did. Where Ed was charming and witty with
women, Peter needed several beers before he could loosen up to speak to
one. They were complete opposites, but their friendship worked.

The weather on weekends that summer was great. We would all
congregate in the cockpit of Bob's boat, while Peter entertained us with
music and we'd drink beer and crack jokes. Women from New York
would invariably be present, so it was a mini-bacchanal adventure. Things
would wind up around 5 o'clock and I'd sail back to Fairhaven while Pete
and Ed would head back to Padanaram; a common sailing bond was being
forged.

I was quite happy sailing around in the outer harbor since I was not
far from assistance should something go wrong. I liked my little boat, but
I was somewhat intimidated by the prospect of sailing too far out into the
Bay. As the reader may have noticed, I have made many references to the
"sou'westerly" on Buzzards Bay. To this point, I had experienced this
afternoon blow on the inner harbor, but by July, this afternoon sea breeze
had diminished to some extent, so that sailing on the outer harbor in the
afternoon was brisk and challenging, but not frightening. Even so, I was
developing a healthy respect for Buzzards Bay and its "afternoon
hurricane". Buzzards Bay, like San Francisco Bay generates waves that
are steep and breaking. When wind driven waves exhibit a crest to crest
period that is equal to the wave height, they are considered to be very
steep. Thus a six foot sea with a 10 second period is a rolling sea, whereas
a six foot sea with a six second period is a steep wave with a breaking top.
San Francisco Bay usually has four foot seas with a four second period;
serious waves. By contrast, it's not uncommon for Buzzards Bay to
generate nine foot seas with four second period, dangerous conditions by
any standard.

I was beginning to become more confident with sailing *Whiskers* and the last thing I wanted to do was to upset my new-found confidence. Consequently, I was not terribly interested in venturing beyond the familiar outer harbor waters where my new found confidence had been won. I was certainly not interested in venturing across the ten miles of open water to the Elizabeth Islands on the opposite side of the Bay.

With all this said, enter my mother, Mary who was confident that her son the sailor could get her over to explore the islands which she had wanted to do since High School. Of course, I continued to present her with a long list of contrived excuses avoid this trip:

"No, the weather doesn't look good this weekend, too much wind"

"No, I need to have the Segull checked, it's been running rough, don't want to venture out without an outboard you know,"

"No, I promised Theresa and her friends that I'd take them day sailing this weekend"

And so it went, I continued to find excuses, Mary continued to fume over her lost opportunity.

Finally, around mid-August she learned from Jane Rustle that the LTYC was planning a rendezvous at Quick's Hole a passage between Buzzards Bay and Vineyard Sound and Bob was going to take Jane and two of her friends. This was too much for Mary, she called me at work in Winchester and demanded that I take her that Saturday, no ifs, ands or buts. She claimed that all I had to do was sail the boat, she would take care of the rest, food, drinks, everything. Oh no I thought, sailing my mother over to meet her friends, great way to spend the day. I agreed to the deal over the phone so she would stop pestering me and let me get back to work. With trepidation, I headed home that Friday, but undeterred, like every other Friday night, I got hopelessly bombed with my friends at the Spinnaker. I dragged myself to my parent's house after the Spinnaker closed at 1AM and collapsed on my bed, fully clothed.

When nine AM arrived, I found someone was poking and prodding me to get up. My mother was fresh as a daisy and rarin' to get going.

"Come'on, get up the day's a wastin'. Everythng's ready, lets' go!"

I groaned and rolled over claiming sickness, but she wouldn't be put off.
"If you hadn't drunk so much last night, you'd be fine now" she exclaimed. "Come on, you promised!"

In fact, I did promise to take her, so I got up, groaned again, stumbled into the bathroom and washed my face, scraped away the woolen blanket that enveloped my tongue, brushed my teeth (Gawd! Crest toothpaste tastes absolutely horrible when you have a hangover) and nearly fell down the stairs to the kitchen. Mary had a breakfast of eggs, toast, OJ and coffee waiting which I picked at after drinking the OJ. We loaded Ramblin' Rose and headed down to the town landing to launch the dinghy and row out to *Whiskers*.

After loading up the boat, we cast off and I started the Seagull, since no wind had yet developed. We "steamed" down the harbor and through the hurricane dike as I bumped around the boat getting the sails bent on. My Mom was steering and beaming at the helm exclaiming what a beautiful day it was, how wonderful everything looked, waving at passersby and generally being obnoxiously cheery to someone (me) who was suffering from a splitting headache and nausea. Fortunately, she did bring some cold beer and after one of those, I began to share her outlook on the day. We steamed along for about 45 minutes and finally the breeze began to fill in from the predictable sou'wes. I raised the main and jib, killed the Seagull and off we went sliding across the Bay towards Quick's Hole. One more beer and I was feeling fine and thoroughly enjoying my exploration of what had been aqua incognita, the middle and south end of Buzzards Bay. It was a truly splendid day and as we proceeded, the water became a deeper blue color and very clear in comparison to the outer harbor of New Bedford.

As we approached Quick's Hole, we noticed fish boats on their way to George's Bank from New Bedford and other headed home to New Bedford from Vineyard Sound. Quick's Hole is one of four passages through the Elizabeth Island chain and is by far the easiest to navigate. This passage is about a half mile wide and is the deepest and least obstructed of the four passages. All of these passages experience vigorous tidal currents that can attain five to six knots under certain conditions. For all of these reasons, Quick's Hole is the most desirable route from Vineyard Sound into Buzzards Bay or vice versa. From the perspective of the LTYC, on this day Quick's offered a tranquil refuge from the sou'wes wind, but also a fine, deep water beach on the Nashaweena side of the hole where the water was warm and the beach was clean.

After transiting the Bay, as *Whiskers* approached the beach in Quick's Hole my Mom and I could make out Rustle's boat anchored off the beach in ten or so feet of water. We waved and exchanged salutations as I dropped the jib and sailed up along side under main alone. Ed was aboard Bob's boat and Peter had sailed his Hobie Cat over from Padanaram. Ed secured my lines to Bob's boat with fenders in between and assisted my Mom over to Bob's boat to begin partying. The reveling lasted a couple of hours, I swam ashore to inspect the beach. After lunch it was getting on toward 4 o'clock and the wind had risen to its customary afternoon strength of 20 knots. I was getting concerned about the trip back and started thinking about reefing the main as I had read about in the last "Sail" magazine article. Being a novice, I didn't realize that I would be sailing back to New Bedford on a broad reach, the most comfortable and safest point of sail on any boat. Be that as it may, Mary was whooping it up with Jane and her friends and I took Bob aside and asked him to take my mom back with him for safety sake. I was getting quite concerned and didn't want her onboard should an emergency occur. He agreed and I roller reefed the main (that was how it was done on this boat) and then cast off and headed downwind. Rustle made some jokes at my expense to all on his boat as I left, but it rolled off my back as I was focused on my task. The boat handled well with a quartering sea of six feet and I made it back okay and sailed to the mooring on the fading afternoon wind. I picked up Mary later at the Rustle's and she was now in the state I had experienced 24 hours previously; quite bombed. She had a wonderful day and thanked me profusely,.......I was just happy that no one had died.

I was now a veteran who had sailed the bay and didn't die and thanks to the prodding of my mother I now had a new appreciation for Buzzards Bay and my sailing confidence was further enhanced. Interestingly, another positive situation emerged from that afternoon. Ed was quite impressed with my resolve and quite angry with Rustle for not accompanying me back across the bay. He decided that he would rather sail with me than Rustle. That day, new friendships had been fostered. After our time at Quicks, Peter also had an interesting experience on his Hobie. Peter had no concern whatsoever about sailing back to Padanaram and in fact, took Bob's sister Susie with him. He sailed a beam reach back and probably made it in record time, but when they reached shore, he found that his windward rudder had dropped off during the trip. Luckily, he sailed all the way back on a port tack. It was a good thing that he didn't need to sail on the other tack that day or a disaster would have occurred.

The next week I heard from Ed and we planned a weekend trip on *Whiskers* to Menemsha on the west end of Martha's Vineyard. Ed planned to bring his girlfriend and I asked a female friend of my sister's to accompany us as well. Rustle planned to take his boat with his girlfriend so we planned to link up in Menemsha Pond on Saturday. I moved *Whiskers* down to Bob's mooring on Friday evening with Ed's help so that we could get a simultaneous start Saturday morning. Unlike other Friday nights, we stayed reasonably sober on this one since we had obligations in the morning.

Saturday morning was gorgeous as we loaded up and began our 19 mile trip due south to the Vineyard. The trip over was pleasant and uneventful as we later transited the channel next to the docks in Menemsha into the Menemsha Pond. The tide was ebbing as we entered and the little Seagull had to earn her pay to get us through the worst of the five-knot rip current. We found Rustle and rafted alongside in the late afternoon. Rustle was considerably wealthier than the rest of us at this point in our lives as he had inherited a small fortune from his grandfather. Bob was one of the last of the Rustle family that had been original homesteaders in New Bedford and had made considerable profits from whaling in the 19th century. My understanding was that Bob was his grandfather's favorite and when the old guy passed on, it was generally known that he had left much of his wealth to Bob. All of this would have been wonderful if Bob had a personality as sterling as his bank account. Unfortunately, this was not the case and, in fact, in my opinion, he was very conceded, cheap and fond of belittling others. To me, it appeared that he had something of a Napoleon complex, but (as we used to say) "beyond all of that he was a really nice guy". Bob was engaged to his girlfriend from New York, Linda who would join in on Bob's sailing trips making matters even worse. Linda was a queen bee and she expected to be waited on by everyone. Bob could do no wrong in her eyes and because she was from "the city" and the rest of us were mere provincials. Linda had just purchased a new stainless steel charcoal grill for Bob's boat and he was showing it off to us. It was mounted on the stern rail and must have set her back $250, a considerable sum in those days. On *Whiskers*, we had an old Coleman camp stove that I had bought for $20 four years before to use on camping trips in my converted Econoline van. It also served as an impromptu heater sitting on the engine cover between the two front seats since the heater in that old van was worthless. The Coleman was very dependable, but frowned on by the New Yawkahs on the Cal 25.

| **Cal 25** | **Rhodes 19** |

Bob claimed that he and Linda would be having grilled hamburgers that night and proceeded to get his charcoal grill started. On *Whiskers*, we were planning on a Dinty Moore stew dinner with all the fixin's using the Coleman.

Bob's grill was the swivel type that had one large bolt holding the grill bed onto the mounting rod. The theory was that when finished, one could loosen this bolt and grill bed containing the charcoal would fall down parallel to the transom dumping the spent charcoal into the sea. Bob got the fire going making jokes about our stew and how good his hamburgers were going to taste while Linda announced from the cabin that the burgers were ready to cook. Bob brought the burgers out on a tray and with pomp and circumstance and placed them on the piping hot grill. He had all of them in place and was about to turn them when the bolt holding the grill suddenly slipped and the whole contents fell into Menemsha Pond,....... charcoal, grill, hamburgers, the whole damned shootin' match. Linda elicited a blood-curdling scream and Bob stood there with the spatula in his hand staring at his dinner drifting off down wind. Ed and I were, at first, transfixed by this scene, but then leapt into action and jumped into our dingy to retrieve the burgers. The fat was keeping them afloat and all we had to do was beat back the seagulls flocking to grab the meat and then pick them up and bring them back to the boat. We managed to save five out of six and returned them to their incredulous owner.

Linda demanded that Bob start another fire and expressed concern about eating meat that had been in the Pond. Bob reported that he couldn't use the charcoal grill because the grill itself was now at the bottom of the pond. Bob's solution to this dilemma was to use his alcohol stove in the galley to fry the burgers. We repaired back to *Whiskers* and about two minutes later, another scream was heard as we witnessed flames leaping inside the cabin of Bob's boat. As with all alcohol stoves, inexperience can be dangerous, Bob had never used this thing and it got out of hand. He quickly brought it up on deck and threw a bucket of seawater on it to douse the flames. Now they were really up the creek. Linda was seething, Bob was in a quandary and the tension between the two was palpable. At this point, as we munched on our stew, we meekly offered our meager Coleman stove as a solution to Bob and Linda's problem. Linda churlishly accepted the offer and the two went below and cooked their burgers on the lowly Coleman. We did receive one or two as payment. The next day, we chuckled about that scene all the way back to New Bedford.

~ *Chapter 6* ~

Buzzards Bay Regatta etc.

Having had had a taste of "cruising" I now wanted to get back to racing to determine if I could improve my skills at that sailing sphere. I signed up for the Buzzards Bay Regatta an annual event that combined the efforts of four Buzzards Bay yacht clubs. The Regatta location shifted each year between the New Bedford Yacht Club in Padanaram and the Beverly Yacht Club in Marion. This exposed sailors to either end of Buzzards Bay on alternate years. In 1974, the New Bedford Yacht Club was hosting the event, so I enlisted Dennis and Geoff to serve as my crew. We agreed to meet on Friday morning at the New Bedford Yacht Club to begin our series of races with the Rhodes 19 fleet. Once again, my inexperience was showing since I was completely unaware that Bob Saltmarsh would be racing with this R19 fleet. Bob Saltmarsh was the Rhodes 19 National Champion in 1973 and was on schedule to repeat his previous title. Scomo Farckle (me, this was one of my nicknames used to denote a dufus) had just begun sailing the Rhodes 19 and, needless to say, there was a better than even chance that I wouldn't be jeopardizing Saltmarsh's effort to repeat his title during this Regatta.

I rose early that Friday morning which was clear, warm and windless. I had prep'd the boat the night before and had lifejackets, gasoline, charts, all ready to go. I brought sandwiches, beer and cold drinks out with me that morning as well as a transistor radio for entertainment should the race get boring. I should explain at this point that since the Buzzards Bay Regatta is annually held on the first week August, all bets are off as to how the weather will be. Usually it either blows like the dickens or is flat calm. There have also been years when fog dominates the competition. Of course, I didn't check the weather forecast prior to my departure, being a novice and all, so I had no disquieting expectations.

I left the mooring and planned to single hand the boat over to Padanaram to meet my crew. I did take the time to obtain the race circular so I knew that my class would race in a circle south of Clark's Point and the first gun was at 11:00. I was underway at 07:30 "steaming" along using the Seagull traveling down the harbor toward the hurricane dike on flat water with no wind. I had used the boat the previous weekend and although I checked on everything before I left the mooring, I hadn't looked in the Seagull's gas tank. All was going well on this warm August morning I tied down the tiller and I was bending on sail as I powered toward the 150 foot opening of the hurricane dike.

New Bedford hurricane barrier, dike gates

Off in the distance, about ¾ of a mile south of me in the middle of the channel I discerned a 200 foot oil survey ship in the middle of the channel headed directly at me. In 1974, the major oil companies were engaged in exploratory work on George's Bank and New Bedford served as their base of operations. The tide was beginning to flood and a three to four knot current was running against me as I started into the center of the dike where the gates close when it is in use. As I transited the center of the dike I was leaning against the boom peering at the oil survey ship headed towards me comforted by the continuous noisy racket of the Seagull. I had just cleared the south end of the gates where the current flushing back into the harbor was most noticeable and I was musing, tempting fate about what would occur if the engine quit at this point. No sooner than when I finished my thought, as had occurred in the past, my world was suddenly enveloped in ....**SILENCE!** I froze,...... OH NO, not again! What happened? I dashed back to the Seagull, and opened the gas tank to find it dry! Oh my God! What an idiot! Now what? I quickly ran forward to the cuddy to grab the gas tank to refill the outboard. As this action unfolded, I found that the oil recon ship had closed the distance to about 150 yards. As captain of that ship began to announce his rights by sounding five short blasts of his horn (distress signal) I fumbled with the gas can. He undoubtedly had the right of way and, at this point, I was an obstruction. With trembling hands, I worked as fast as I could, but the flooding tidal current was sucking me back into the gate area of the dike. All while this was occurring, the oil recon ship continued to blast his horn as he closed in on me at 10 knots. Finally, as I passed the southern opening of the gates, I managed to get fuel into the outboard and get it started (being careful to DISENGAGE the choke). With a thrust of the propeller, the boat managed to get ahead of the oncoming tidal current and push itself out of the gate area off to the west side of the channel. Just as we cleared the gates, the oil recon ship came steaming through the channel and entered the gate area of the hurricane dike. Once again,...disaster averted, how many lives had I used up at that point? Hopefully there were enough left to get me through the first sailing season.

After recovering from this near calamity, I chugged a beer, to steady my nerves and powered down the channel for about two miles and then made a right turn toward Padanaram. The wind was still nonexistent, so I continued "steaming" until I past the Padanaram breakwater into the harbor, headed toward the yacht club. Padanaram is a fine harbor, delightful to behold and is protected on three sides. The mouth of the harbor opens to the bay at the south and, as such, is exposed to sou'eas winds. Hurricanes arrive with winds from the sou'eas so this makes the harbor quite vulnerable. A granite breakwater constructed in the 19th century helped to moderate the seas emanating from the sou'eas, but not the winds and most certainly not the storm surge.

The name of the village came from one of the original settlers Laban Thatcher who was a successful merchant and a pillar of the community. Mr. Thatcher was a Quaker and saw parallels between his life and that of the biblical Laban who dwelled in the plains of northern Mesopotamia known and Padan-Aram. The harbor itself is about a mile long and is of sufficient depth to accommodate many moorings, consequently the recreational fleet in Padanaram is quite large. Fringing the harbor are many large, expensive homes of classic New England design. The New Bedford Yacht Club calls Padanaram home after it was relocated from New Bedford harbor following the destruction of the club by the 1938 hurricane. The NBYC has a large membership and provides launch service throughout the harbor using two or three diesel-powered launches.

As I powered along at five knots, I noticed that one of the yacht club launches was headed out into the harbor, crowded with people. It was progressing in my direction and in the crowd of faces onboard the vessel, I noticed two who were quite familiar. The attire of the majority of passengers onboard was typical boating wear, T-shirts, banlon shirts, shorts and the like. However, I noticed one of the familiar fellows, a tall blond guy dressed in a white shirt with a black bowtie. He was conversing with the launch operator when suddenly the launch swayed from its course and headed directly toward me. I slowed and as the launch approached and I saw that it was Geoff standing next to the launch operator and next to him was Dennis. A quick glance at the two confirmed my initial observations as each was dressed in white, oxford cloth, button-down shirt with black bowties and tan Bermuda shorts. In addition, each had white ankle socks and deck shoes. They were my "crew" they announced. The launch pulled alongside and the two stepped aboard *Whiskers* carrying yet another cooler filled with beer.

This display was a big hit with the Yachties on the launch who apparently expected these two "dapper" crewmen to board a vessel of substantial proportions, but instead witnessed them climbing down from the launch onto a 19-foot daysailer. The irony (and absurdity) of the moment was not lost on the launch passengers nor on the "captain" of *Whiskers*. We all thanked the launch operator and I came about and we headed back out toward the race course. We all had a good chuckle about their ruse at my expense and Geoff explained that he had told the launch operator that he and Dennis wished to board *Whiskers* (the operators are trained to ask their passengers which boat they are bound for). When they spotted me headed toward the yacht club, Geoff casually walked up to the launch operator and asked him to "cut him off at the pass". This was a clear indication of the level of maritime expertise that would be found with me on this day. Needles to say, *"cut him off at the pass"* isn't exactly a common nautical phrase passed around the yacht club on a regular basis. Oh well, you get what you pay for, we all had a good laugh over Geoff's comment and then proceeded onto the course.

By this time the sou'westerly had begun to build, so I instructed "my crew" as to how to raise the sails and with this done, I killed the engine as we began sailing toward our designated racing area. Neither of my crew had any sailing experience, so besides being the captain, I was also the most experienced sailor onboard....God help us. Upon arriving at our racing circle, we sailed by the committee boat to check in and we were immediately directed to don life jackets as the wind was rapidly building to 20 knots and the seas were likewise growing. I bore off away from the committee boat after scribbling down compass courses posted on the race display board. As we headed down wind, I asked Dennis to scrunch down into the cuddy and grab three life jackets to comply with the committee's command. Little did I know before this request that Dennis was hypersensitive to motion sickness. No sooner had he bent forward to obtain the jackets, than his pallor turned from pink to green. He doned his jacket, as did Geoff and me, but Dennis did not look good. We came about and headed back to the starting line;.... late. As the gun sounded we watched three Rhodes 19s execute a textbook crossing of the starting line and begin sailing to weather. We came along about three minutes later and waved at the race committee as we trailed way behind the leaders on the race course. We cleared the windward mark five minutes behind the leaders who now were broad reaching toward the leeward mark under spinnakers. As we sailed along on a broad reach, well behind the leaders, the wind had built to more than 20 knots and Geoff asked if we were going to set the spinnaker. "No Freekin' Way" was my response. The seas had built to about four feet at this point rolling us along toward the next mark.

About then, Dennis found it necessary to pull himself to the leeward rail and began a lengthy conversation with one of the lesser god of the sea; Ralph. He then proceeded to "ralph" his way along that entire leg of the course until we reached the next mark. Situated just to weather of this mark was the committee boat and as we rounded it, I tried to bear away on a starboard tack. However, *Whiskers* was not answering her helm in the sloppy sea that had now built to five feet. I tacked the boat and we headed in the opposite direction getting ever closer to the committee boat. At this juncture, the bulk of the fleet was approaching the next windward mark as *Whiskers* and her stalwart crew wallowed in the sloppy seas downwind from the committee boat. I fought the helm and tried to keep her nose to the wind as Dennis puked over the side and Geoff was doused in seawater with each successive breaking wave. We were all getting drenched and not making much headway as we moved closer to the committee boat. Finally, in the lee of the committee boat, Whiskers was blanketed and uncontrollable. Then slowly, as if we were sleep walking in a bad dream, we moved inexorably toward the committee boat until ....we collided, bow on into committee boat's port side leaving a silver dollar-sized ding in the planking. The committee fended us off and we tacked over and increased our speed away from the stationary vessel avoiding further collision danger. Once again, I had screwed up, the committee boat was anchored, I was underway, my responsibility was to do my utmost to avoid a collision.

As we sailed off on a starboard tack, several more six-foot seas broke over the bow, soaking us all and leaving a substantial quantity of water in the cockpit. That was it for me, I yelled out above the rising wind, "DONE,…..we're outta heah!" Both Dennis and Geoff nodded in tacit agreement we tacked over and I set a course for the Padanaram breakwater, once again withdrawing with notice.

We entered the harbor and I grabbed a vacant mooring near the yacht club, not knowing who's it was and, and that point, nor caring. Although the temperature was in the seventies, Dennis was beginning to shiver uncontrollably he was probably dehydrated from the vomiting and beginning to exhibit hypothermia from his seawater soaking. Fortunately, I had dry clothing stowed in garbage bags in the cuddy, so I was able to get some dry clothes onto Dennis and Geoff. I had a slicker on during all this, so I was fine. After we cleared the gear, we each popped a beer and waited for the launch; so much for the Buzzards Bay Regatta day one.

On day two, Dennis decided to let discretion be the better part of valor, so Geoff and I headed out to the course to try our hand at racing once more. Geoff had wisely chosen to wear more conventional sailing attire that included a slicker; of sorts. As luck would have it, on Saturday the weather was more cooperative with sou'wes winds of 10-15 knots and a two to three foot chop. We headed toward the race circle, but as we approached, before assembly, fog began to cover the course. I took a visual bearing on the committee boat and we sailed a compass course toward it observing as all the race committee members running for cover. Within 100 feet of the vessel, like a phantom it suddenly disappeared in the clammy mist leaving us dumfounded. We sailed a reciprocal course to try and recover the starting pin, but once again, nothing. After ten minutes, I was getting concerned, so I had Geoff pull out the four-foot square chart of Buzzards Bay that I had purchased that week, so we could get our bearings. He did so and I unfolded it as we sailed along under main alone. I was beginning to ascertain where we were and where needed to go when a gust of wind came from nowhere and blew the chart out of my hands and over the side!

- "Oh freekin' great!" was Geoff's response to this event, "Now what?"

Fortunately, I had some sense of the location of the breakwater and using the compass we managed to find it without further incident. Once again, we had retired with notifying the committee boat. The only trace left of us on the race course was a chart of Buzzards Bay floating on the waves like jetsom. I later learned that the committee boat counts the participants and when one is missing and hasn't checked in, it is their responsibility to locate the missing vessel; at least for a time. Those poor old bastards must have cursed me up and down searching the circle after the race trying to find that Rhodes 19 with no number on its sail.

We found the mooring that I had arranged to use for the weekend, dropped sail and "licked our wounds". I uncovered the transistor radio that I had brought, hoping for some music to soothe our tired minds, but it had been sloshing round in the bilge and was totally worthless. Over the side it went and we proceeded to drink beer and eat the seawater dampened sandwiches from the cooler. We stowed gear, straightened up the boat and headed ashore to drown our sorrows at "Julia's Whale's Tale" in town. After several beers, the world looked much brighter.

Geoff headed home and I set out to find Ed, Peter and Rustle who had been racing Rustle's Cal in the PHRF class that day. I found them at the yacht club and we proceeded to have a few more brews, before heading off to get a bite to eat at a local restaurant. Over dinner we shared stories about the day and as it turned out, they hadn't fared much better than me; a little solace for me.

Since Linda was in town, Rustle had planned to sleep ashore that night as had Peter. The last day of racing was Sunday and I was fed up with the Rhodes 19 class, so Rustle invited me to join them in the PHRF class the next day. Ed offered to stay on Bob's boat that night and invited me to join him. I agreed and we caught the last launch out to the Cal. *Whiskers* was settled in on an adjoining mooring as Ed and I sat in the cabin hoisting a few more before turning in, me in the quarter berth, Ed up forward in the V-berth. I removed my hearing aid and I was out in no time. As it turned out, a cold front began coming through that night and the wind picked up and blew 25 to 30 as we slept unconcerned. At around 02:00 I could feel (couldn't hear anything without the hearing aid) banging above my head up on deck. I awoke, rolled out of my sleeping bag and walked up into the cockpit. There on the port deck was Ed and some stranger fending off a second boat that was banging against the Cal. I moved forward and helped out as we mounted fenders between the two and attached spring lines and bow lines to securely raft the two boats. This was accomplished in about fifteen minutes and then the other boat's crew repaired to their boat as Ed and I made our way below on the Cal. I fished my hearing aid out of my bag and put it on so that I could find out what occurred.

Ed was chuckling as he recounted that our mooring had dragged in the wind and we were hitting the other boat, so one of the crew came down into the Cal and was shaking me violently yelling "Your boat's hitting my boat!" He said the guy couldn't get anywhere with me, so when he saw Ed up forward he began yelling the same thing at him. Finally Ed, rolled over and in a half-asleep daze looked at the guy and said "Its okay its not my boat" And it wasn't, it was Rustle's. I guess the guy then gave up and began trying to remedy the problem himself during which he made so much noise that it finally roused Ed to action and eventually me. Fortunately, no damage occurred to either boat. We went back to bed about 03:00 and then did manage to get some rest.

Later that morning the crew of the Cal assembled and we headed out for some exhilarating sailing in 30 to 35 mph winds and ten-foot seas out at the mouth of the bay. We didn't finish vey well in the fleet, but I was hooked on blue water sailing.

Chapter 7

Martha's Vineyard

That evening I discovered that Rustle, Peter, Ed and I all had the rest of the week off, so we hatched a plan to sail over to the Vineyard on the morrow. Bob and Linda would be in the Cal, Peter, Ed and I would rendezvous with them sailing in *Whiskers*. We all headed home that night for some well deserved rest and in the morning my crew and I assembled our gear for our weeklong adventure. All of our clothes and bedding were stowed in plastic garbage bags to try and keep them dry and we bought canned food, baloney, cheese and bread for sandwiches and as much beer as we could safely stow (there was tacit agreement to jettison the bread if necessary in favor of beer). We trucked my dinghy over from Fairhaven and I secured an extra five-gallon can of gasoline inside, firmly tied down between the seats. We loaded the Rhodes and headed out around 11:00 as the wind was still fairly brisk from the sou'wes at around 20+ knots. We were all clad in slickers as we passed by the Sandspit off Round Hill and then we bore the full force of wind and sea. The wind was gusting to 25+ and the seas were running at around eight feet with occasional breakers. We were sailing on a close reach headed for Quick's Hole, taking seas over the starboard bow with occasional green water over the foredeck. Peter was at the helm, Ed on the rail and I occasionally slumped down to the port side to pump out accumulating waster using my new stationary bilge pump, she was a beauty; 15 gallons per minute!

It was a long wet slog across the middle of the bay, but we made good time and eventually came under the lee of Cuttyhunk and the Penekese way up to windward of us. This helped to tame the seas, although the wind was still piping up quite well, and bought the wind more on the beam allowing us to bear off on a close reach to the hole. We transited Quick's Hole with a foul current and fell off downwind headed east in Vineyard Sound towards Woods Hole. The wind was dead aft as we sailed our intended course hoping to pass Middle Ground to the north since the *Eldridge Tide and Pilot* book described the rip current at that shoal as being quite nasty in a foul tidal current. We were dead reckoning using new charts that I had bought that day for the trip and in a bouncing, wet nineteen-foot sailboat, this wasn't an easy task. The current was running against us at around three knots and the wind was dead aft at 20 knots, so the result was a large breaking seaway with seas of eight to ten feet. It was quite impressive, particular since none of us had ever sailed the length of Vineyard Sound before. By our reckoning, the tidal current would ease as we moved east and would slack off by the time we reached Middle Ground; a good thing.

Middle Ground is a shoal that runs roughly east to west from Norton's Point, just west of Lambert's Cove, to West Chop a peninsula that juts out into Vineyard Sound. The dynamics of this shoal have been described in detail in the 1960s (J.D. Smith, Geomorphology of a Sand Ridge, *The Journal of Geology* Vol. 77, No. 1 (Jan., 1969), pp. 39-55). Middle Ground is fairly shallow especially off West Chop ranging from six to nine feet over a mile long section that's about one-half mile north of West Chop. The water depth on either side of this shallow region is fifty feet or more. The location of this shallow is such that much of the water racing around West Chop is funneled directly at Middle Ground. Here's the interesting part, the tidal stream running at four to five knots rushes up from the fifty foot depth to six feet which compresses the phenomenal mass of water and increases its velocity; in effect, a Venturi . Even with no wind, waves form on the shoal as a result of this effect. When a breeze is blowing, the waves become quite impressive in size and often confused in nature. What further complicates any navigation near this

> *The weight of seawater is 64 pounds per cubic foot. (Freshwater is 62.4 pounds per cubic foot.) The density of the male human being is (170 lbs./2.8 cu ft) is 61 pounds per cubic foot.*

shoal is that once over it, this racing tidal stream falls over into yet another fifty-foot "sink". The result of this is the development of whirlpools and even more aquatic consternation. Fishermen love this place, because large stripers will lurk in the deep water on the back side of the shoal waiting for dinner in the form of a squid, mackerel or alewife to be pulled over the top and dropped into their lap. We were headed toward this shoal and we wanted to give it a wide berth.

Middle Ground, note the high water velocity at West Chop

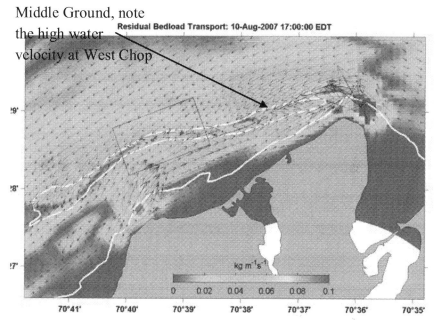

http://cstms.org/index.php/CSTMS: Community Sediment Transport Modeling System

We rigged a preventer on the boom in the event that we unexpectedly jibed and each of us kept an eye out for traffic and cross-seas. I was at the helm at this point focused intently on keeping the boat on course and doing my utmost to avoid a jibe. This was rigorous work since breaking seas would occasionally slop over the transom and they constantly tried to force us into a broach. As we sailed along with the dinghy on a short hawser, it continuously surfed down waves behind us banging into the transom and the rudder. Expecting imminent damage, I complained to Ed and Peter who found more line and strung the dinghy fifty feet behind us. With the high seas, there were many occasions when we would be on one side of a wave and the dinghy would be out of sight on the other side with the hawser burrowed directly through the wave. I was a bit concerned, but had the dinghy swamped, we all agreed to cut the line immediately.

This solution to the dinghy problem worked and I could then concentrate on my helmsmanship. Halfway down Vineyard Sound the seas moderated a bit and we relaxed a little. As we sailed along I occasionally caught a glimpse of something off to port with my peripheral vision, but when I looked turned to my left to focus it was gone. Finally my timing was correct, I looked to my left at the precise moment that the apparition appeared and there was the dinghy surfing down the same wave as us, about thirty feet away to port! What a sight! Kind of like the "Flying Dutchman" surfing along with a "bone in her teeth", but no one in command. It was still intact and I took some solace in that.

We proceeded down the sound and, in fact, headed a bit north of West Chop and witnessed the effects of a dwindling tidal current on this nautical pitfall. The whirl pools and eddies on the backside of the chop were nothing short of amazing. Here we were 300 yards north of the worst point of the shoal and we could easily see why it had earned its name. I could well appreciate what the sea conditions would be like right on this shoal when the wind and current were directly opposed to one another.

Once around West Chop, we hardened up and headed for Vineyard Haven harbor to rendezvous with Rustle and Linda. At this point, we also shortened the dinghy hawser and surprisingly found that she had not shipped much water during the trip down the sound. Vineyard Haven is a pretty, little town and is the main island terminus for the Steamship Authority ferries. In 1974 there were three or four ferries that made the seven mile crossing from Woods Hole on a regular basis. Consequently, the town was quite busy in the summer with day-trippers and vacationers coming and going. There were some attractions in town for shoppers, but at the time, Vineyard Haven was a "dry town" meaning that restaurants served no alcohol and there were no packages stores. This was a remnant of the repeal of Prohibition in the late 1930's when local jurisdictions were empowered to decide whether alcohol could be legally sold in their municipality. Vineyard Haven was the only dry town on the island and tourist retail traffic was minimal. Most everyone got off the boat and drove four miles down the road to Oak Bluffs where liquor was readily available. I believe that the locals in Vineyard Haven liked it that way; it certainly was a far quieter town after the last ferry arrived.

During the nineteenth century, Vineyard Haven was a harbor of refuge for the myriad of coastal schooners that sailed the coast from Maine to Florida. Schooners were the nineteenth century equivalent of today's tractor trailers moving goods of all description from port to port along the New England coast. All of these vessels were required to transit Pollock Rip Shoals near Chatham if headed north toward Boston and Maine or west toward Rhode Island and Connecticut. Like most of the narrow, shallow passages around the Cape, Pollock Rip was notoriously dangerous, especially in winter. All of these coastal schooners were exclusively powered by sail, so there was no thought of relying on an engine if trouble arose. As a result, a savvy seaman paid close attention to the weather and to their coastal Pilot. Waiting out the weather was a common occurrence in those days and safe, easily accessible harbors were far and few between. Vineyard Haven was a perfect stopover as the harbor was large enough and deep enough to accommodate many vessels. In addition, the harbor ran from nor'wes to sou'eas offering some protection from nor'eas gales and great protection nor'wes winds which predominate during winter storms. As a result, there were many schooners anchored in Vineyard Haven harbor at any time of the year awaiting favorable conditions for transiting Pollock Rip or any of the other dangerous obstructions in and around Cape Cod and the Islands.

Vineyard Haven

We entered the inner harbor of Vineyard Haven behind the granite breakwater, found Rustle and rafted alongside. We hung out our wet slickers to dry and Bob invited Peter to stay aboard the Cal that night which freed space for Ed and me on *Whiskers*. None one bothered to go ashore as we new it was a dry town. We sacked out and awoke to a fine day and planned our next leg sailing down the Vineyard coast to Edgartown. The day was fine and the visibility excellent, so we could relax as we picked off the buoys marking Squash Meadow, yet another shoal off Oak Bluffs and then the buoys off Middle Flats marking the entrance to Edgartown Harbor. Rustle had left before us under power to save time as Linda wanted to "get there" and do some shopping. This was fine with us as, once again, Rustle would grab a mooring and we would raft to him when we arrived. Before leaving Padanaram, I had been in contact with my sister who planned to join us in Edgartown with her friend Nina. They would take the ferry *Schamonchi* from New Bedford to Vineyard Haven and then a bus from there to Edgartown.

Edgartown is a very famous, wealthy town a summer playground for the rich and famous. Here we were the poor and obscure about to take the place by storm. Edgartown was a small (by New Bedford standards) whaling port in the nineteenth century. It has a fine, protected harbor running roughly north – south and is protected on all sides by bluffs. It is about ¼ mile wide, around a mile long and averages 20 ft in depth accommodating many vessels on mooring and anchors. One enters the harbor at the Edgartown light and then proceeds roughly west past the town docks and the venerable Edgartown Yacht Club which is perched on a dock jutting out into the harbor. On route, you pass the "Chappy" ferry which plies the ¼ mile trough between Chappaquiddick Island (cf Senator Ted Kennedy and his infamous joy ride) and downtown Edgartown. Entering the harbor is usually quite a spectacle as there are always people beautiful people and beautiful boats to behold.

We found Rustle about half way down Edgartown harbor and rafted alongside, then made plans with him to have dinner in town that evening. Linda was ashore shopping, so the boys had a few beers before heading into town. The town owned the moorings and rented them for $5/night which included launch service to the town landing. We hailed the launch that was being run that day by the town's harbormaster, Mr. Prada. Mr. Prada was a native who had been born and raised in Edgartown. He was a bit reticent, but he became friendly and as we headed to shore and he quizzed us as to our whereabouts, when I mentioned Fairhaven, he exclaimed that he had a sister who lived there. As it turned out, his sister and her family lived across the street from my parents and I knew them all very well. I knew that they had roots on the Vineyard, but Mrs. Rezendes never informed me that she had a brother in Edgartown. We hit it off after he found that I knew his sister and her family and he took note of us.

He suggested that we patronize the "Kafe" for dinner as the food was good and reasonably priced. This we did, but on our way there, we bumped into my sister and Nina who had just arrived on the bus. Now we had a large crew and headed toward the Kafe for dinner and madness. As you might expect, the Kafe served "adult beverages" and we made the most of it. Peter produced his kazu and after dinner, over more drinks, he entertained everyone in the place with renditions of old songs including many of Tony Randall's "disaster songs". Tony claimed these songs were written to commemorate great events which, unfortunately, went sour, they became known as "smash flops". The inevitable ending of these events was (he claimed) that these songs were resigned to obscurity. Tony Randall was a regular on Jonny Carson's "Tonight" show which Peter

121

viewed religiously. Consequently, Peter knew all of Tony's "disaster" songs by heart as did Ed and Bob. The repertoire consisted of "Bon Voyage to You New Titanic" supposedly written to be played on the arrival of the ship from her ignominious maiden voyage, "They'll Be A Hot, Hot Night in Lakehurst New Jersey" which turned out to be a lame celebratory refrain about the arrival of the Hindenburg at the conclusion of her flight and the last song was "When Amelia Earhart Circles the World" which rounded out the routine. By the time we left at 10:45, the place was rocking. We would have stayed longer, but we had to catch the last launch before 11:00. At the dock next to the Edgartown Yacht Club, Peter and I stepped in to the bar to grab a "nightcap" before the launch arrived. We began talking with two women at the bar when it was announced that the last launch was about to leave, Pete bolted for the dock with me in pursuit and in the process I spilled my beer on the floor. In an instant, the Yacht club carabinieri were on me, hustling me out the side door to the launch dock. I had been physically ejected (thrown out) from the Edgartown Yacht Club, a badge that I would wear proudly from then on throughout my sailing career.

    Rustle and Linda had gone out earlier, so there were five of us waiting for Mr. Prada when he showed up and as we boarded his launch he asked each of us which boat we were bound for. One after another we responded "*Whiskers*". With each successive response, Mr. Prada looked increasingly more perplexed. Finally, as I boarded and responded to his question with the same response, he burst out,

- "*Whiskers?.. Whiskers?.....Whiskers* is a Rhodes 19, this is the last launch, are you sure that's where you want to go? I won't be coming out to get you later....you'll all have to sleep on that damned thing!"
- "Yup, that's right, we'll figure it out" I said,
- He just mumbled something under breath to the effect of, "now I've seen it all" and backed out of the slip and we were on our way.

As luck would have it, Peter bunked aboard the Cal once again, but the Deb, Nina, Ed and I bunked out on *Whiskers*. Two up forward, one each on the cockpit seats and all reported a good night's sleep the next day.

In the morning, a dip over the side was the method of choice for morning hygiene requirements, we then we headed ashore once more for breakfast at the Kafe. Bob and Linda elected to stay another night in Edgartown, but the rest of us needed to get back, so we headed out towards Woods Hole under an increasing overcast with a building southerly breeze. The latter was fortuitous as we could broad reach on our rhumb line toward our destination. We had a three to four hour sail to Woods Hole and inevitably, the ladies eventually had need of "the facilities". As could be expected, there were no "facilities" on a 19 foot daysailer, but that was fine with the male crew which was anatomically-adapted to the conditions. It was quite a different matter for the female guests, so we did our best to accommodate them. Onboard we had a collapsible canvas bucket that, when partially filled with seawater, was placed in the cuddy as an emergency female waste receptacle. A beach towel draped over the cuddy entrance provided a modicum of privacy for the participant. The male crew members became aware that the "bucket was being used when, on occasion, a scream would be emitted by the user as the boat lurched and cold seawater splashed up on her bottom from the bucket. Deb and Nina were good sports about the whole thing and our answer to their call of nature seemed modest but adequate. As the afternoon wore on, it was clear that a rainstorm was approaching and the tidal current in Woods Hole was foul, so we headed for Falmouth, just east of Woods Hole expecting to wait out the weather until the next day.

Falmouth has a long narrow harbor that serves a few commercial day fish boats, many recreational boats and two or three commercial ferries that make the Vineyard run. We entered the harbor and headed to the north end where we found a town landing that we could use for the night for a nominal charge. What was even better, we found the "Beef and Brew" restaurant that was about 50 yards from the landing. We buttoned up the boat and carried our personal gear into the restaurant. It was about three in the afternoon when we settled down to a late lunch or early dinner (your choice) of steak, potatoes and pitchers of beer. After a few hours and many pitchers of beer, we stepped out to check the boat and found that the monsoon had arrived, ….. it was pouring! It was obvious that five people would not be sleeping on *Whiskers* that night. Fortunately, Peter had a company credit card (a rare item in those days) and was able to secure a double room at a local Hilton. His plan was to keep the cost low by checking in as a single in a room with patio access; the rest of us would then sneak in through the patio door. We hailed a cab and headed over to the Hilton. Pete checked in and came back out to the cab purportedly to pay the cabbie, but in fact to give us the room number. Pete returned to the motel with a small bag and headed for his room. We exited the cab in the rain, ran around the back of the building and Pete let us in through the patio. The girls got a bed to themselves, Ed and I doubled up on the box spring of the second bed and Pete got a mattress on the floor.

In the morning we reversed our previous night's footsteps and upon crowding into a cab headed back down to the harbor. The rain had ended, bit it was a still misty morning. We peeled back the boom tent, bailed the boat out, started the Seagull and headed for Woods Hole, checking the Eldridge to determine what the tidal current was up to in the "hole". We found that it would be against us, but only at three knots or so. Before entering the hole, we stopped and I topped off the Seagull's gas tank, ……..ANTICIPATE!

The town of Woods Hole is home to the world renowned Woods Hole Oceanographic Institute, the National Marine Fisheries Service, the Marine Biological Laboratory and Coast Guard Station Group Woods Hole. It's also the mainland terminus for the Steamship Authority and (at the time) their major ferry terminal. The town has played many a part in my life as I will detail later.

Woods Hole passage is undoubtedly the most treacherous of the four passages between Buzzards Bay and Vineyard Sound it is also the most heavily trafficked.

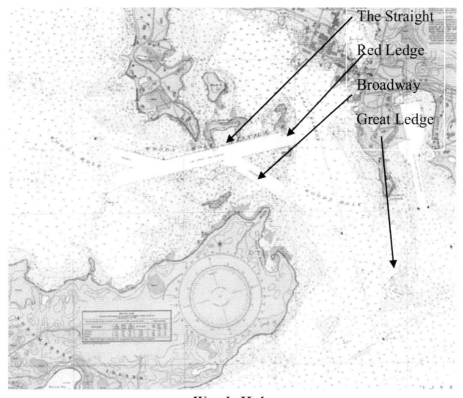

The Straight

Red Ledge

Broadway

Great Ledge

Woods Hole

As shown in this rendition of the NOAA chart of Woods Hole passage, the channel is a double dog leg with obstructions everywhere. The infamous "Red Ledge" is located at the intersection of Broadway and "The Straight", when the current is flooding, it sweeps down the main channel from Buzzards Bay and over Red Ledge. When you approach Can 3 at the junction of Broadway and the Straight, you need to make an instant decision (if not made beforehand) which way you're going to go, should you hesitate, there's a good chance the four knot current will sweep you over Red Ledge. What's more if you choose Broadway, you'd best stay to the right side of the channel until you clear Red Ledge. Many a yacht has come to grief on Red Ledge because of tardy decision making by the helmsman. The current in the hole can reach speeds of five knots at certain times of the year. When the sou'wes or nor'wes wind whips down The Straight, there's usually a four foot standing wave in the middle of the channel between can 5 and nun 6. Can 3 has recently been replaced with a steel day shape that is embedded on the sea floor, because can 3 had a nasty habit of being sucked underwater by the current and thereby disappearing for short periods of time.

Can 5 on The Straight, note new day shape replacement for the infamous can 3

This was fine if the helmsmen kept a sharp lookout when transiting the passage, but as I mentioned, you need to hug this nav aid to keep clear of Red Ledge. There were frequent instances of a skipper frantically looking for can 3 only to have it suddenly rise up under his boat striking the bottom and causing a great deal of damage. Can 3 was one of the larger nav aids in the channel the larger size was required for sufficient buoyancy to keep it afloat in the swirling current at that juncture of the channels. As a result, if it popped up under a boat, it usually resulted in a general alarm and frantic efforts to stem the resulting flooding onboard from the hole in the bottom of the boat. On summer weekends events such as this would occur as 10 to 15 boats were simultaneously traversing this narrow waterway. In short, transiting Woods Hole passage was always an adventure.

Since we're on the subject of Woods Hole, I will now divert from my *Whiskers* narrative to describe my adventures with Capt'n Charles G. Mitchell and the Tug Jaguar in and around Woods Hole. I'll pick up on the *Whiskers* account further down the line.

Tug Jaguar

As I detailed back at the beginning of this book, Charlie Mitchell had a yearning to become a tug boat captain after mustering out of the Navy and subsequently reading Farley Mowat's excellent book "The Grey Seas Under". This is a fascinating account of the Canadian ocean salvage company called Foundation Marine and their chief ocean salvage tugboat the *SS Foundation Franklin*. The book recounts astonishing depictions of high seas salvage operations during two world wars by this tough little vessel and her equally resilient crew. As I recounted, Charlie cut his teeth with Sanchez Towing Company and then bought, restored and worked his first tug, the *Fort Phoenix*. Charlie had some interesting adventures with that old boat including his endeavors to corral floating containers in a mountainous seaway off Hens and Chickens reef near Westport following the grounding of a container that spilled its contents into the bay. Tug *Jaguar* was built in 1978 as a replacement for the aging *Fort Phoenix* and she was gradually fitted out over the years as funds became available. This was typical Yankee bootstrap thrift and ingenuity. *Jaguar* has two 671 GM diesels (350 hp each) and her twin screw power and Charlie's uncanny capability to handle her often caused observers to inquire if *Jaguar* had bow thrusters.

In 1979, my wife Carole and I bought a house on Fort St. in Fairhaven and two years later, Charlie, with whom I interacted over the years, bought 26 Fort St, three houses south from us. We socialized regularly for the next couple of years as neighbors and friends and on occasion I would help Charlie on *Jaguar* with docking jobs and even one small salvage operation on Red Ledge in Woods Hole. Around February of 1982 Carole had taken our baby girl Julie to visit Carole's family in Oregon and I was left to "bach it" for a couple of weeks. At the time, Charlie was dating his future wife Janine and on a blustery, cold Sunday afternoon, they invited me to join them for a lamb dinner at their house. I headed down toward their home at 16:30 and I was literally pushed down the street by the building nor'wes gale. The mercury in the thermometer was sinking with the sun as the air temperature approached 18 degrees.

In contrast to the chilly weather conditions, I was warmly welcomed by my hosts and dinner was nearly ready as the VHF radio in the sunroom crackled with conversations between fish boats out on the bay and their counterparts tied up in the harbor. Since his profession was towing and salvage, Charlie needed to keep his ear to the radio to be sure he didn't miss any potential opportunities. Consequently, the VHF was always on, which served as a bit of an annoyance to some. I liked it though, because I also relished possibility of some seaborne action.

After dinner, over coffee, the wind was increasing and the night took on an increasingly malevolent quality. Like our house, Charlie's was on the water side of Fort street and bore the brunt of a nor'wes wind as the harbor was wide open to the north for nearly a mile. We'd been sitting in the sunroom listening to a developing "case" as they're called, of a fish boat named the *Connie F* that had been homeward bound to New Bedford from Quick's Hole when her crew discovered she was shipping water in the foc's'al and engine room. She was an older 65' eastern rigged trawler and had been pounding into a head sea all the way back from George's Bank. It appeared that she'd opened some seams below the waterline from the punishment she had endured and now she was paying for it. Interestingly, the *Connie F* was the first job Charlie had with the old *Fort Phoenix* towing her in with engine trouble; he had a soft spot for her. In her heyday, *Connie F* had been a "high liner", waterfront lingo for a very productive and profitable fish boat. But in 1982, those glory days were well behind her and the crew had all they could do to pay off expenses and hope to see a pay check. In that atmosphere, boat maintenance often suffered, such was the fate of an older wooden eastern rig and on this bitter, windswept night in February, the piper had been paid and the *Connie F* was going down.

The Coast Guard had dispatched a forty-four foot motor lifeboat from Woods Hole to supply two-inch, gas-powered pumps to the *Connie F* to stem the flooding. The CG had sent the 44, because the conditions in the middle of Buzzards Bay that night were too extreme for their 41-foot utility boats. The 44 was a self-righting, surfboat that can withstand breaking seas and high winds, but they were not nearly as fast as the 41. The 44's have since been replaced with the aluminum hulled 47-foot self-righting patrol boats.

44 foot motorlifeboat

The 44 was one rugged vessel, but so too was *Jaguar*. As we monitored the "on scene" events, it became evident that the situation was getting worse. Charlie called it beforehand when he predicted that the CG pumps wouldn't work. This was surprising to me, because as I discovered later, the CG tests their pumps beforehand, fuels them up and then they're stored in water-tight, half-sized 55 gallon drums with a sealed top. In this manner, they're always ready to use. When I quizzed Charlie about why they weren't working, he simply replied, "They never do".

As we heard the coms back and forth between CG Group Woods Hole and the *Connie F* it became increasingly clear that things were beginning to go down hill fast. The flooding was escalating as she settled and the crew couldn't get the pumps working, because they were quickly clogging and shutting down. It then became clear what Charlie meant, the CG pumps had no screens on the pump hose intake, so they quickly clogged with the debris that normally resides in the bilge of a fish boat, especially on an old boat like the *Connie F*.

Charlie picked up the microphone of his sunroom VHF and broke into the conversation between the CG and the *Connie F*:

-"Break, break….Connie F, Tug Jaguar, ….Connie F, Tug Jaguar, come back"
- "Tug Jaguah, …Connie F, .ovah"

- "Yeah, Skip (Capt'n's name) what's the situation?"
- "(long pause) Well, Chahlie, doesn't look good, lot a watah up fo'wahd and in the engine
   room...pumps are, ah.......(long pause)... Coast Guahd pumps are clogged...we've got one wourkin', but the watah's makin' up pretty good,... ovah"
-" Okay Skip, we're headed down to the boat should be out there in forty-five minutes, can you
   hold on?"

There was another long pause on the other end of the microphone,
-    "Yeah Chahlie, I think we can hold on till then, but......ah,...(another pause)...I don't have any money Chahlie and I'm not shuah the insurance will covah you"
Charlie then keyed in the mike and said:
   -   "Yeah Skip, but you want to save the boat, don't you?"
   -   "Yeah Chahlie, I want to save the boat"
Charlie replied:
   -   "Okay, then, we'll be out there in forty,...no, thirty minutes"

Charlie, looked at me and asked, "Are you in?" I replied immediately "Are you kidding, of course I'm in".

Connie F

At that point he called his mate, Dick Searle to alert Dick to get down to the boat and then Charlie and I bundled up and jumped into his car to make the short ride down the street to Fairhaven Shipyard. When we arrived, Dick Searle was already onboard, firing up the engines. Charlie yelled down to inquire if Dick had switched from shore power to the generators and upon getting an affirmative yelled to me to clear the shore power chord and stand by to cast off. I completed the order and stood on the dock shivering slightly from the minus twenty degree wind chill or adrenaline or both. Finally, Charlie lowered his window in the wheel house and motioned to me to clear the bowline and make ready the stern line. The dock was quite slick with ice as I jumped about clearing lines. With the bowline thrown aboard, I moved aft to find Dick on the after deck, I cleared the stern line and tossed it to him and Charlie began powering Jaguar forward, tensing the spring line so I could remove it and holding her to the dock. I lifted the slackened spring line off the piling and stepped aboard, Charlie put Jaguar in reverse and we steamed stern first away from the dock and into the night. At this point the wind was up to thirty knots in the harbor and the temperature had dropped to single digits, surprisingly, I was not cold. I was wearing blue jeans, a turtleneck woolen sweater and a lined jacket. I had one pair of heavy woolen socks and topsiders for footwear. As we turned and headed for the dike, I entered the deckhouse, closed and dogged the door and climbed the four spoke ladder from the cramped by efficient galley up to the wheel house.

Charlie and Dick were already there and Charlie was a whirlwind of activity talking almost simultaneously on two VHF radios while poking buttons on the Loran set and peering into the radar hood. We wasted no time as Charlie increased our speed toward ten knots as we passed through the gates of the hurricane dike and out into the bay. I hadn't met Dick before, so after a hasty introduction, he and I sat back quietly listening to the radio chatter and awaiting instructions.

By the time we cleared Butler's Flat lighthouse, Charlie had sufficient information from his radio conversations to formulate a plan. He instructed Dick and me to ready two four-inch pumps for transfer over to the *Connie F* once we arrived on scene. He also instructed us to retrieve the pump screens from the lazarette and fit these to the intake hoses on each pump to prevent pump clogging. He then told us to come back up after finding and ready the equipment for instructions. We proceeded down to the engine room, found the pumps, hoses and screens, made all ready for transfer and headed back to the wheelhouse. By then, we were approaching the casualty way south of Brooklyn Rock, about halfway across the bay. The breaking seas were running around seven feet at this point and *Jaguar* was rolling 25 degrees from side to side. When we returned to the wheelhouse, Charlie was still in conference with the CG and the captain of the *Connie F.* After a several minutes he turned to us and explained the game plan. He would pull *Jaguar* up on the leward side of *Connie F* and hold there while we transferred the pumps and then he would stand closely by while we got the pumps going and began pumping the boat out.

Although she was going down, *Connie F* was still maneuvering under her own power and she had electricity as she slowly made progress toward New Bedford. However, this would not last for long as the rising water was threatening her main engine and generator. Under these conditions, we were instructed by Charlie that in no uncertain terms if we could not make progress against the incipient flooding, we should call *Jaguar* immediately and Charlie would pull up close to get is all off;......leave the equipment.

Charlie pulled *Jaguar* up to the *Connie F* and kissed her starboard aft bulwark with *Jaguar's* port bulwark, a textbook example of proper ship handling under very difficult circumstances. I boarded the fish boat behind the wheelhouse and Dick began handing the pumps, hoses and jerry cans over to me. *Jaguar* has around three feet of freeboard at her stern, so what I found amazing was that I had to step down about two feet to get aboard the *Connie F*; she definitely was sinking.

Besides the crew of five, *Connie F* now had two CG personnel and two *Jaguar* personnel onboard fighting against the elements. Dick quickly set up one intake hose in the engine room and placed the pump on the rail telling me to hold it there so that the output would flow over the side. He instructed the engineer to clear the hose periodically, he started the pump and then moved forward with the second one to begin working on the fo'c'sal. The engine of the pump roared away as water blasted out over the side at an amazing rate. I held onto the pump with two hands, one of which was situated near the engine spark plug. The pump and frame weighed about fifty pounds, but most of the weight was borne by the rail, I just had to hold it there.

Over the next hour, the pump worked frantically and on occasion when the boat rolled, my hand would touch the spark plug and give me one hell of a jolt. I was in the middle of the "fog of war" existing in my little world of bilge pump, wet feet, cold air and noise, not knowing if we were winning or losing this little war against the sea. Occasionally, *Jaguar* would circle by and I could make out Charlie in the wheelhouse with the radio microphone in his hand. It was comforting to know that salvation was not far away should the situation become desperate. Finally, I began to notice that the sea was a bit further down the side of the boat from where it had been when I first boarded. After an hour or so, the engineer emerged from the engine room to tell me to kill the pump, because the water was under control. I did so, placed the pump on deck and headed forward to the fo'c'sal.

There I found Dick and the Mate working away in the bilge still pumping water. Dick finally emerged and motioned for me to follow him aft. We entered the wheelhouse to find the Captain talking to Charlie on the VHF. He reported that the flooding had been stemmed and they would proceed to Pier 3 under their own power. Charlie confirmed the transmission and said he'd standby until *Connie F* reached the dock; the 44 stood by as well. Dick and I stood in the wheelhouse chatting with the captain who was very appreciative of our efforts. I noticed there was a small forced hot water radiator on the back wall of the wheelhouse that was pumping out some heat and ambled over toward it. We steamed along slowly at about five knots as the wind continued to whistle, but the seas moderated as we came under the lee of the New Bedford shoreline. We transited the gates of the hurricane dike headed up the harbor and finally tied up at the Fisherman's Coop dock.

It was around midnight and there were a dozen people at the dock as we tied up. These were families of the *Connie F* crew and as I watched, an impromptu celebration erupted as we finished making her fast to the dock. As the crew climbed up on the dock, they were met with hugs and kisses and an outpouring of emotion. It was then that it hit me, these guys were in real trouble and their families were extremely worried about them. It gave me a warm feeling inside, I didn't say anything to anyone, but I realized that I had been part of a rescue. What a nice feeling it was to have a really positive effect on a stranger's life. I didn't dwell on it, and I didn't feel that I'd done anything special, but it certainly was a nice feeling. It became clear to me at that point why Coast Guardsmen, Policemen and Firemen do what they do.

Dick and I reboarded *Jaguar*, which had pulled up alongside Connie

F, and upon reaching the wheelhouse Charlie announced that coffee and burgers were on their way from MacDonald's. He'd contacted a crewmen who missed our departure and this fellow was on his way to us with the food. When the food arrived there was plenty for everyone (compliments of tug *Jaguar*) the CG, us and the *Connie F* crew. We chowed down, except for Charlie who crossed over to the *Connie F* to work out the business arrangements with Skip. The crew of the 44 got their grub and after expressing appreciation, headed back to Woods Hole across a highly turbulent Buzzards Bay.

At around 01:00, as I listened to tales of the previous rescues, Charlie suddenly swung open the deck house door and ran up the ladder to the wheel house exclaiming "The *Northern Edge* is up on Great Ledge". He dashed over to the VHF and responded to Woods Hole CG asking for confirmation of the casualty and what the captain had requested for assistance. After finishing his transmission, he turned to us and said that the scalloper *Northern Edge* had grounded on Great Ledge in Woods Hole and needed assistance. Were we willing to go out again? At this point, we were all a bit beat, but what was the alternative? Where was he going to get a crew at that ungodly hour? After a few minutes, the owner of the *Northern Edge* agreed to have *Jaguar* render assistance, so off we went, back out in 40 knot winds and air temperatures of five degrees….oh what the hell!

The trip across the bay was one to remember. *Jaguar* is known to roll considerably in a following sea as she is not of deep draft, but that night was amazing. I was standing on the starboard side of the wheelhouse near the ladder, holding on for dear life while I looked down below my waist at Charlie on the port side of the house. The boat was rolling 35 degrees to either side with each sea. The waves must have been enormous in the middle of the bay, but I couldn't make them out for the spume and blackness of the night. As we came under the lee of Weepecket Island, the seas diminished appreciably and we steamed directly up The Straight and into Great Harbor. Charlie was busy most of the way over checking the tidal currents, and charts, the weather and interacting with the CG and the captain of the *Northern Edge* over the VHF. Once again, he had a plan in place for this salvage before we arrived on scene. The CG provided a 41-footer as an assistant since the weather conditions at Great Ledge were acceptable for this boat. The CG met us as we arrived on the scene and awaited instructions from Charlie.

Dick and I headed down the wheelhouse ladder to prepare for the next step in this rescue. Dick flipped the "dogs" (hinged levers on the side door that seal it shut) on the wheelhouse door and tried to push it open. It wouldn't budge because there was a thick layer of sea ice coating the whole wheelhouse and the door was sealed shut. We both put our shoulders against the door and banged it open breaking free the ice that coated it. The deck was a solid sheet of ice from bow to stern and we both needed to hold tight to the handrail that is fixed to the wheelhouse and walk gingerly on the slick deck. Dick moved aft and began breaking up the ice covered three-inch polypropylene hawser that was coiled on the lower section of the wheelhouse just aft of the stack. I moved forward to take a line form the 41 footer. Sea ice has physical properties that are very different from fresh water ice; it has a texture similar to frozen treacle. Although not nearly as slippery as fresh water ice, sea ice can still be dangerous. We were instructed by Charlie to be very careful on deck that night since the water temperature was just above freezing (27°F) and if we fell in, we wouldn't last long. It was somewhat comforting that the 41 was there in the unsavory event of such an accident.

As we pulled to within 200 yards of the casualty, I noticed that the crew had deployed the six man inflatable life raft which was tied up alongside the fish boat. She was listing slightly to starboard with her stern toward us and it was evident that she was stuck good and proper. She went up just after flood tide, so it was important to connect and start pulling before the tide went out completely if we were going to prevent any more damage to the vessel. Although there wasn't a large seaway running, because the wind was nor'wes, occasionally a huge swell would roll in from Vineyard Sound and violently break over the stern quarter of the boat sending white water over her after deck. I now understood why the crew had deployed the life raft. She had grounded with her stern to the prevailing wind, so we would need to extract her in the same direction. This strategy placed the prevailing wind on Jaguar's port bow which would push us toward Great Ledge while we waited for the hawser to be connected to the casualty. The 41 would take the hawser in and then we would pass a one inch line to the 41 which would pull our bow to windward until the hawser was securely connected and we were on a course away from Great Ledge.

These tasks were completed and as the 41 pulled on our bow, Charlie put the "pedal to the metal" and we pulled for all we were worth on the casualty. After about ten minutes, we dropped the line to the 41, no longer needed, and continued to hank on the casualty. Forty minutes later, just when it seemed as though nothing would happen, the captain on the *Northern Edge* announced over the VHF that he felt her move. We continued to pull and then heard more positive reports over the radio. Finally, after about an hour of pulling, she came free with a bounce and Charlie immediately backed off on the throttles. We pulled her about 300 yards away from Great Ledge and then Dick and I ran back aft. As Charlie backed down toward the casualty, Dick and I pulled in the floating polypropylene hawser and laid it on the after deck. As a last measure, the Hawser was run forward and we towed *Northern Edge* into Great Harbor where she was made fast to the dock. It was four thirty in the morning. Charlie found me a ride back to Fairhaven where I showered and ate breakfast at Margaret's restaurant. This is a local waterfront eatery and hangout, so I was able to regale the local maritime cognizantě with the tales of daring do from the previous night's outing. Following this, I headed off to work and after a brutal day, I crashed at five PM.

There is footnote to this tale, I believe the *Connie F* fished for a number of years and then she was retired, too old to continue her battle with mother nature and the elements. My understanding is that she was sunk off the south coast of Long Island as an artificial reef. So, even in death, she continued to help fishermen. *Jaguar* and Charlie continue to work the New Bedford waterfront and the coast of New England. A sad fate finally befell the *Northern Edge*. In December of 2004, she capsized in heavy seas off Nantucket in the middle of the night. The lone survivor recalled how he clung to the vessel's life raft for nearly an hour before being rescued by a second fishing boat that was nearby. He was extraordinarily lucky to have been seen and rescued considering that the seas were running eleven feet and the water temperature was near freezing. Five men lost their lives that night which made this accident the worst since the *Andrea Gail* sank in the Perfect Storm of 1991.

Back to Whiskers

So, to recap, there were five of us onboard my Rhodes 19 *Whiskers* headed from Falmouth through Woods Hole passage into Buzzards Bay. The only time any of us had ever transited Woods Hole was onboard a ferry from New Bedford. We knew it was a difficult and potentially treacherous channel and we knew that we would be fighting a foul current, albeit fading as we transited the passage. As I mentioned before I digressed from this tale, I had filled the gas tank of the Seagull outboard knowing full well that we would be reliant in this device to get us through the passage. We sailed up to the mid channel mark north of Great Ledge and then I started the Seagull as we began to be effected by the foul current. I started the engine (being careful to disengage the choke , (ANTICIPATE!) and I opened the throttle half way.

We cruised along under main, jib (the wind was light) and "iron sails" until we started up Broadway at which point I gave the engine more throttle. We rounded can 3 at full throttle and inched our way into the The Straight. We powered along and finally dropped the jib as it was hurting more than helping and inched along as vessels passed on either side of us. There were times when I thought we were losing ground and everyone else also looked a bit concerned, but finally we began to speed up against the onrushing water and made it out of The Straight headed into Buzzards Bay. It took us about 40 minutes to transit the passage and the current was fading as we went through. I would not have wanted to make that passage against a neap tidal current. The Seagull had finally redeemed itself as we were able to shut her down and sail on our way. I tilted the engine forward and checked the gas tank......empty! We had finished the passage on fumes.

We sailed nearly due north headed for Nina's parent house on Mattapoisett Neck. Nina's family controlled the My Bread backing company in New Bedford the signature product of which was Sunbeam bread. Nina's grandfather had founded the company and, she being the oldest granddaughter, was claimed to have been the inspiration for the product's iconic logo Little Miss Sunbeam. My sister and Nina were schoolmates, beginning with kindergarten, and now as adults still maintained their friendship. My sister is fond of telling the story of how she and Nina enjoyed sailing Nina's bettlecat in the summer when they both were teenagers. The story went that they used to sail out to Butler's Flat lighthouse which at the time was manned by Coast Guard personnel. This lighthouse was a bunker-type structure that stood singularly on a shoal next to the ship channel in New Bedford. It was about one-half mile to the nearest shore and the personnel that were consigned to the light required transportation from shore and subsequently had no means of egress once aboard.

Enter these two little mischievous vixens in a beetlecat; just for fun, these two would remove their bikini tops and sail around the lighthouse taunting the poor twenty year old Coast Guardsmen. One can only imagine the torment inflicted upon these hormone-ravaged young men at the tantalizing scene of two half-naked young women just beyond their reach. Apparently, this scene occurred more than once, but I didn't learn of the miscreant episodes until my sister was in her mid-twenties. What a couple of rascals!

We sailed across the bay and up to the dock at Nina's parent's house where we were warmly welcomed. Nina and Deb unloaded their belongings and we bid them farewell as Pete, Ed and I headed east toward New Bedford. By then, the faithful sou'wester had piped up and we were in for yet another salty excursion. All went well until we were approaching the bell outside West Island which we needed to observe in our transit back to New Bedford. We had checked all of this with our new chart of Buzzards Bay (the reader will remember that I lost the first one during the BBR) because, once again, we were all novices at navigating these waters. As we beat upwind to the bell, I slumped down into the cuddy and retrieved baloney sandwiches for everyone from our cooler. I was sitting in the shelter of the cuddy when Ed sarcastically (He still is very sarcastic) asked if he could have some salt with his sandwich. No sooner had he made his request when a huge dollop of seawater broke over the rail and drenched him and his sandwich. He sat there dumfounded with a drooping, soaking wet sandwich in his hand staring at me in amazement. I looked back from the shelter of the cuddy and without missing a beat I asked "would you like some pepper to go with that salt?". We sailed on and reached New Bedford late in the afternoon. We were now tired, salty veterans of a weeklong cruise across some nasty waters in a very small boat.

The last chapter in the *Whiskers* saga involves an end of the year get together at the LTYC. One of their last social events in those days that was called "The Steakout" and as the name suggests, it was a steak cookout at the club, usually held in late September on the club grounds. Ed, Peter, Rustle and I all signed up and attended. I wasn't familiar with very many of the club members, but most of them were well acquainted with Rustle and Ed, since they had grown up in the South End of New Bedford. As we stood in a group drinking draft beer in plastic cups, Ed introduced me to one of his acquaintances. He, of course used my full name, Scott Morris, during this introduction. No sooner had he finished saying my name than a middle-aged gentleman who was close by in another group, walked over to us and remarked "Scott Morris, Scott Morris…which one of you is Scott Morris?" Of course, I immediately owned up to my personage to which he said in consternation:

"Do you realize that you broke EVERY RULE in the book while racing this summer?"

Everyone in our circle looked at me, rolled their eyes and chuckled, but I just let it roll off my back.

"Well" I responded, "you have to start somewhere and I can only get better from here"

He let out an uproarious laugh, patted me on the back and bought me a beer.

The remainder of the season paled by comparison to that week of "pocket" cruising, it was clear that we all enjoyed our time that week and wanted more. We realized that we would soon be adhering to Roy Scheider's advice in "Jaws"……. "We're going to need a bigger boat" so we began to hatch plans to find a suitable replacement that winter.

This was the beginning of the next sailing yarns and the birth of the *Circadian Rhythms*.

~ Chapter 8 ~

To Marblehead to follow Chief Brody's advice

After the Hobie cats and *Whiskers* were hauled out for the winter, Pete and Ed would occasionally drive up to Boston and the three of us would prowl boat yards looking for a new boat. Ed and I agreed to be partners on the new purchase and would sell our current vessels as part of the down payment expecting to finance the remainder. One particular Saturday in late January 1975 found this trio in Marblehead driving along the waterfront, sampling the offerings of the numerous yacht brokers. We were looking for a used boat in the 23 to 25 foot range, but after reviewing the available listings and speaking with several brokers, we were satisfied that their inventories lacked what we were seeking. As we ambled along one of the crooked streets near the harbor, we noticed three brand new sailboats sitting in a parking lot next to the brokerage Sailboats Northeast. These three were exactly alike with the exception of color, one was red, one yellow and one was cobalt blue. They looked gorgeous, so we decided to stop in and see if the brokerage had any used boats like these for sale.

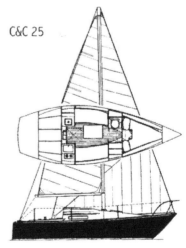

C&C 25

As we walked into the office, there we were met by the ever affable Peter

Specifications:
L.O.A.: 25' 2" (7.67 m)
L.W.L.: 20' 8" (6.30 m)
Beam: 8' 9" (2.68 m)
Draft: 3' 10" (1.17 m)
Displacement: 4138 lbs. (1880 kg.)
Ballast: 2090 lbs. (949 kg.)
Sail area: 306 sq. ft. (28.45 m²)
Motor: ususally 9.9 hp outboard.
Headroom: 5' 8"
Berths: 4

Rating (PHRF-LO) : 213

Haines. Peter was about our age, very well groomed and knowledgeable about boats and …..people. We explained our objective, which was to find a comfortable used sailboat of 23-25 feet with a price tag in the five to eight thousand dollar range. He listened carefully and pulled out his used listings book, but as he did, he noticed Ed dreamily admiring the three new C&C 25s in his parking lot. He began to tell Peter Richards and me that he didn't have much in that price or size range and then he stopped himself mid-sentence and looked at Ed and said "Would you like to step outside and have a peek at one of the new C&C 25s that just arrived?" As he directing his question at Eddy he added "Just to eliminate them as a possibility, you understand." Ed remarked. "Oh, sure, why not" as we all got up and headed for the door. Now this was one of those rare days in late January when the air was quite chilly and there was frozen aged snow all about, but the sky was deep blue, as was the hull to which Ed immediately gravitated.

The sun was shining and the parking lot was clear of snow as we climbed up the viewing staging next to the three boats. We boarded the blue one and Peter Haines opened the cabin for us to step inside. Immediately, we were all hopelessly smitten. Peter Haines showed off the various aspects of the cabin and although he was a very good salesman, the boat was doing the selling. We finished our tour and he dragged us away, back to the office to look at the numbers….just to eliminate this as a possibility. He ran through the numbers figuring what he could allow for Ed's Hobie and my Rhodes and came up with the final number. I believe it was around $10,000. He had financing immediately available (of course), and then he broke the payments down by the month and asked the age-old question; "Now you single guys can afford $135/month to sail this beautiful boat can't you?" I was a little hesitant at first, so he then

144

suggested that we head down to a waterfront pub to talk it over in private and then let him know. We headed across the street into the pub on the harbor and there sitting on a mooring right in front of the pub was the same exact boat, all rigged and ready to go. Man, what a sly salesman, he knew all along that boat would be there. We had a couple of beers and finally agreed that you only live once. So, we headed back up the street at Peter Richard's urging (he wasn't in on the deal, but he would be sailing with us) and agreed to the deal. Peter Haines had us fill out bank loan forms, in case we couldn't get a better deal, then we signed all the papers and we owned a boat….the blue one.

We went out one more time to have a look as the light was fading and then it was time to head back to my apartment in Cambridge. We were walking on air back to the car and when we got back to Boston, the first place we stopped was the Bull and Finch pub on Beacon St. This was the place that was made famous by the TV show "Cheers". I still believe that the converse was the case as Cheers was popularized by the Bull and Finch, since it had been in Boston for a very long time. So, we got drunk and called our parents and friends and anyone else who would listen to tell them the news that we'd bought a boat. That night we were kicking around names for the new boat and out of the blue I suggested *Circadian Rhythm*. Neither Peter nor Ed had heard the term before, but Ed liked it. I had learned this term from a graduate animal ethology course that I'd taken at U Mass Dartmouth a year or so before. It describes the natural routine than any animal exhibits during a normal day, such as waking, hygiene, hunting for food, eating, sleeping etc. The root of the term is from the Latin circa (about) and diem (day). As it turned out, after a few minutes of thought, an agreement was reached and the boat was dubbed *Circadian Rhythm*. With each call we made, when the question of "what will you name it was posed by the call recipient, we would all shout in unison "CIRCADIAN RHYTHM!". It was quite a night followed by quite a hangover on Sunday. Ed later claimed that the name reminded him of a new British rock band "Sir Cady and Rhythm".

During the following week, we firmed up transfer of funds for the boat, obtained the bill of sale and made arrangements for delivery of the C&C and the transfer of the traded boats. The delivery was set for early February and Leo Murach had agreed to store and subsequently launch the boat for us. There was about three weeks of anticipation as we prepared for the delivery during which we made trips to marine stores for boat parts and to Manchester Sail loft in Padanaram to commission the building of a suit of sails for the boat. We provided Gary Ledoux, the manager at Manchester, with the boat specifications and he obtained the sail specifications from C&C in Ontario. I found a ten hp Mercury outboard on sale at a marine store in Winchester and bought it then Ed and I bought a compass and associated deck hardware for sail handling. We also bought three single speed Lewmar winches to mount on the cabin top so that sail hoisting could be accomplished from the cockpit. The winter was a bit milder than usual, without much snow which was a good portent from our perspective.

Finally, the chosen Saturday came for the delivery. It was scheduled for late morning and we had a small contingent of followers with us as the tractor/trailer arrived with *Circadian Rhythm* aboard. Once in the boatyard, Mr. Murach fired up his travel lift and gingerly lifted boat and cradle off the trailer and set them down next to one of the other stored boats. He then lifted *Whiskers* and set her on the trailer and then Ed's Hobie cat. Peter Haines was on site with all the paper work and a bottle of champagne. After we provided him with bills of sale for our old boats, he gave us the one for *Circadian Rhythm* bid us good luck, fair winds and farewell. We found a ladder and clambered aboard toasting *Circadian Rhythm* with beer at 11:30 on a cool (35 °F) clear morning in Fairhaven anticipating a whole universe of new, exciting adventures.

Over the next couple of weeks we installed gear, bought more gear, corrected mistakes, redid installations, bought more gear, redid installations and in the process consumed prodigious qualities of beer. We scurried about boat stores with lists in hand during the week and converged on Murach's boatyard on the weekends to carry out the work on the boat. This was always weather-dependent, but we managed to get the work done before the launch date. On Saturdays, after finishing work, the three of us (Peter Richards was working right alongside) would repair to a restaurant for something to eat and then on to the Spinnaker bar for entertainment. By the time we arrived at the Spinnaker, we were a bit "popped" and after a few hours of dancing, drinking and socializing, we'd managed to talk a small group of people into accompanying us back at the boat sitting on a cradle in Murach's boatyard to continue the party. This was usually after the Spinnaker had closed for the night (1:00 AM). Everyone that came along was very pleased with the boat's layout and very happy to be drinking for free. I'd crank up the old Coleman stove to heat up the cabin and Peter would break out his Sony cassette player and the party would commence. There were times when we had eight to ten people crammed into the cabin of *Circadian Rhythm* singing, yelling and drinking at 02:30 in the morning. Poor Mr. Murach, he lived in a house on the property that was not more than 50 feet from the transom of our boat. He was a good sport about the whole thing and didn't call the police about the noise until the third party. The situation that ensued was classic, the police showed up in two squad cars (no lights or sirens) and one of them climbed up the ladder, gun in hand, transited the cockpit and then knocked politely on the companionway boards.

Peter was seated on the stoop just below the companionway, so he removed the boards to see a uniformed police officer standing there. His first response was "Good eeffening occifer, hoo can I help you?...... (hiccup)" The cop was somewhat stunned to see eight or nine people sitting in a boat on dry land illuminated by the glow of a Coleman stove with beer cans in their hand. He hesitated a bit and then stated that a noise complaint had been received and we needed to break up the party. Of course, we were always hospitable and invited him and his colleagues in to join us, but he declined and claiming that they were on duty and that we needed to call it a night. To which Peter immediately responded "Hokay" as he shut off the cassette player and we began to close up shop. I think this was the first time that the Fairhaven police had been called to break up a noisy party on a boat that was on dry land, I would have loved to have seen the "police log" for that weekend.

Finally, following several weeks of preparation, to the great relief of Mr. Murach we were going to launch the boat; this was on or about March 10th. I told Mr. Murach that we didn't intend to moor the boat at any of his slips that spring and with that he seemed to be even more enthusiastic about getting us in the water and away from his facility. The launch was set for Saturday morning to coincide with the tide so, like clockwork, Ed and I planned to begin the weekend at the Spinnaker on Friday night. My sister, Deb had come down from U Mass in Amherst for the launch. I found some old merchant marine officer's caps that my Dad had stored in the attic and armed with these, we headed off to the Spinnaker. Deb was wearing a nice dress for the occasion, Ed and I wore blue blazers and Ed sported a white turtleneck. We showed up at the door speaking with a phony British accent claiming that we were celebrating the launch of our

"Yacht" in the morning. Ed really played it up smoking his pipe and all and I referred to him as "Reggie", he called me "Freddy" and Deb was "Leslie". As we became more intoxicated, the theatrics further increased. We knew several of the people in the place and they got a big bang out of our play, but there were many strangers in attendance who truly believed that three wealthy English yachties were launching a boat in the morning. It was great fun…….until the morning arrived and we had to be at the boatyard by nine AM.

We had all slept at my parent's house on Cherry St, which was only a couple of blocks from the boatyard, but Ed and I were running on adrenaline as we headed down in his car to the boat. Deb was still asleep and we left instructions with my Mom to get her up, dressed and down to the yard as she was going to christen *Circadian Rhythm* before the boat hit the water. Fortunately, the morning was windless, clear and fairly temperate for that time of the year.

When we arrived, Peter Richards was already there with our mutual friend Bob Jones who was an extreme extrovert and had a fixation on media broadcasting. Bob was very hyper so he convinced Peter to help arrange a mock radio broadcast of the launching event they would record. Bob played the part of the radio interviewer/announcer and was dressed in a turtleneck and blazer and Peter was the "media guy" in the booth. Bob was walking around the yard with a microphone attached to his tape recorder trying to interview people and on several occasions, he approached Ed and me. We each paid him lip service, because there were far more serious issues on our agenda that day and we both had wicked hangovers. There were around fifteen people on site for the launch which, fortunately, didn't create too much confusion. Mr. Murach moved his small travel lift over and grabbed the C&C from her cradle and moved her over to the travel lift dock and began to lower the boat into the water. Just in the nick of time, my sister Deb showed up in a white flowing gown, the quintessential "vestal virgin", "Leslie" was now ready to christen our "yacht".

We opened the champagne that Peter Haines had given us at the delivery and Deb sprinkled some on the bow as the boat's keel kissed the harbor waters. Following this, she was quickly whisked away to the "broadcast booth" (Jonesy's VW minibus) where she was interviewed at length about her association with the enterprise. Meanwhile, Ed, Peter and I got on with the launching which included stepping the mast. Mr. Murach's travel lift was "jury rigged" for mast stepping and he was not used to such a large boat with such a tall mast. There were some fits and starts and at one point the truck of the mast nearly punctured the forward Plexiglas hatch, but finally, we got the rig secured and moved on.

After launching we loaded on sails, sandwiches, gasoline (we wisely mounted the engine on its transom mount while on dry land) and, of course, beer. The three of us with a few other friends (Deb went home and to bed) headed out for the maiden, shakedown cruise. After clearing the New Bedford-Fairhaven swing bridge, we "steamed" down the harbor while trying to figure out the sails. The main was no problem and had been bent on at the dock, but the first try with the genoa resulted in the tack being hoisted as the head; we finally got it straight. This was early afternoon, so the sou'wester was making up as we cleared the hurricane dike gates and headed out into the bay. Finally we had sails set and I killed the outboard and Oooooohhh, how sweet she sailed! We were in heaven, tacking upwind in 12 knots of wind healed over about 18 degrees and lovin' every minute of it. We sailed around in the outer harbor for a couple of hours and then headed in to tie up at the Coast Guard Auxiliary gas dock for the night. It had turned cooler and damp as we reluctantly secured and locked the boat. Our spirits improved as we headed up to 13 Cherry St for a launching party.

My mother had gathered friends and relatives and we had music and dancing as we toasted *Circadian Rhythm* and danced and sang the night away. My seventy-five year old grandparents were in attendance and I danced a jig with my grandmother. Around 11:00 the famous Nummy stopped by and I stood in the hallway listening to him banter on in a monotone as my body began to cry out for rest. I listened patiently standing at first, then leaning on the radiator, then stooping and finally lying on the floor as Nummy bantered on completely oblivious to my slowly sinking body. I finally made my apologies to him and dragged myself upstairs to a bed. The last I saw of Nummy he was still bantering at me as I headed up the stairs and disappeared in a bedroom.

We sailed again on Sunday even though the weather had deteriorated. The bloom was off the rose for our acquaintances and family, who, in light of the rotten weather, chose to stay ashore. So, the three of us spent the day becoming more accustomed to our boat. We finished in the late afternoon and that evening tied to our mooring with the Coleman pumping out heat in the cabin, we sat in silence and total satisfaction. We finally shut off the stove and headed ashore around 20:00 as I reluctantly headed back to Boston for work on Monday.

The weather had spared us that late winter, but it came on with a vengeance in the early spring. It seemed as though there was some sort of a snowstorm each weekend that year until late April and it was unusually cold. Nevertheless, Pete, Ed and I were on the boat each Friday evening getting ready to sail the next day despite the weather. The Spinnaker bar was always on the agenda for Friday and often we would drag a few people back to the boat and run a rowboat ferry service to get them all out to the boat. The party would ensue and unlike Murach's boatyard, we didn't need to worry about waking the neighbors or intrusions by the police. These impromptu parties would usually break up by three AM and the *Circadian Rhythm's* crew would call it a night and sleep onboard.

Most of our sailing in March and early April consisted of day sailing or overnight trips to Padanaram. The weather was generally cold and nasty, so we didn't venture too far offshore at first. We did spent many a weekend sailing in the snow and on one occasion, an announcer at the local radio station that was housed on Pope's Island mentioned that he could see those crazy sailors in that blue sailboat leaving the harbor once again in a snow storm. We were smitten and that was that. We would also take friends and relatives out for day sails during those first months and Ed had purchased a bottle of "Old Mister Boston" brandy to warm us and our passengers in the cabin during these cold sails. It was kept in a small wooden cabinet that Ed had attached to the main saloon bulkhead. When a guest came below and complained that it was terribly cold outside, one of us would swing open the cabinet and grab the bottle of brandy and present it to the dissident as a remedy for their complaint. They would then open the bottle and take a deep swig which immediately produced the exclamation "OH MY GOD!" This stuff was so bad that it produced the same effect on everyone who sampled it. It did have the desired effect of warming them, so we changed the name to "Oh My God Brandy".

The weather that spring led to the nearly complete consumption of that brandy as it was cold, windy, snowy and foggy. Not all at the same time, mind you, but we did experience many of the weather conditions, of which windy was the most prevalent. More than once, when we arrived at the mooring, we were required to shovel snow off the deck before setting sail. We were a common sight sailing in the harbor in snow squalls. Once a radio broadcaster at WBSM whose studios were on the water at Pope's Island announced to his audience on a Saturday afternoon:

"Well, its 33 degrees in New Bedford, it's snowing and there goes that crazy blue sailboat again, headed out"

We had bought and paid for this thing and by God, we were going to sail it….weather be damned!

Ed and Peter had maintained loose contact with Bob Rustle and discovered that he too had bought a new boat. In his case it was a Pearson 30 of which he took delivery in Rhode Island and had it transported to New Bedford. He had a crew of friends that pledged to help him with his boat (called *Rustler*) and was planning to moor it in New Bedford as he had with the Cal 25. He was in the water by early May and we would raft up with him on weekends as in the past.

~ *Chapter 9* ~

Meeting Carole

In May, *Circadian Rhythm* would be the catalyst that would change my life forever. As the weather improved we longed for new sailing experiences so we planned a trip to Nantucket on the third weekend of May sailing in company with the *Rustler*. The plan was to depart early Saturday morning, but I would not be making the initial passage as I had been invited to attend a wedding in Barnstable that Saturday and would be forced to catch the ferry thereafter to meet up with the boats in Nantucket. My gear would transit to Nantucket with Ed and Peter so that my sole task would be to get from Cape Cod to the island. I planned to meet my sister Deb, Chris Renfree and some of Deb's friends who would be riding over on the ferry as well and spending the night at a guest house. I attended the wedding, and took a cab from Barnstable to Woods Hole at the dear cost of $25 which was a steep sum in 1975. Arriving early for the ferry, I chose to patronize a local bar on the ferry dock to await my sister and her friends. I had a couple of drinks at the wedding and a beer or two while waiting, so I was feeling fine by the time Deb and Chris arrived and we boarded the boat. The weather was comfortable in the high 50's and sunny as we departed Woods Hole on the *SS Nantucket* which was the last steamship operated by the Steamship Authority. She was also the largest vessel of the Steamship Authority's fleet, built in 1957 and retired in 1987. Once we had departed, Renfree, of course, encouraged me to have a few more beers over the course of the two and a half hour ride. It became a bit brisk on deck with me attired in khaki pants and a blue blazer, but the cool air helped to keep me lucid.

By the time we began our approach to Nantucket at 6:30 and I was feeling no pain. Nantucket is so low in the water that you don't actually see the island until you're about five miles from it. The harbor is protected by a long breakwater that forms the entrance channel. Once past Brant Point, the steamer made a sharp right turn and pulled up to the dock. Ed, Peter,

Rustle, Dave Barclay and Tommy Joseph were standing on the dock looking up at us as we pulled in. I gave a rousing cheer and Renfree and I walked down below to join Deb and her friends and disembark. As we stepped onto the dock, I was highly conspicuous as the only passenger clad in a tie and jacket. We had a fine reunion and then headed up Broad Street toward the Jared Coffin House and the Brotherhood of Thieves, a local pub. Nantucket has been well preserved so that it looks pretty much as it did in the early nineteenth century with cobblestone streets and fine brick buildings lining Broad St. As one walks up the street, there is a slight incline until you reach the Coffin House.

Jared Coffin House

The Brotherhood is a local tavern and restaurant located in the basement of the Jared Coffin House. The building was originally a residence built in 1845 by Mr. Coffin who had been one of the most successful ship owners of the day. The house was a mansion and one of the most stately and largest buildings on the island then and now. Eventually, the home was converted into a hotel and the Brotherhood of Thieves was established in 1972 by Arthur Krause in the basement of the building. The name of the bar was taken from a pamphlet published in 1844 by Stephen S. Foster of Nantucket. This document was a vigorous attack on those who continued to support slavery as the tide of abolition was rising. Nantucket enjoyed a somewhat schizophrenic existence with regard to slavery in the mid-nineteenth century. The population was predominantly Quaker and their philosophy forbade slavery and human usury in general. The Quaker and Puritan religions formed the basis for the cultural life of most of the New England cities and towns of the era. However, the entreprenural spirit and profit motive of the New England ship owners lured them to the easy profits offered by the triangle trade of the day. Slave transport was one of the legs of this triangle and offered obscene profits to those willing to take the risk and participate in this obscene enterprise. Some of the most prominent names in colonial and subsequently early American history were involved in the slave trade. Timothy Fitch of Medford was one who owned ships that plied the ports of New England including Nantucket and was intimately involved in transporting slaves as were many of his contemporaries. At the same time, free blacks were openly welcomed on Nantucket and were involved in the business of the island. For example, Absalom Boston was a free black who became a successful whaling captain.

Entering the Brotherhood, one immediately became aware of what it was like to have nefarious dealings in the 19th century. You took two steps down (sort of like the Dipper in New Bedford) and the place had low ceilings and was dimly lit by candles on the walls and tables. It was somewhat dark, but not foreboding. The boys and I entered and found the place mostly vacant with the exception of a table up against the back wall at which sat two lovely young creatures. I was pretty well lit and the general character of the place got me to start belting out sea shanties. Of course the other guys didn't have a clue what I was singing (I think it was "the Dreadnought") but they quickly cued in on the two single girls at the table and immediately pulled up chairs and sat down. I took a seat at the end and continued my solo until one of the staff politely asked me to pipe down. I complied as I was hungry and not interested in being ejected, so I listened to the other guys trying to enchant the two young lovelies. I was immediately taken with the blonde who was really cute and coy, but not at all shy or reserved. She was bright and smiling with a very thick, shock of beautiful nearly platinum-colored blonde hair. Her cheeks were rosy, her complexion clear and she was very open and friendly. Not what I had been used to in New England women. Her associate looked very much like her, but was more reserved. As it turned out, Carole and Wendy were sisters who were over nighting on the island, but they were originally from Oregon. This explained why they were so completely different from local women; they were from the far West. Carole was a dietetic intern at Massachusetts General Hospital in Boston and her sister Wendy was visiting her for a week. The two had decided to spend the weekend on Nantucket and were staying at a local guesthouse. We immediately dubbed them "the oregenos", since none of us had ever been to the Northwest and knew nothing about it. We enjoyed dinner with them and they joined us on the *Rustler* for a nightcap.

What I failed to appreciate at the time was that I was very attracted to Carole. I didn't let on to this as I was overshadowed by the more demonstrative Rustle and his friends. I discovered later that Carole found me to be more interesting that the rest, precisely because I was content to stay in the background. We failed to directly connect at this first meeting, but we would cement our relationship in Boston as I detail later. Carole would become my beloved wife in 1977 and has been for the past thirty-four years. *Circadian Rhythm* was the vehicle for this mutual life altering experience.

Following our nightcap, we bid Carole and Wendy farewell and we all retired to our respective boats. The next morning, we bumped into them again at the "Downy Flake" which was the only place in downtown Nantucket open for breakfast at that time of the year. Over breakfast, Rustle asked if they wanted to sail back to the mainland rather than take the ferry. Wendy was hesitant, but Carole spoke right up and said "Sure"

My sister and her friends and Renfree were also at breakfast, after which Deb and Chris headed for the ferry and Deb's two friends joined Peter, Ed and me to sail back to the mainland. We all wended our way back to the boats and made preparations to depart. I instructed our passengers about safety procedures (in the event of a sinking, put your head between your legs and you're your ass goodbye) and suggested that they stay below to remain dry. Secure preparations were needed since the wind had clocked to the nor'eas over night and it was blowing 30 with higher gusts. Both boats pulled away from the dock and hoisted the mail'sal in the relatively protected harbor. We both passed Brant Point Light and headed up channel under power in a heaving seaway. The breakwater was helping to break up the bigger seas, but there was still a five foot chop which we had to contend with in the channel.

Brant Point Lighthouse, Nantucket

Once past the breakwater, we each hoisted our 100% jibs and began a starboard beat toward the nor'wes. The seas were running about ten feet with occasional breaking crests and it was cold, around 48^0 F. Onboard *Circadian Rhythm*, the crew (Ed, Pete and me) were fully suited up in slickers and bib pants with wool turtlenecks and sea boots, so we were fine. Our passengers, Deb's friends, had no foul weather gear, but they were wearing jackets. They were confined to the cabin to stay dry and as is well known, when you put a lubber down below in a seaway you're asking for trouble. When we traded tacks with Rustle, we could see Carole and Wendy standing in the companionway and all seemed fine on the *Rustler*. After about two hours of sailing toward Tuckernuck Shoal, we noticed the ferry *Nantucket* coming up from behind us. As the ferry passed within 200 yards, we could see two figures on deck waving frantically; Deb and Refree. They later reported that our two boats looked like little corks bobbing on a huge, undulating sea.

SS Nantucket

Onboard *Circadian Rhythm* we began to notice that our passengers were acquiring a green pallor about them as they sat gulping in cool fresh air at the foot of the companionway. This status quo was maintained until Peter leaned down from the rail and asked one of them to please reach into the icebox and grab him a beer. The "go for" was in the process of fulfilling this request when, upon opening the icebox, she apparently got a strong whiff of a long dead baloney sandwich. That was it; she dropped the cover and dashed for the marine head up forward. Once one of them was gone, it wasn't long before the other one followed suit. Now we had two cold, seasick, useless passengers on board and we were still a good six hours from landfall at the Cape. The crew talked it over and decided that since we were not as yet at the point of no return it would be faster and easier to head back. Otherwise, once we reached the Cape, it was going to be very complicated trying to explain away the two frozen corpses lying on the sole of the main cabin. On the next trade of tacks, we notified Rustle of our intentions and he too decided to come about. The distance we had achieved in three hours of sailing from Nantucket we now covered in less than an hour on a broad reach back into the harbor. We tied up again at the boat basin and witnessed a miraculous recovery by our passengers. They headed into town to thaw out and find the next plane back to the mainland. Carole and Wendy were stuck with us, since the last ferry had left and they had no place to stay in town.

We all made the best of it and after dinner in town made accommodations for the ladies on Rustle's boat and we all settled in for another night on Nantucket. The next day, Carole and Wendy caught the early ferry and *Circadian Rhythm* and *Rustler* made another attempt to depart the island. The Nor'easter had moderated and after we left, it backed more to the west which aided our trip home. Even so, it was ten hours before we finally tied up at Fairhaven Marine.

I headed back to Boston the next day and I had a call from Carole who wondered how we had made out. I reported all went well and then asked her if she would be interested in dancing with me on the Jazz Boat in Boston harbor that Thursday night. She agreed, so I picked her up at her residence on Commonwealth Ave and we had a great time. She was living in a common house (a mansion) owned by Mass General with 25 other female interns. When I reported this to the guys at my office at GEI, I suddenly became very popular. Carole and I hit it off and after 34 years of marriage we're still soul mates and I like to think that we still like each other. That's the true indication of a successful marriage. It was a completely serendipitous and unlikely meeting which appears to have been preordained. I, for one, believe in luck.

That was the beginning of great fun in the summer of 1975 and I had a girl friend to boot.

Back in New Bedford, we registered to race with the LTYC in the first Sunday series which was held in June and I managed to recruit Billy Mee who was a very experienced sailor and the son of one of my mother's close friends. Billy was my sister's age, he was sandy-haired, short in stature (about 5 feet) but he more than made up for his diminutive size with his outgoing personality, sailing expertise and the glint in his Irish eyes. I'm only 5' 7" tall, but what's funny about Billy is that (like Chris Renfree) I never thought of him as a little man, probably because he was one of those people who is bigger than life. I'd known Billy for a few years on and off and we'd met many times at the Spinnaker, in fact, he introduced me to Ray Andrews, who in turn, instructed me in the use of the spinnaker on *Whiskers*. Billy was quite excited about sailing *Circadian Rhythm* and quickly agreed to help us with racing. He'd had been involved with boats for many years I believe he attended the Apprendiceshop in Rockland, Maine to learn boat lofting and marine architecture. Thereafter, he was a regular on the Mattapoisett waterfront and sailed with many of the wealthy yacht owners as crew in club and offshore races.

He also helped to deliver boats with Ray Andrews in New England and to points south including the Caribbean. He'd been around and certainly had far more experience than we did. Ed and Peter were overjoyed that Billy had agreed to help teach us about racing and help us to campaign CR that summer.

Billy brought along a friend of his to also help us out, his name was Joe Donnelly. Joe was as tall as Billy was short, he must have been 6' 5" which made him a giant amongst we Lilliputians. Ed and I were 5'7" and Peter was the "the big guy" at 5' 8". The other interesting aspect about this duo was that as agile and quick as Billy was, Joe was clumsy and ham handed. To that extant, whenever we went sailing or racing, Joe would, without fail, shed blood. In fact, it happened so often that we coined the phrase "another good day of sailing,.....blood was shed". Although Joe was somewhat inept on the fore deck, he was an incredibly affable individual a good sport and better yet, he was a cook at the Mattapoisett Inn.

This latter attribute turned out to be a god sent to us as it provided a new destination for our weekend sailing. Joe informed us that the town dock in Mattapoisett didn't charge transients for overnight dockage, because the town dock was used only sparingly by them. Well, we were about to change that policy. With the warmer evenings of June, we developed the habit of meeting at the Spinnaker bar by seven o'clock and after some reverie we would retire to the boat by ten or eleven. Around 10:30 Ed would ask me:

"Well, what are you planning to do now?"
To which I would respond "Not much,…… you?"
He would then counter with "Wanna go sailing?"
And I would say "Do you have a boat?"
He would quip "Yes, I do"
And I would respond "Well, what are we waiting for?"

With that, we would grab Peter and trundle off to *Circadian Rhythm* and set sail for Mattapoisett, from which we had traveled not more than 20 minutes before.

Peter would turn on his cassette player and we'd head out into the night sailing east to Mattapoisett. More often than not, the moon would be out and we'd be navigating by moonlight and the flashing of the channel markers on our way east. We did this so often that by mid-summer I knew all of the light characteristics for the marks between New Bedford and Mattapoisett by heart. By the middle of July Ed reasoned that we were defying the name of the boat, because since we'd bought it, our normal circadian rhythm was out of whack; to wit, we'd sail by night and sleep during the day. We would usually pull up to the Mattapoisett town float at the end of the main granite pier around three of four in the morning. After securing the dock lines, we'd all crash and wake around ten. In the morning we'd amble on up to the Mattapoisett Inn to find Joe and get some breakfast. Joe lived in one of the Inn rooms and had the key to the kitchen. This was yet another major advantage as he would let us into the kitchen in the morning or in the dead of night and we could always count on him to be a good shipmate and provide for the crew.

A word here about the Mattapoisett Inn; it is still in operation under a different name, it is now called the Kinsale Inn (BIG MISTAKE). Built in 1799 it is the oldest continuously operating seaport inn in the country and is still occupies the original structure. As one might expect, the walls are not plumb the low ceilings sag and the floors creak, but the structure is still sound. The town of Mattapoisett was originally a shipbuilding town and the whaler *Wanderer* was the last whale ship built there in the late 19th century. Main Street faces the expansive harbor that points sou'eas and like Vineyard Haven is safe from all points of wind save the sou'eas gale. There are two granite wharves that jut out into the harbor, I have been on those wharves in a fall sou'eas gale when the grey beards are breaking over them; it's no place to be in a hurricane. The main part of town is sufficiently elevated to be unaffected by high water, but the seas and spray are another matter. All in all, though, it's a very pleasant small seaport with a beautiful harbor and a lively town inn; the stuff of New England postcards. We spent many an hour at the "Matt Inn", but more on that later.

After a Saturday in Mattapoisett, we'd sail back to Fairhaven for the Sunday LTYC races where Joe and Billy would meet us. We did reasonably well in the first LTYC Sunday series and took second place overall in the four race series. Even though we had limited spinnaker experience we were able to score well enough to secure a second place. Our main competition was a modified Bristol 24 owned and very aptly sailed by Mr. John Malcolm a math teacher at Fairhaven High School. John had sailed his Bristol *Witch of Agisi* for quite a few years and knew the boat very well. We felt quite smug that to have challenged him as we did on our first try and succeeded. What was important was that we were becoming a crew and we were learning the intricacies of racing and spinnaker handling from Billy and Joe. We made plans to enter the Buzzards Bay Regatta in August hoping to do well.

Our trips to Mattapoisett on the weekends were becoming more frequent, and the Matt Inn was becoming a second home to us. We were spending our share of money at the bar, so the owners were pleased to see us. One other place in town that we frequented was a small bar on Route 6 called Brad's. This was a local hangout that served beer in 6 ounce glasses at 25 cents per glass. The building was something of an afterthought as it was little more than a one-story rectangular box in a parking lot with a side door and a front door. Apparently, the owner had delusions of grandeur as the sign above the front door actually read "Brad's, Inc." Brad's incorporated, ...whoa! I mean what was this guy thinking, a board of directors, stockholders annual meetings, 10k reports, SEC filings? Oh well, everyone deserves a dream, eh? The front door was located about 40 feet from US Route 6 which bisected the town. Besides beer and a full service bar, Brad's also featured a television and a bumper pool table that was located in the middle of the main floor of the place. It was the centerpiece of the establishment, because the 4' x 8' table occupied most of the 20' x 30 ' room; Brad's was a pretty small place.

The pool table faced the front door and on one memorable evening that summer, with the temperatures in the eighties and humidity hovering around 85%, Ed and Joe Donnelly were engaged in a hotly contested bumper pool game while Peter, Billy and I observed from a safe distance. There was no air conditioning in the bar, so both the front and side doors were open to provide some cross ventilation. The two opponents were wagering rounds of beer on the game and Ed was ahead. Joe was becoming agitated until Ed finally handed over the cue having missed a crucial shot. Joe lined up the cue ball and as he prepared to make the pivotal shot, I noticed beads of sweat were beginning to roll down his forehead. Just as he thrust his pool stick to make the shot, one of those beads apparently landed in his eye, because he overshot the cue ball which bounced off the rear bumper went over the end of the table and onto the floor.

Now, in and of itself, this would have been a forgivable sin, but since the front door was open, the cue ball continued on its way, powered by the momentum that Joe had imparted. To our collective astonishment, it proceeded to travel unimpeded across the floor, down the two front steps, across the parking lot and onto Route 6. Joe stood there mouth agape and when the cue ball subsequently collided with the front wheel of a passing car, he looked at the rest of us and exclaimed, "Drink up, time to go!"; which we did before the bar keep could ascertain what had occurred. We hustled out the side door laughing like fools as we departed.

As mentioned, we spent a great deal of that first summer sailing at night between various ports as well as entertaining passing boats and ourselves with our antics and our onboard kazu band. Here's a picture of our usual attire before the start of a race.

Prerace preparations onboard Circadian Rhythm

It's plain to see from this photo who the serious sailor was in our crew, note Billy standing at the helm behind Ed's hands in this picture. Ed was wearing the light-up nose and working out on his kazu while Peter sang through the megaphone and I played the harmonica. This was a common sight that summer at the beginning of all the races that we attended. We became instant celebrities, not necessarily for our sailing expertise, but because we knew how to have a good time. I think Billy got a little tired of it after a while.

Peter kept a log of our exploits that summer and he kindly lent it to me for this book. It has been invaluable in rekindling my memory of the events of that year. Our nighttime sailing was really special I've excerpted a short section of Peter's log to better describe these events.

[Sunday, May 25, 1975[- New Bedford – Quick's Hole

.........After dinner Scott decides it's a good night to sail to Menemsha
– Pete agrees, but others aboard had reservations.....Well, so does Gay
Head! (*reference here to the Wompanoag Indians*) So, we're off @
10:30 PM . Best night yet for sailing. (yes it beat out Friday night (5-
23-75). Full moon, good breeze out of the S.E. and visibility is
unbelievable! Scott's working the tiller & winches alone for quite
awhile as Pete below to cop a few "Zs". It was fairly brisk out, temps.
Around 50-55°. Arrived @ Quick's @ 2:30 AM & Scott's tired now so
we dropped anchor and stayed there for the nite. Only one other boat at
the Hole, a catamaran (open) w/ people sleeping outside under a tarp!!
Crazy people!!

And so it went, many a night time sail was had that first year as we
worked hard to squeeze every penny of our investment out of that boat.

In late June we participated in the annual Clark's Cove Challenge
Cup race which is traditionally held on a Sunday and pits the best racers of
the LTYC against those from the NBYC. This was a team race with only
the top finishing ten boats receiving points. Until I reviewed Peter's log
book I had a piecemeal memory of this event, but now it's all quite clear.
Our crew for that day included Ed, Billy, Joe Peter and me. We left the
dock at Fairhaven Marine at 12:00 noon and headed toward the racecourse
which was south of Clark's Cove about two miles distant. This day was
warm in the 70's and the wind was from the faithful sou'wes blowing at
25 -30 kts. Once we cleared the hurricane dike we proceeded south
staying just to the west of the channel. As we sailed along just south of
Butler's Flats lighthouse we caught sight of a capsized sailboat with one
man hanging on to the centerboard. The seas were running about three
feet as we altered course in his direction. Upon arriving at the scene, we
dropped our jib and maneuvered under mains'al alone. The boat was a

Flying Dutchman that this novice sailor was trying to singlehand in high winds and waves. Not a wise decision on his part and he ended up in major trouble. As we circled the boat we could see that he was getting very tired from his exertions of staying with the boat and he needed help, quick. Peter took the helm from Billy who then dove into the water and swam over to the stricken vessel and her crew. The boat's skipper was then washed off the upturned hull by a breaking wave and he became separated from Billy and the boat with only a life cushion for flotation. At this point Ed dove in to help rescue the stricken skipper while Joe and I began making arrangements to pull the poor fellow aboard CR once we reached him.

Several private powerboats then arrived on the scene offering to assist in the effort. This was fortuitous since the powerboat offered lower freeboard and was therefore better suited for retrieving the tired sailor. This was accomplished and the occupant of the boat was then safe....thank goodness. There still was the boat to deal with, but in the highly capable hands of Billy aided by Joe, who by now had traded places with Ed in the water, the two were able to flip the Flying Dutchman back over. Joe used his bulk to pull on the centerboard and over she came. With that, Joe and Billy then sailed the boat to Davy's Locker restaurant a half mile away where they pulled it up on the beach and rejoined CR climbing aboard from the end of the pier near the restaurant.

With this highly auspicious beginning to the day, the reunited crew then headed toward the start of the race, not knowing if we would make it. As luck would have it, the start was delayed until 14:00 so we just managed to get to the line as 16 boats from the NBYC and 21 boats from the LTYC commenced the race as one unified class in 30 kts of wind; it was an exhilarating beginning.

A side note is needed at this point in advance of the remainder of the narrative. When Ed and I bought the boat earlier in the year, I, having been raised by Mary and Benny to be a considerate, responsible person had purchased a life insurance policy to cover my half of the boat's mortgage should misfortune befall me. Ed, on the other hand, was pleased to learn of my purchase noting that if I died, he'd own the boat for half the cost. As you might imagine from his attitude, Ed did not reciprocate by buying a policy to protect my interest; he obviously had not been raised by Mary and Benny. These facts will have a bearing on what next unfolds.

The first windward leg for the 37 boats was very wet and exhausting. We executed many windward tacks attempting to gain an advantage on our opponents. Sporting a main with one reef and working jib this was still very hard work as we moved along toward the first mark. As we approached the windward mark we were in company with many boats and most of them were far bigger than us. We came up towards the mark on a port tack and just barely cleared a Bristol 39 that was on a starboard tack without fouling her. The mark required a starboard rounding and our plan was to sail just beyond it on port and when we reached the rhumb line, flop over to starboard and round it with our nav rights intact. The Bristol was on the rhumb line, but had pinched too much (headed too close to the wind) and just as they rounded the mark, her port quarter struck the mark in clear view of all onboard CR. We were within their earshot, so Billy (who was at the helm) yelled "Protest" at the Bristol. Apparently striking the mark discombobulated the skipper of the Bristol, because no sooner had this occurred than he swung around the mark on a port tack and headed right for us! We'd barely cheated death two minutes earlier and now here we were facing this beast once again! We had tacked and now were on starboard, but this guy must have been spooked, because he continued to bear down on us at breakneck speed. We were closing with him at 12 kts! Ed was on the foredeck preparing the spinnaker and he was a sitting duck as the Bristol would strike him first. As Peter relates in his log:

> - Scott was yelling one obscenity after another in rapid fire - not because he was afraid of the eminent collision and probable damage to the boat – but because Ed doesn't have life insurance yet and (*Scott*) is going to be left alone with the payments!

At what seemed like the last possible moment, the helmsman of the Bristol apparently regained his senses and bore off missing poor little CR by inches as we passed starboard to starboard. Ed later claimed that he saw our jib touch the Bristol's spreader as we passed. At that point, protest screams were flying from everyone on both boats as we continued the race. Billy claimed that this was the closest he'd ever come to a catastrophic collision. There's no doubt that given the speed of the two boats and the weight of the Bristol that had we collided, someone would have been grievously injured.

The rest of the race was less stressful, but even the venerable Bob Saltmarsh had trouble when he capsized his Rhodes 19 while flying the chute. This was a tribute to the severity of the conditions that day. When the race finished, the NBYC had beaten the LTYC soundly. According to Peter's log:

> - As we headed back to F.M. (*Fairhaven Marine*) Scott was having Ed sign a life insurance
>   policy he worked up below deck while on the last leg (*of the race*).

Peter; always the comedian.

~ *Chapter 10* ~

The Mattapoisett Inn Challenge Cup and other races

As our racing experience with the LTYC improved, thanks to Billy and Joe, we began to get a little cocky. As Joe and Billy were standard fixtures at the Mattapoisett Inn they found that the Inn was planning to sponsor the first (and as it turned out last) sailboat race to help drum up business. The owners reasoned that many of their customers were sailors and if they sponsored a race with a dinner thereafter, it would increase sales for them that weekend. We, of course, entered and made preparations for the race which was scheduled for mid-July. Since we had been in Mattapoisett every weekend since early June, we decided that we may as well compete in the race. The rules called for a staggered start, which means that a boat's handicap is awarded at the start of the race rather than at the end. This allows the slower boats to get a head start on the faster ones. In addition, with a staggered start, each boat knows where they stand in the race at anytime during the race. Another twist that added to the interest of competitors and spectators was that one crewman was chosen from each boat to run from the Inn to Hiller's beach (about one half mile) and then board the boat's dinghy and row to their boat which was anchored about 100 yards off the beach. This constituted the start of the race, but the finish was similar, in that after completing the course the boat was once again anchored off Hiller's beach and the same crewman had to row ashore, run up to the Inn and chug a draft beer before the boat was officially granted a finish. I was chosen to perform these duties since I was the only crewman who could run fast and row well. Beer chugging was a talent that the entire crew shared.

There were about fifteen boats in the fleet and one of them was a 1928 Herreshoff S-boat that had been restored and looked terrific. The S-boat was twenty-eight feet long (overall) with low freeboard, a wineglass transom and extensive forward overhang. The most outstanding characteristic of this vessel was its huge, heavily raked mast that sported a huge main'sal. The boat's jib was comparatively tiny which further emphasized the size of the main'sal.

S-Boat

We had raced against this S boat once before and they'd beaten us badly, but Billy maintained that CR only needed to worry when the winds were light. The S-boat was a flyer in light airs, but we believed that we could beat her if the afternoon sou'wester piped up. The S-boat was our primary competition that day. Billy was otherwise committed that race day, so Joe, Ed, Pete and I convinced two locals Obie and Bessie to help as crew. We didn't expect to win and decided to just make the best of it and have a good time that day.

Since the S-boat had a PHRF rating of 201 and we rated 225 we would start 24 seconds before them, meaning that they would have to play catch up. The day of the race was clear, warm and windless. The start was scheduled for 11:00, so we left the town dock and powered the 1/2 mile over to Hiller's beach with dinghy in tow. After setting the hook, I boarded the dinghy and rowed to beach, secured the boat and walked up to the Inn. I sauntered up the small hill on Main St. as calls of encouragement from my crew rang out until I turned the corner toward the Inn and was no longer in sight. I entered form the front door and headed for the bar where the race committee was waiting. I signed in and gave the name of my boat which prompted the committee person to assign me my start time. The ship's clock behind the bar was the official time piece for this race, so I took note of its location and checked the current time against my wrist watch….the bar clock was slow. I was to start running for the beach at 11:22:30 as there were quite a few smaller boats that would start before us. The S-boat runner would be 24 seconds behind me. I was in fairly decent shape, but my competition appeared to be much better at chugging beer than running. I felt pretty confident that I could make some time on him on the trip down to the beach, but if there was a photo finish at the bar I might be in trouble. At 11:00 the first participant ran out the side door headed for the beach. At various intervals this process was repeated until there were only three or four of us left at the bar. As we stood waiting to start, we could see the smaller boats heading out of the harbor under the light nor'wes zephyr.

Finally my start time drew near and I became transfixed on the bar clock. As the minute hand closed on 11:22 I guess the bartender approximated when next 30 seconds transpired as he abruptly yelled "GO!" at me as I stood in the doorway. With that, I was off, sprinting down Main St lined with townspeople who came out to watch the start. I ran as fast as I could and reached the beach in about two minutes flat. I grabbed the dinghy and pushed it hard down the beach and into the water. I jumped in, grabbed the oars and began rowing like a madman to the yelling and cheering of my crew. The rules stated that sails could not be hoisted until the crewman was onboard, which we observed.

As soon as I hit the boat, the crew was hoisting sail and Ed grabbed the dinghy painter and made it fast to the anchor line. We were under sail in 90 seconds, free of the mooring and headed down the harbor. As the crew congratulated me for a job well done, we looked astern to see the S-boat crewman, just reaching Hiller's beach, we had the head start we wanted, now we needed to maintain it. The wind was still light as we broad reached on a starboard tack past the moorage area and then hardened up a bit to head south by west past Ned's Point and then out into the bay. At Ned's Point we could see the S-boat was now chasing us and beginning to close the gap. As we hardened up, our speed increased and we set a course for the first rounding mark. Overall, the course length was about 12 miles, so we would be out on the bay for quite a while. We chose not to set the spinnaker since the wind was forward of the beam, but the next leg would be more down wind and we hoped that out larger chute would better equalize our chance against the S-boat. As we rounded the first mark, the wind was still nor'wes and light, but we had a good set and the S-boat was still behind us. They rounded about one minute behind us and set their handkerchief-sized spinnaker and headed our way. Since the race start, we, and the S-boat had passed just about every other boat in the fleet and it was quickly becoming a two-boat race.

On the downwind leg, we increased our lead a bit so that when we turned the downwind mark we were two minutes ahead of the S-boat. We chose to stay on the left side of the course as we tacked into the fading nor'westerly expecting that the sou'wester would soon replace it. As we sailed along, we were all remarking that the S-boat must have an electric motor powering it as she continued to chew away at our slim lead. We stayed on the left hand side of the course even though it was not the rhumb line to the last mark, but it would be the preferred side if the wind backed. The S-boat sailed the rhumb line and continued to chew away at our lead. After about ten minutes, the wind dropped and we could see a new wind line forming from the sou'wes. By now, the S-boat was technically in the lead, but was poorly situated as the sou'wes wind began to fill in and build. Our hunch had paid off and we were able to fall off as the wind built and close reach toward the last mark. As we did, we could see that the S-boat was pinching to make the mark with far less boat speed than ours. As we turned the last mark and headed for home, we were beam reaching with a 20+ knots of breeze pushing us along. The S-boat rounded about one minute behind us, so the issue was still in doubt. Even so, we were confident that we could beat them with our bigger jib and beamier boat. We were lucky again as we were the first boat to arrive at the mooring.

As the anchor line was snagged, sails were dropped and I immediately jumped into the dinghy and once again rowed like crazy, this time toward shore. I hit the beach, pulled the dinghy up about five feet and then hit the beach running. Again, the crew urged me on with hoots and hollers and as I ran past well-wishing spectators, I glanced over my shoulder to see the S-boat crewman just reaching the shore of Hiller's beach. I picked up the pace, rounded the corner and dashed through the Inn's side door to a waiting mug of ice cold beer at the bar. I quickly raised the glass and downed its sweet contents in three gulps. *Circadian Rhythm* was then officially declared the winner of the first Mattapoisett Inn Challenge Cup!

I sat at the bar savoring the victory, sipping more beer as the rest of the contestants began spilling into the bar. My crew squared the boat away and brought her back around to the town dock and then ambled up to the Inn. Once they arrived, the party began. We were delirious with glee over the unexpected victory consuming much beer in celebration. By this time, all the crews of the participating boats had arrived and the place was bedlam with laughter and stories and backslapping. Quite a few rounds of drinks were bought for us as the winners and we reciprocated as we could. After about an hour or so of celebrating, everyone was pretty-well toasted from wind, sun, seawater and booze. The dinner was ready, so we all sat down to feast on lobster, clams and steak along with many of the other race participants. Peter had linked up with Bessie during the race and in Peter's boozy condition they were becoming increasingly amorous sitting opposite Ed and me. Peter was far more interested in French-kissing Bessie than eating his steak and as their performance proceeded Peter acted increasingly agitated and weird. I was quite bombed at this point and found this spectacle across from me to be quite humorous, but didn't think much of it beyond that. Later, I discovered that Bessie, who was known locally as the "town pump", had been providing complimentary digital stimulation service to Peter, under the table. Following her performance with Peter, Beesie made the rounds that summer for most of the crew except me it seemed I was always otherwise engaged.

Following the Matt Inn cup race, we proceeded to Edgartown the next weekend for the Edgartown Regatta. The boys took the boat over on Friday and I joined them Friday night by taking the *Schamonchi* ferry from New Bedford to the Vineyard. I took a cab from Vineyard Haven to Edgartown and as we passed through Oak Bluffs, there were hundreds of well-dressed people thronging the little movie theatre in the center of town. I asked the cabbie what was going on and he mentioned that it was the premier of a movie shot on the Island the previous year; it was called *Jaws*. I responded that I vaguely remembered hearing about that last summer; I wondered out loud if it would be a hit. Once again, we didn't do very well in that racing venue, but we did get to see Mr. Prada once again, he was pleased to see we had a bigger boat. I think his response went something like

"What the hell did you clowns do, win the lottery or rob a bank?" He was his usual understated self.

After the Edgartown Regatta, we sailed part of the third LTYC series, with spotty attendance as cruising was now interfering with the weekend racing schedule. We made several trips to the Vineyard and Cuttyhunk and planned a week of cruising to Block Island with some additional friends at the end of July.

The last week of July arrived and Pete, Ed and I were joined by two old school chums of Peter's Mike Rowley (known as "Pineapple") and Frank Pleshea. Peter, Mike, Frank and I had all been in the same class at Fairhaven High and although I knew the three of them, we didn't move in the same circles. Peter was close friends with Mike and Frank as all of them lived in the south end of Fairhaven. These three had attended the same grammar school and had known one another for years. I lived on Cherry St which was considered to be part of North Fairhaven. Like most New England towns, Fairhaven was very provincial in the 1960's and is still today. The part of town that you hail from is your identity. People from the "fashionable" south end of Fairhaven seldom hobnob with those from North Fairhaven and, of course, would never be seen with someone from East Fairhaven. It's all very petty, but important when you live there. I was happy to see Mike and Frank, but provincialism would inevitably intrude in our relationship. Frank was an extrovert and Polish to boot, so he was happy and loud and good company. Mike was reserved and soft spoken and his head looked like a pineapple, hence the nickname. They both lived in Coco Bach Florida and were still close friends. Mike and Frank were in Fairhaven as part of our class's 20th reunion that had taken place the night before our planned departure. Peter and I also attended and we were both under the weather the next morning. We'd been sailing and partying on Saturday with classmates and at the outset of the reunion we consumed quite a few more beers. The result was predictable, during dinner Peter actually fell asleep in his mash potatoes and I spent most of the evening sleeping in a friend's car in the parking lot. It wasn't much of a reunion for us.

Our sailing plan for that week was to head for Newport, stay the night and then on to Block Island as our western terminus, then back east to the Vineyard, onto the Cape and then back to Mattapoisett prior to the beginning of the BBR scheduled to be held in Marion that year.

We all gathered at "C" dock at Fairhaven Marine on Sunday morning with provisions for a week of sailing. We had cleaned the boat up for this trip including a thorough scrubbing of the 20-gallon polyethylene water tank located forward under the V-berth. We were experiencing an unprecedented heat wave in Fairhaven that weekend with low humidity and temperatures exceeding 100 °F. These conditions seldom occurred and the five of us were itching to get loaded and away from the dock. Everyone was sweating profusely as we loaded the boat and after Ed filled the clean water tank, he dumped in a bag of ice to cool the water; ice water on tap, for a while anyway. We finally pushed away from the dock and "steamed" out of the harbor into Buzzards Bay headed west. Around 12:30, the faithful sou'westerly finally filled in albeit feebly. This allowed us to hoist sail and provided much needed respite from the oppressive heat. With the eight knot breeze the air temperature decreased five to ten degrees. We made decent progress west as the modest wind didn't provoke much of a seaway and arrived at the dock at the Treadway Inn in Newport around 19:00. Newport had cooled off a bit, but it was still sultry. We made the boat fast and headed into town for drinks and sustenance. I won't bother to describe Newport as I'm sure most of the readers of this narrative have visited the place at some point. Let it suffice to say that it is a rowdy place in the summer and a haven for yachties and those who wish to see and be seen. We enjoyed the evening and somehow managed to accommodate five male adults in a rather small cabin on *Circadian Rhythm*, I recall sleeping in the cockpit.

The next morning, after breakfast, we settled our account with the dockmaster and headed on our way toward Block Island. Once again the day was warm, clear and windless as we "steamed" past Castle Hill and out into Block Island Sound. Peter entertained us with selections from his cassette player and as we reached the halfway point, we noticed the approach of Providence steam ferry *Yankee*.

Yankee

She was "headed for the barn" and we were set to pass her on our starboard side within about 100 yards. As she came abeam we could clearly see many of the passengers waving happily to us on this clear warm late morning. At the prearranged signal, four of us dropped the back of our bathing suits and "chucked moons" at the *Yankee*. All of us participated except "Pineapple" who ran below and hid to preclude being identified with us. Pineapple worked for the IRS in Coco Beach Florida and he was deathly afraid that someone onboard the *Yankee* would identify him during our antics and he would be reported to his superiors. Talk about absurd paranoia, what were the chances than someone on that boat would recognize any of us let alone Pineapple and report him to his boss? *Yankee* steamed on, we covered our butts and had a good laugh over that one.

After arriving in New Harbor, we pulled up to the dock to be directed to a mooring and we were met by two plain clothes US Marshalls who were looking for a fellow named Michael Rowley who was reported to have been sighted with four obscene young men and now Rowley was wanted for questioning, because he was a federal employee. The Marshalls were attired in black suits, wearing dark glasses as they escorted (actually hustled) Mike off to a black sedan that was waiting on the dock with the engine running. Mike dutifully entered the back seat of the vehicle and off they sped up island. A few minutes later, we witnessed a black helicopter lifting off from the island and heading north towards Newport.

Apparently the chopper landed at the Navy base in town and Mike was taken to a witness area and told to enter a "lineup' room. The room had a stage with bright lights facing the stage and Mike was one of four other male "suspects" standing at the foot of the stage awaiting instructions. Like all "lineup" rooms, this one had a very large a one-way mirror facing the stage. The "suspects" were instructed to walk up onto the stage and then to turn around facing the wall with their backs to the mirror. At the appointed moment, the "suspects" were instructed to loosen their belts, drop their drawers and bend over with their butts facing the mirror.

A group of complainant witnesses from the *Yankee* had been assembled in the witness room behind the one way mirror. As luck would have it, Mike's worst fears had been realized. Unbeknownst to him one of his neighbors Coco Beach had been aboard the *Yankee* that afternoon and was peering through binoculars at *Circadian Rhythm* as we passed the steamer earlier that day. This neighbor had managed to just catch sight of Mike as he retreated down into the cabin passing by the glistening white flesh of his crewmate's bottoms that were hoisted towards the *Yankee*. It was really quite amazing that this neighbor had recognized Mike with the sun reflecting off those upraised buttocks, but such is life.

Mike and the other "suspects" held their pose for several minutes while the witnesses viewed the display. Finally, the "suspects" were told to cover up and were escorted from the room. Luckily, none of the witnesses could identify the offending bottoms and Mike was finally released following a harsh warning to be more discriminating in choosing his friends. As it turned out he was safe since he hadn't chucked a moon and no one could have possibly recognized his butt.

Since he was now stranded on the mainland, Mike was provided a ride to the Pt Judith ferry, but he had to pay for his own fare back to Block Island. He made his way back to New Harbor and we laughed till we cried listening to his account of his brush with the Law at our expense. As might be expected, Mike was very nervous for the rest of the trip and would quickly disappear down below at the slightest provocation.

We brought Mike to "The Oar" a dockside bar which became our home away from home for two days. I'd like to provide a description of Block Island as this was my first visit, but unfortunately, I didn't see much of the island. Once we found The Oar, we never left the place, they had food, showers, booze, entertainment, women and everyone in New Harbor passed through the place at some point during the day, because it was right on the dock. We had arrived on a Monday and as we discovered, Monday night was dead on the Block Island. When we discovered this, I told Pete that we should pull out all of the stops, so I returned to CR and obtained one kazu, three harmonicas 3 silly hats one megaphone and Peter's light-up Groucho glasses. Armed with these weapons of entertainment, the CR crew headed over to the piano player and began our accompaniment. Within a few minutes we had the place rockin'. Peter became the hit of the place when he did two encore performances of "dueling banjos" with his kazu and a real banjo player accompanying him. As the evening progressed, the noise from our playing brought more and more customers from their boats who wanted to join in. The waitresses claimed that Monday night was the busiest she had seen in two or three years.

We had some wild times that two days. On the second day, we presented an oar to the bar at "The Oar" with our five names carved into it. This was the tradition and throughout the inside of The Oar there are literally hundreds of oars from boats that have stopped at New Harbor over the years. On our final evening we were all pretty tanked and headed back to the boat early as we were leaving the next morning. The evening was completely calm there wasn't a ripple on the water. As we sat in the cockpit sipping beer we noticed the schooner *Bill of Rights* anchored 100 yards away and she was crewed primarily by women. Harvey Gamage built the the *Bill of Rights* in South Bristol Maine; she was launched in 1971. The Gamage yard also built many of the wooden eastern-rigged trawlers and scallopers in the New Bedford fleet during the 1960s and 70s. The *Bill of Rights* was a Fredonia-style, 129 foot, gaff-rigged, topsail schooner. *Bill of Rights* was one of several similar schooners that plied the southern New England coast in summer with paying customers. All of these vessels then headed to the Caribbean in winter to continue their sail-for-hire work.

Bill of Rights

We five we a bit tipsy at this point and so we decided to board the two-man pram and paddle over to serenade the ladies on the "Bill". We piled all five of us in the dingy and with one oar (the other was at "The Oar") we slowly paddled over toward the Bill. We had about one inch of freeboard as we slowly paddled around the schooner doing our renditions of "Irene Goodnight" and "Sentimental Journey". Our efforts produced the desired result and within five minutes there were ten eligible females hanging over the bulwark applauding our feeble singing activity. As we paddled along, one of our admirers became a bit to exuberant and dove over the side swimming in our direction. As she moved toward us, we exhorted her to stop since her bow wave was about to swamp us. She slowly approached and ever so light grasped the gunnel of our dinghy which caused much consternation to Pineapple. She introduced herself as did we and after introductions and small talk, she and a few of her friends launched a boat and joined us on *Circadian Rhythm* for a nightcap.

The next day we were off for Martha's Vineyard and sailed in limited visibility, but warm temperatures and a steady sou'wester all afternoon until we fetched Menemsha Bight in the early evening. We sailed along most of the afternoon listening to tapes of "The Bob and Ray Show" and "Imus in the Morning". Peter had hours of these programs in his collection. He had recorded them while living in Manhattan and, in the same manner as his music tapes, these radio programs were archived in impeccable order in his two carrying cases. The weather was changing, but we pulled into the salt pond and had a hearty dinner of beans and hot dogs and beer. The next morning the wind was up and the weather was overcast and cooler as we planned to transit Robinson's Hole and head to Mattapoisett in preparation for the BBR.

Robinson's Hole is the worst passage in the Elizabeth Islands for a transit between Vineyard Sound and Buzzards Bay. It is poorly marked, littered with rocks and granite ledges it has a narrow channel and a strong current. We decided to try it since it was shorter than going through Quick's Hole and it would be a new experience. The current would be with us, so, as the old saying goes, "it seemed like a good idea at the time". We set a course for Robinson's from Menemsha and arrived at the hole at peak flood current. I was on the helm, Peter and I were sharing navigating duties, Ed was napping, Pineapple was in the cockpit and Frank was sitting on deck at the bow. As we headed into the channel, Peter had the chart out and he noted that there was a ledge to starboard on the right hand of the channel. There were only two markers in the crucial part of the channel and I chose to hug the can. We were broad reaching with main and genny and with the four knot current *Circadian Rhythm* was making about nine knots. All was well, until suddenly there was a resounding BANG as the 4200 lb. boat was stopped dead in the water. The boat stopped, but Newton's first law of motion was obeyed as I was immediately hurled forward and caught my fore head on the hatch lock hasp (the external countervailing force as it were). I fell onto the cabin sole, dazed, but conscious. Everyone else was knocked silly as well, fortunately, Frank was not

> **Newton's First Law:**
>
> **Every object in a state of uniform motion tends to remain in that state of motion unless an external force is applied to it.**

thrown over the side. The boat slid off the rock and we drifted down stream through the channel and avoided any further obstructions. I clambered back into the cockpit, blood streaming down my face, Peter was at the helm and I helped get the boat back on course.

We took stock of the situation and realized that we'd clobbered a rock with our keel, but there were no leaks, the mast was still standing and outside of my wound, everyone else was fine. I was all for continuing on to Mattapoisett, but the wound was bleeding pretty well, so we chose to put into Eel Pond at Woods Hole where Frank's parents had a summer house. We arrived at the dock and Frank called his dad who drove me to Falmouth hospital The gash took five stitches to close after which we headed back to Frank's house for dinner and then to the boat for the night. While at Frank's we arranged for Brownell Boats Systems to haul us out the next day (Friday) to inspect and repair the damage. We had the get the boat repaired before Saturday if we were going to race her that weekend.in the BBR. We called Billy and he and Joe made the haul out arrangements and would be ready for us when we arrived. We left early the next day with a nor'eas storm beginning to build. The wind was on the nose most of the way back to Mattapoisett, but the boat held together with no leaks, so we hoped the damage would be minimal.

Once we hit the town dock (very familiar territory by now) Joe had his SCUBA gear and immediately dove on the boat to check out the damage. When he surfaced, Joe informed us that the damage was minimal, but she needed to be hauled to do the repairs. At Billy's direction, Brownell hauled us using their hydraulic trailer (which was invented by Mr. Brownell) and left us on the trailer to be launched the next day. We had 24 hours to assess the damage and fix it. Billy and Joe got under the boat and found that we clipped the rock about four inches from the end of the lead keel. The rounded portion of the keel at that point was flattened and the fiberglass hull behind the keel was fractured. Apparently, the keel crushed the fiberglass which absorbed the force of the collision and subsequently fractured. The solution was prescribed, grind out all of the broken glass, dry with a heat lamp and then fill in the hole with resin-saturated fiberglass. We also planned to round off the flattened lead keel using an industrial grinder. The rain had begun by then so we improvised a shelter using plastic tarps. The Matt Inn was the base of operations, supplying extension cords and heat lamps as well as dinner and sleeping accommodations. We bid farewell to Frank and Mike as they would be in the way from here on in and got to work. We worked into the evening got the job done and let the heat lamps go to work curing the new glass. While she was out of the water, we cleaned the bottom and applied a fresh coat of bottom paint. She would be more than ready to race the next day. Finally around 19:00, we had done all we could for the casualty, so we repaired to the Inn for dinner and drinks.

It was 19:30 and the wind and rain outside were as boisterous and rancorous as the singing, yelling and drinking inside the Matt Inn. We were having a great time with Peter on the Kazu with Joe and me harmonizing tunes, when the side door nearest the bar flung open and in walked Renfree and Carole. She had Chris's phone number and managed to get a ride down with him for a weekend at my parent's house while I raced. I was very happy to see her and called my mom to be sure that she had a bed for Carole that night and over the weekend. Carole questioned me about the bandage on my head, but I sloughed it off and we all got back to partying. About half an hour later, the door flung open once again and as six soaking sailors blew into the bar together with wind and rain as they struggled to close the door. The ambled up to the bar and ordered whiskey all around. They then told us their story. They had just finished sailing two Shields from Newport to race in the BBR that weekend. They told a harrowing story of bailing like madmen to keep the boats afloat as they sailed up Buzzards Bay and into Mattapoisett. The Shields is a 30 foot one-design sloop and is raced as a class. The BBR usually includes a Shields class since a local boat builder (Cape Cod Shipbuilding) in Wareham is still turning out these beautiful, stately vessels. Although the Shields is very fast (it has been claimed that it is the only thirty footer that can beat a forty footer) it is an open boat subjected to swamping with consequent sinking in rough conditions. With this in mind, it was very surprising to us that these two boats had sailed from Newport in a nor'eas storm and had actually arrived in Mattapoisett. Listening to their tale, it was apparent that they had a very difficult passage and were forced to keep one person manning the bilge pump on each boat for most of the trip up Buzzards Bay. They were visibly relieved to have made it to port safely, without any damage to boats or crew. We bought them a round in celebration of their success. The party was really cranking up by the time Carole and I left for Fairhaven at 22:00.

Thanks to Carole, I enjoyed the luxury of a hot shower and a bed with sheets that night so I was refreshed and ready to go the next morning when I was again deposited on the dock in Mattapoisett for the BBR. The weather had broken and it was a beautiful, warm day. *Circadian Rhythm* was bowed, but not broken by her insulting experience at Robinson's Hole. The repairs looked good the glass was fully cured as Brownell slid her back into her element. We all boarded and headed out to the PHRF starting area near Bird Island off Marion. Billy gave us our marching orders and we began plotting our strategy based on the scratch sheet of competing boats that Saturday. We'd just bought new sheet lines for the spinnaker which included large stainless snap shackles attached to the business end of each sheet. The snap shackles would (in theory) help with quick spinnaker take downs when we arrived at downwind marks. Unfortunately, the new sheets were a bit short and did not run two lengths of the boat. Our normal technique for dropping the spinnaker at a leward mark was to raise the jib, turn the mark, ease the spinnaker pole forward to the head stay and then pull the pin on the foreguy snap shackle which would cause the "chute" to deflate and flag behind the genny. We would then pull the spinnaker in from under the jib as we headed upwind.

We arrived at the starting line and managed to get a good start, and stayed with the fleet to the first mark. We had some trouble with the chute but got it set as we headed down to the next mark. Here's a shot of us with chute and Joe's Hobie 16 "tall boy" recut jib being flown as a staysail.

Circadian Rhythm, with a bone in her teeth

Things were going well on this first downwind leg until we reached the turning mark and attempted to doff the chute. The new snap shackles were too sticky and in out haste to leave the dock, we hadn't rigged lanyards on the pins, so Joe, who was the "deck ape", couldn't pull the pin to release the clew. As a result, we were headed up wind with the chute pulling us sideways, so Billy yelled to let the foreguy go, which I did and the "short" line ran through the pole and flagged twice at the end of the chute. This action succeeded where Joe had failed and the snap shackle opened letting the line and shackle fly off into the air landing in the water 50 yards away from us.....gone! There was quite a bit of cursing, but we recovered and rigged a lanyard on the pin of the remaining spinnaker sheet, we tied a new line to replace the lost sheet. All of this unproductive activity caused us to lose a lot of ground to the competition, but we pressed on to the next windward mark. The chute was repacked and we made ready for the last downwind leg. Turning the last windward mark, in last place, we raised the chute and immediately had an hourglass halfway up. Billy was beside himself, Joe and Ed lowered the chute, cleared the hourglass and we raised it again and off we went. We turned the last mark and despite the pin lanyard, Joe's attempts to pull the pin on the foreguy a second time were met with the same degree of obstinacy from the second snap shackle. Once again we were pulled sideways until I released the foreguy and once again the short line fed through the pole, flagged for a second at the end of the chute and then sailed off into the ethers to join its sibling in Davy Jones' locker. That was it for Billy, he handed the helm over to Ed and walked below, he was mortified. We finished dead last as Ed headed us back to the dock in Mattapoisett.

We arrived back in Mattapoisett under power and Ed proceeded to try docking the boat, but continued to have difficulty. Billy offered some advice, but he was at the end of his rope (no pun intended) with that day's events, so he finally yelled he'd had enough and dove over the side and swam the 20 yards to the dock. He didn't race with us the next day, or ever again for that matter. I couldn't say that I blamed him, but he'd taught us the basics and he introduced us to Joe who sailed with us for the rest of that summer. We sailed in the BBR the next day, without Billy and did poorly, but we finished. Although we did well in club racing, we couldn't seem to repeat that success in the big regattas.

The first season with *Circadian Rhythm* was drawing to a close, we has learned many a lesson and acquitted ourselves fairly well in club racing at the LTYC. Carole was finishing up her residency at Mass

General and would be going back to Oregon and I was slated to travel to Iran for four months to work on a project for GEI. I obtained my passport, visa and shots and awaited word about eventual transit to Iran to begin the job. Carole and I were becoming quite serious, but neither was sure where developments would lead with her scheduled to return home to Oregon and me expecting to be spending five months in Iran. In the meantime, the boat had developed a few warranty-related problems and Peter Haines, our sales representative, had moved from Sailboats Northeast in Marblehead and established his own C&C business in Warren, Rhode Island. We contacted him and arranged to have out boat serviced over the winter in Rhode Island.

We planned to sail the boat over on one of the last weekends of September with Joe and Carole onboard to round out our crew. As was our usual routine, we didn't bother to check the weather as we had a schedule to keep, weather be damned. We left the dock in Fairhaven under leaden skies and proceeded west toward Rhode Island. As we rounded Clarks' Point in New Bedford, we were beam reaching under a freshening sou'eas wind headed toward Rhode Island. At the mouth of the bay, the wind had risen to 30 knots and the seas had built to ten feet with visibility diminishing in rain squalls. We were all dressed in slicks at this point and enjoying the exhilarating ride on breaking seas off out port quarter. We had reefed the main two points and had our working jib pulling us along at a crisp ten knots with higher speeds as we surfed down the face of the building wave fronts. As we sailed past Sakonnet Point, the seas had built to fifteen feet and we were fast becoming Lilliputians in a field of watery mountains. The rain squalls were intense, but brief and the wind seemed to build to a climax and then began to diminish as we approached Brenton Reef to the south of Newport. We had been reaching on a port tack since departing Buzzards Bay and now we needed to make a decision. In order to turn for Newport we had to either jibe or tack to put the wind on our starboard side. We discussed this for several minutes as no one wanted to make a mistake in those conditions. Finally, we chose to tack and put the nose of the boat through the wind to lessen the chance of an all standing jibe. I sent Carole down into the cabin and we executed a flawless tack and headed off toward Newport on a starboard beam reach in large, but diminishing seas. What a ride! In retrospect, I was a fool to bring Carole along, even though she had the time of her life. The conditions were really too severe to risk any injury to her and I regret having been so imprudent.

We tied up at the Treadway Inn where we had docked back in July and I immediately consigned Carole to the sauna to warm up. I later discovered that my Dad had phoned the Coast Guard to inform them of our situation as he was concerned about our safety. I phoned him after our arrival and after chastising me, he called the Coast Guard to apprise them of our safe arrival. Did I learn my lesson? Yes, from then on I tried my best to be prepared and not knowingly place those in my charge in a dangerous situation. I was learning to be far more cautious about sailing and I tried to follow Geoff's advice and anticipate the situation in advance to minimize the potential danger. Danger is always present in nautical pursuits, but if one is properly prepared and thoughtful, these dangers are manageable.

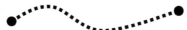

In the same vein of managing potential calamities, after our fateful voyage to Newport, a we discovered that Joe had made the same voyage later a few weeks later as a volunteer crew on *Cotton Blossom*. *Cotton Blossom* was 72 foot William Fife designed yawl (yawl-rigged at the time, now she's a cutter called *Halloween*) that found herself in New Bedford in need of a pick up crew to accompany her professional skipper on route to Newport for some repair work and thenceforth to the Caribbean for the winter. According to Joe this trip took place in mid-October with the conditions a bit chilly and breezy. Joe described how the short voyage went bad early on with equipment failure left and right as they made their way along the coast to Rhode Island. Apparently, *Cotton Blossom's*

owner was scrimping on maintenance and the skipper was accomplishing the herculean task of keeping this 40 year old "woodie" in one piece while sailing her to her winter quarters. Joe described how the trip started in the late afternoon and as they proceeded on to Newport, the nor'wes wind continued to build as *Cotton Blossom* bowled along like a wild mustang on the open range toward their destination; she was a "yar bot"!. All was under control until they began their entry on a broad reach into the harbor under full main, mizzen and a storm jib. As they passed the Ida Lewis Yacht Club, the capt'n attempted to start the big diesel engine to no avail.....SHIT! was exclaimed several times as the skipper made repeated tries to kick over the beast. No luck and time was growing short. At this point in Joe's story, he became quite exhilarated as he proceeded to explain the next incredible portion of this yarn. Joe explained that the capt'n next ordered that the jib be dosed and the anchor be made ready to drop at his command. *Cotton Blossom* proceeded to charge down wind across the harbor at 7 knots toward the Brown and Howard Wharf. As she approached the wharf and came within 60 yards of its end, the skipper suddenly put the helm hard over turning the vessel hard unto the wind which removed most or her way. At the precise moment that her forward momentum ceased, the capt'n yelled over the howling wind "**DROP IT**"! And drop it they did, the anchor chain whizzed out of the hawse pipe and the big hook hit bottom and apparently grabbed as *Cotton Blossom* began backing down toward the wharf. It was a hell of a gamble and everyone onboard (one assumes the capt'n as well) held their breath to see of the hook would hold. Finally after about 60 second of drifting backwards with main and mizzen flogging like banshees in the wind, *Cotton Blossom's* aft cap rail just kissed the edge of the wharf and she stopped. The crew immediately dropped all sail, paid out more slack on the anchor rode and then made the vessel secure to the dock. What a ride! Joe jumped ship at Newport, apparently he'd had enough excitement for one year.

We laid the boat up for the winter, and I was slated to be off to Iran for work while Carole planned to finish her internship and head back to Oregon. While we wiled away our time in October, the Red Sox had played themselves into the pennant race with the Cincinnati Reds and the "there's no tomorrow" game six was held in Boston. I was now living on Anderson St. at the foot of Beacon Hill as my lease on the apartment in Cambridge had expired. It was not unusual for people in Boston to move from place to place when leases expired. This was due to the very annoying habit of Boston landlords to automatically raise the rent when a tenant's lease expired. The demand for housing in Boston had always outpaced the supply, so landlords had long been in command of the going rate of rents. I could no longer afford the Cambridge apartment so I needed to move. I found a third floor four-room walkup in one of the seedier sections of Beacon Hill, and Dennis agreed to be my "absentee" roommate. He was still living with his fiancée and, once again, required a "cop out" living arrangement when her parents were in town. As a result, Carole and I were home on Beacon Hill the sultry October night when Carlton Fisk hit his famous two run homer that won the sixth, tying game for the Red Sox in that incredibly dramatic 1975 AL pennant series. My apartment was about a mile from Fenway and we had all the windows open as the weather was very warm. The game was blacked out and of course one couldn't get tickets, so we sat watching some program on TV when, at around midnight (in the 12th inning of the game), we heard an enormous low roar from the direction of Kendall Square which sounded as if the heavens were about to open. In fact, it was the crowd at Fenway as they reacted in unison to Fisk's hit that remained in fair play (just to the right of what is now called the Fisk pole) and exiting the park over the Green Monster in left field. We knew something huge had occurred which was verified on the TV news a little later. Of course, the Red Sox lost the next game, but the improbable "cardiac kids" of 1975 had once again borrowed into the hearts of Red Sox faithful who would realize their ultimate reward some 29 years later.

Carole's sister Wendy arrived in Boston to accompany Carole back

West, they had planned a train trip to New Orleans and then a flight home from there. During our last night together in Boston, I treated the girls to dinner at the Marliave restaurant on Boswell St in the oldest section of Boston. The Marliave is a quaint European café dating back to 1875. The food was very good, the atmosphere charming and the prices reasonable. It was a wonderfully memorable evening and the girls were on their way the next morning. I was quite blue after Carole left, but I got on with my job. As luck would have it, within a week of my intended departure, the Iranian job was terminated. The Shah (no relation to the Dipper) was still in power in Iran at the time, but even then, the official Iranian position was condemnation of Israel. The Iranian government had discovered that one of the principals at GEI was Ron Hershfeld and cancelled the contract which was very ironic, because Ron Hershfeld was not Jewish. As late autumn arrived, my contact with Carole became more frequent with letters, notes and phone calls. She was looking for employment and I encouraged her to apply in Massachusetts so that we could be together. In the meantime, it became clear that if I wanted to advance at GEI, I would need to obtain an engineering degree. I wasn't that interested in civil engineering, so I did some investigating and found a new job with a startup chemistry company in Waltham. I made the move, to Giner Inc. in December and Carole found a dietician's job in New Bedford expecting to start in March. As a precondition to my new employment, I would be allowed ten days vacation to visit and retrieve Carole from Oregon. Giner Inc. was a strange little company located on the second floor of an old mill building next to the Charles River in Waltham, Mass. The company took its named after its founder, Jose Giner, who started the company after he and one of his associates had been laid off from Tyco Industries. Tyco had begun chasing the fuel cell rainbow after NASA chose to use fuel cells to provide electric power for the astronaut capsules in the Apollo program. The *Bacon Cell* based on the use of sodium hydroxide solution as the electrolyte was the fuel cell technology of choice for this program. However, as time wore on, United Technologies became the favored NASA contractor for fuel cell technology and Tyco's program fell by the wayside. This resulted in a RIF (reduction in-force) for a number of Tyco scientists and it is my understanding that Jose received a "golden parachute" from which he was able to found Giner Inc.

Jose was an electrochemist and although I wasn't particularly enamored with electrochemistry, it seemed to the right job at the right time. My previous exposure to electrochemistry had been in an Analytical Chemistry class at SMTI that focused on the technique known as polarography. This procedure involves the use of a dropping mercury electrode for the analysis of metals in solution. I hated the technique and never could get the hang of it, …..pun intended, (get it? dropping mercury electrode,……hang of it).

I liked Jose very much he hailed from Valencia, Spain and was a "bon vivant". He liked good living and was very fond of good cigars. He spoke impeccable English and had a great sense of humor. One of his drawbacks was that he procrastinated when faced with a deadline. I participated in the proposal submission process on several occasions while employed at Giner Inc. and each time it was a whirlwind of effort by the staff in which all other work at the company ceased. Since I was a neophyte, I came to expect that this was the normal process for preparation of federal proposals by a private company. Little did I know that usually there was a period of a month or more that was normally allotted for proposal preparation, but Jose would leave his until the last ten days of the allotted time slot. Consequently, everyone in the company would be running at flank speed to get the document assembled and throughout this process, Jose would be puffing away on his cigars appearing like a steam locomotive powering down the tracks toward the deadline. His office was a fog of cigar smoke and the greater the pressure to perform, the more he puffed on his cigar. The final outcome of the process was a frantic taxicab ride for one of the clerical staff to Logan airport who, upon arrival at National (now Reagan) Airport would grab a second taxi and hand carry the proposal to the select federal agency with no more than 20 minutes to spare before the submission deadline. A telephone call from the company courier to our office in Waltham informing Jose that she had made it before the five PM deadline would result in a grand celebration with the popping of a champagne bottle and great exultation. After witnessing this frenetic process on several occasions, it seemed to me that it could be greatly improved upon.

My job at Giner was that of a bench chemist and I was assigned to work on a new project, the development of an electrochemical glucose senor for diabetics. As time went on at Giner, this project took on increasing importance and we obtained funding from the National Institutes of Health. We were partnered with the Joselin Diabetes Foundation and one person who took a personal interest in our work was Mr. Ken Olsen, founder and CEO of the Digital Equipment Corporation (DEC). As is well known, DEC invented the minicomputer in the 1960s. This device was anything but "mini" requiring a 6'x4'x4' metal frame to support the CPU and associated equipment. It was a game changer in its day and the company thrived as a serious competitor to IBM. Mr. Olsen's son had juvenile diabetes and this was the source of Mr. Olsen's interest and financial support. I had the pleasure of meeting Mr. Olsen on two occasions and found him to be a very pleasant, amicable person. The work was interesting, but the variables that we were trying to control in the system were far too daunting. Eventually, the program ended, unsuccessfully. What's ironic is that the ultimate answer to the problem of developing an artificial pancreas was solved using microprocessors and small implantable pumps. So, in the end, it was Mr. Olsen's technology (electronics), not electrochemistry that provided the solution.

After I started working at Giner, I flew west to meet Carole's parents and bring her back to Massachusetts to (hopefully) begin her new life. In 1976, the airlines operated under rather strict federal regulations. Consequently, unlike today with a myriad of discount airlines driving down ticket prices, flying was still fairly expensive and beyond the reach of most Americans. My round trip ticket from Boston to Eugene, Oregon was about $650 which would be equivalent to around $2500 today, quite an expense at the time. I hadn't been in an airplane since I was five years old when Mary, Butch and I flew from Providence to Albany in a DC-3 to meet Benny. So, for me, flying cross country in 1975 was a real treat. Along with the steep prices came better services. The stewardesses (not flight attendants) were civil, friendly and helpful the seats were wide and comfortable even in coach class. The plane I flew on was a reconfigured stretch DC-8. It had two service areas located in the middle of the cabin and on this flight we were provided with a buffet lunch with a variety of cold cuts and breads, potato salad and coleslaw and iced up cans of soft drinks. Each passenger sampled the buffet, made their choices and returned to their seats. It was very good and very civilized especially in light of today's coach amenities or glaring lack thereof.

I landed in Eugene a little worse for the wear and after deplaning, I was greeted by Carole, her mom Brenda and two of Carole's friends Jim and Becky. Jim and Becky had driven over from Klamath Falls to meet me in person which was quite gratifying. Following initial introductions, the group broke up, boarded two cars and drove to an Italian restaurant in Eugene for dinner. We ordered and the waiter asked if we would like wine. Carole differed to me and I ordered a bottle of Cabernet Sauvignon and did my utmost to pronounce it with my best French accent (High School French was finally put to good work). As I finished my order, Carole's mom Brenda who, like her daughter, is a hopeless romantic exclaimed "You said that just like Maurice Chevalier". I knew I had Brenda at that point. My stay with the Gardner clan was wonderful. Brenda drove Carole and me up to Portland and then down the coast and back to Roseburg where the family homestead was located. We stayed overnight on our coastal jaunt as the distances were quite significant and the roads windy and primarily two-lane. I was very impressed with Oregon having never been west of Albany, NY in my twenty-seven years. I met Carole's Dad John and her sister Susan which rounded out my introduction to the Gardner family. John and Brenda were low key, but extremely pleasant and friendly. I hoped that the feeling was mutual as I was about to steal their daughter from them and bring her back east.

The week passed quickly and before I knew it, Carole and I were on a plane flying back to Boston. Although it was February, it had been mild and damp in Oregon when we departed. Our arrival in Boston was just the opposite, cold, windy and dry. Carole had all of her worldly possessions packed in two steamer trunks and I had to find a taxicab that could accommodate our luggage. I found one of those "checker" cabs at the end of a long line and had that taxi driver pull up to the front to load the trunks. As usual, it was bedlam at the United terminal at Logan airport, and the cop who was directing traffic lost it and began screaming at my taxi driver to get back in line. Meanwhile I was screaming at the same driver to pull up for the luggage. I was finally able to talk some sense into the traffic cop as the driver loaded the trunks and we finally headed for my apartment at one o'clock in the morning; Welcome back to friendly Boston.

After a day or so, my mom drove up from Fairhaven and got Carole settled in a friend's rental apartment in Fairhaven. She started her job a week later and I would travel down from Boston to spend the weekend with her. Carole is very resourceful and resilient and she settled right in to Fairhaven and her job at a local hospital. With the arrival of spring, we began getting the boat ready for launching. At that time, Ed and Peter both drove matching company cars, Ford Granadas....a couple of rear wheel drive "boats". They were doing better than me at that point as my Rambler had died and I was "a foot". This was inconvenient, but an advantage for one living on Beacon Hill as there was virtually no parking anywhere for a personal vehicle. Boat work required traveling to Rhode Island on Saturdays to polish the hull, clean the interior and paint the bottom. This was invariably a good time as Carole would come along with us and we would then make an evening of it a local restaurant after out boat work. Warmer spring weather also brought neighbors out of there houses and with that we discovered that Paul and Nancy Bertouli were living next door to Carole in Fairhaven.

I'd known Paul for years and he was a hell raiser. Nancy was a really good influence on Paul as she was more level headed and placid which is what an emotional Italian fellow needed to keep him on course.

Paul and his older brother John were in the same age bracket as

Butch and me and we had grown up and gone through High School with them. Their mother was also named Mary and her maiden name was Howland, another old Yankee family that became wealthy from whaling in the 19th century. Their father, John, was a second generation Italian immigrant who grew up in Boston and was an extroverted highly artistic, emotional Italian gentleman. The progeny of this marriage of a stern Yankee and an emotional Italian was something to behold. With two years separating John and Paul, sibling rivalry was rampant throughout their adolescent years. They seemed to go out of their way to outdo one another and at times this rivalry took on a riotous quality. One incident in particular is memorable. In the center of Fairhaven sits an old two-story building dating back to the 1830's. Upstairs is the now defunct grange hall and the first floor housed the Brown's Pharmacy. In the 1960s, the main attraction for most of us adolescents in Brown's was the soda fountain and on summer days, there usually was a large number of youngsters and teenagers enjoying an ice cream soda, a cherry coke or a lime rickie.

Paul and John and their contemporaries were regulars at the soda fountain and it could become quite crowded especially after basketball games on hot summer days at Roger's school not far from Browne's. Imagine 15 to 20 sweaty, hot teenagers all crowded around the fountain yelling commands at the poor soda jerks all demanding their lime rickie at the same time. Eventually, the testosterone in the place would get the better of a few of these youths and personal rivalries would surface evoking taunting and teasing of the younger members of the group by the older ones. John began to taunt his brother (as older brothers will do) and all was fine until he apparently touched a nerve with Paul who swung around on his fountain stool and lunched a fist at John. Luckily, John ducked in time to miss the punch, but he retaliated and pulled Paul of the stool and the "donnybrook" began. Before anyone knew it, the two were on the floor rolling over one another trying to obtain an advantage. Of course at this point all of the other teens in the place were urging the two combatants on rooting for their favorite in this contest. Rather than calling the police, the storeowner ran down the street to find Paul's mom to get her two sons to break up their fight and get them out of his store. Fortunately, Mary was readily available and she hurried to Browne's and managed to separate her two sons just about the time that John was attempting to push Paul's head under the greeting card display case. The fight ended as Mary scolded the two boys and ordered them home they obliged, but continued sniping at each other all the way home. The reason why the storeowner (Bob Browne) ran to get Mary rather than the Police was due to the fact that this sort of thing happened on a regular basis with the Bertouli boys and their mother was the far more effective at breaking up these altercations than the Police.

Paul and John were standouts, but by no means the singular eccentrics in the large group of adolescents that claimed the "Center" of town as their territory. In the 1960s, the central and peripheral members of this loose knit social network numbered around 100. Most were male, but females were also allowed. Everyone was enrolled in school and in the summer nearly everyone worked. The center of town with Browne's Pharmacy as the focus was a natural place for teenager to congregate since it was at the intersection of two main thoroughfares witnessing a constant flow of traffic. In the days before the internet, cell phones and all of the attendant paraphernalia, face-to-face contact was the main social medium and one could always find someone else hanging around in the center. It was where contacts were made and news and gossip was exchanged. The merchants had witnessed a long line of adolescent "townies" over the years and the list of eccentric adolescents was extensive including Steve Bouley, "Nappy Holmes", Tommy Mendell, Tony Richards (Peter's brother and one hell of a nice guy) my brother Butch and the Mitchell brothers. These "elder" townies were then followed by my age group including Brucie Silva, David Butcher, Bob Jones ("Jonsey"), "Mimmie" Silvia, Charlie Newton (aka Chuck Farley) and David "Tex" Anderson to name a few. Tex was quite a character and was a Maryland resident before moving to Fairhaven to attend High School. He had a bit of a southern drawl, so of course my highly provincial, geographically

197

challenged associates dubbed him "Tex", because they considered anywhere south of the Mason-Dixon Line, or south of Fall River for that matter, to be Texas. We had many funny raucous times which should be the subject of another book at another time.

Now that Paul and John were adults, their passion for settling their differences with fists had cooled significantly, but they still wore their Italian emotions on their sleeves. Paul was a born salesman and as Nancy would often comment, "he can break a pencil in two and sell you half". As spring wore on to summer, Paul and Nancy became regulars with our group and often sailed with us in company with Bob Rustle during our weekend excursions in the waters of southeastern Massachusetts.

Several incidents from that summer standout among the many memories of our shenanigans. Since it was 1976, the two hundredth anniversary of the founding of the United States with the signing of the Declaration of Independence, we all knew that this July 4th would be special. The International Sail Training Association was planning a big blowout in Newport which was on the route of the square rigged training ships (Tall Ships....I hate that term, much too generic) tour of the east coast. So we planned to be there for that. However, before that date we had weekends to burn on the Vineyard and the weekend before the fourth of July, we sailed to Oak Bluffs together with the *Rustler* and managed to get there early enough to obtain two slips at the bulkhead on the main drag. That summer, there was an almost endless list of colonial balls and parties being held at every waterfront venue along the coast as inns and restaurants tried to cash in on the 200th anniversary. I would hazard to guess that costume suppliers were also doing a brisk business as the managers of these inns required their staff to wear colonial period attire in keeping with the theme of the event. As luck would have it, this particular weekend the Wesley House a Victorian–era hotel in Oak Bluffs was hosting an island colonial ball.

Rustler and crew tying up across the street from the Wesley House

The Wesley House was located directly across Lake Street from the boat basin and, to the misfortune of its management, directly across from the scruffy crews of the *Rustler* and *Circadian Rhythm*.

Wesley House, Oak Bluffs, MA

It all began very innocently, the crews (fairly well juiced after a hard

199

day of sailing) were enjoying their dinner standing on the dock with their food situated on the bulkhead, when Peter (that rascal) happened to notice several colonial soldiers dressed as "Redcoats" standing guard at the entrance to the Wesley House. Besides traveling with his omnipresent kazu (also his clarazu, combination of a kazu and clarinet) and Sony cassette player, Peter was also known to have on hand an old New Bedford High School cheerleader megaphone and also Willy Talk. Willy was a small ventriloquist dummy that Peter carted everywhere, although he never tried to use Willy for his intended purpose.

Having had a few beers, Peter began shouting jeers at the Redcoats and after a few minutes they took up the taunting. In good fun the Redcoats (obviously locals playing the part) began shouting insults at the colonial rebels and Peter took up the challenge.

Here's Peter, note t[hat] he's wearing a button-down, oxford cloth shirt and bermudas, always dressed well

Rustler and CR crews across from Wesley House 1976

As Peter's enthusiasm for the exchange of invectives increased, he began to enlist the participation of others in our group and eventually we were all involved making up tongue-in-cheek insults to throw at the surly Redcoats. Eventually, the situation escalated as the Redcoats made a mock charge down the slight hill toward our position on the other side of Lake St. Well, that was all it took, suddenly crewmates were scampering aboard both vessels looking for whatever equipment was available to turn our ragged group into the semblance of a fighting unit. Bob immediately grabbed his ensign mounted on a three-foot long mahogany staff, our flag. Ed grabbed the boat horn to use as an auditory bazooka, Paul wrapped a bandana around his head and fitted a roll on his shoulders simulating a Revolutionary War soldier. He also grabbed his high school trumpet that he had brought along as part the CR band and began blowing the Calvary charge. Peter, who started the whole thing, stood off to the side and yelled commands through the megaphone performing like a pageant director, that sly dog.

Our motley crew assembled on the bulkhead and with Rustle in the lead (with the flag) we made several mock charges at the Redcoats position on the hill blasting boat horns and yelling as we charged. Each mock charge was repulsed amid shouts and laughter. Our efforts stopped the busy traffic on Lake St. as passersby stopped to gawk or take pictures. Ed and I grabbed Peter's megaphone and held the boat horn at the mouthpiece to increase the effect of our auditory bazooka. The "raid on the Wesley House" lasted about fifteen minutes, but was the hit of the overall event as Ball attendees laughed and snapped pictures of the two "warring" sides. We shook hands with out Redcoat counterparts at the end of the "raid" and got back to our dinner. I'm told the entire incident was reported on that week in the local newspaper which claimed that the local militia had valiantly beaten back consistent charges by a group of marauding boaters.

The day following the Wesley House raid, the entire crew assembled at the Martha's Vineyard airport to welcome Carole's sister Wendy who had flown in from Oregon for a visit. Wendy popped in during the middle of the weekend and had to spend the next day and a half with the whole gang before we sailed back to Fairhaven allowing Wendy to unwind from her transcontinental flight. She was afforded this brief respite, before we launched her into the next foray which took us all to Newport, utilizing ground transportation, for the American Sail Training Association gathering of ships, better known as the "Tall Ships" event; oh how I hate that term. Lord knows, a three-masted square-rigged Barque such as the USCGC Eagle is not in any way similar in sail plan to a fore and aft rigged schooner like America. However, generally speaking, these details are lost on the average spectator and do not lend themselves well to a mass advertising campaign, hence the abhorrent term "Tall Ships". So, we were all off to Newport to take part in a small intimate gathering of some 300,000 people on hand to witness the last leg of the 1976 trans-Atlantic training ship race. This was a major part of the Declaration of Independence Bicentennial celebration.

Our group consisted of around 15 people so we approached this experience like a military exercise. We used three cars to transport the "platoon", we dressed accordingly (it was hot and humid that weekend in mid-July) took plenty of water, hats, kazus, Groucho glasses and Peter took his megaphone. We parked way outside of town in a designated lot and took the bus transportation into Newport. To ensure that no one would be lost, Peter assigned a number to each and made us count off periodically to ensure that we were all together. When we emerged from the bus, the throngs in town were treated to a sight to rival any that day. As we marched down Thames St. with Peter in the lead wearing Groucho glasses, he would periodically stop and yell for a count down from our group. Dutifully, all would yell out their number in sequence until Peter heard "FIFTEEN" and then he would signal for the troupe to continue the march Occasionally, we would all take out our kazus and play Colonel Bogie's March (Bridge over the River Kwai) during the longer marches between piers, this really worked up the crowds as we marched along. No strangers to Newport, we traipsed all over town from one dock to another to board the vessels with Peter demanding a count down before and after our inspection of a vessel. Of course, periodic stops were made for liquid refreshments at waterfront establishments like the Black Pearl, Bowen's Wharf, The Moorings……..the list goes on. At the end of the day, Peter was slurring his count down request and some of the participants were beginning to forget their number. Finally, after an exhausting day, we all staggered back aboard the transport bus, arrived back at our cars and headed for home. It was a rewarding, if tiring day and we were all inspired to greater sailing heights (no pun intended).

Carole and Wendy would accompany Rustle later that week to witness the departure of the sail training fleet from Newport. Rustle had the week off and I think Carole played hooky from work. I was forced to miss this event, but he pictures looked great.

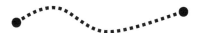

That summer, Carole's parents John and Brenda paid Carole a visit and we saw to it that they spent a fair amount of their visit on the water. Brenda was very happy sailing along with we goofy guys on *Circadian Rhythm* since she could enjoy being on the water wearing only a light sweater. The coast in Oregon is often quite chilly as the California current which is a Pacific Ocean Current that begins off the coast of British

Columbia and sweeps south along the coast to the Baja. The California Current is part of the North Pacific Gyre a large swirling current that occupies the northern basin of the Pacific. As this current sweeps south along the west coast, it carries cool water from the north Pacific that causes the coastal areas to be cooler than comparable east coast locales at the same latitude. This current regulates the temperatures along the coast maintaining them in a narrow range throughout the year.

On the east coast we have a countervailing current, the Gulf Stream that brings warm water from southern latitudes to northern waters. This helps to warm the air in the summer and with longer days the shallow waters of the bays heats dramatically to the mid-seventies. Brenda was enjoying these warm temperatures while being on the water, a new experience for her and John. Both Brenda and John were quiet, low-keyed folks, but I think they enjoyed the antics of the *Circadian Rhythm* crew. We more or less behaved ourselves, but Peter and Ed were always the cut ups with one-liners, silly songs and Bob & Ray routines. John owned timberland in Douglas County, Oregon and worked that land thinning out his trees and taking them to market. His dad (Rex Gardner) had been a timber cruiser in the 1920's and had purchased large tracts of timberland in the Northwest when he was partners with the publisher of the Portland Oregonian. According to John, Rex's "silent" partner would stop by Rex's office on occasion and ask for a "checky" as his portion of the partnerships profits. John claimed "Dad got a little tired of having to write checkies for someone who wasn't doing much for the business, so he finally bought out his partner". John's land in Douglas County was very productive yielding much high grade Douglas Fir, the best wood for construction.

Brenda had an equally interesting background having been born in Alberta, Canada and then immigrating as a child with her family to Glendale, California. Her dad (Papa) had a Type A larger than life personality, the patriarch who ran a very successful loan company in Glendale. That he was able to successfully survive the Great Depression as a banker with a large family is a tribute to his business acumen. Likewise,

John's father Rex was a shrewd businessman since his business not only survived the Depression but apparently thrived. I really enjoyed my conversations with John and Brenda since their life experiences out West were so different from mine. I've come to know and love these two soft spoken, gentle, incredibly kind and generous people and I'm very proud to be their son-in-law.

Once again, in late August of 1976, we experienced another heat wave with temperatures hovering in the 90's and humidity in the 80% range. One Saturday during these conditions, Paul, Nancy, Carole and were the only available crew as Ed and Peter had other commitments. The four of us boarded the boat and started out toward Quick's Hole hoping to beat the heat, if only for a few hours. Once past Clarks Point, the sou'westerly kicked in and we were bathed in a cooler, but very humid sea breeze. We sailed for an hour or two and finally fetched the beach at Quick's. No sooner had we furled the main and dropped the hook than Paul was over the side cooling off in the swirling waters of the passage. As you might expect, with the prevailing weather the anchorage was quite crowded with others trying to beat the heat. There was one particular powerboat off to windward who hailed us on his loudspeaker and announced that we should be aware that a hammerhead shark had been spotted in the passage five minutes earlier. Paul was the only one in the water from *Circadian Rhythm* and he overheard part of this announcement and with that swam over to the side of the boat to clarify what had been said. I mentioned to him that there was something about a shark sighting and with that……….he yelled "Shark?" and literally clawed his way up the side of the boat to get out of the water. Can't say that I blame him, I think that if I had been in his place I would have acted in the same manner.

As might be expected, sharks are a constant presence in and around the waters of southeast Massachusetts, particularly in the summer when they follow the pelagic fish north. Sharks are so common in the summer that a shark tournament is held each year on the Vineyard. Generally speaking, blue sharks or "blue dogs" are the most common species found in and around the Cape and Islands and at the mouth of Buzzards Bay. These sharks are usually found to be in the five foot range and can weigh in at up to 50 lbs. They are curious, but usually not aggressive

Hammerheads are also occasionally sighted in Buzzards Bay and in a very rare occurrence a large (18 ft) female Great White shark began frequenting the waters of Woods Hole and Hadley's Harbor in the summer of 2004. She caused no harm, but was a major spectacle for about a week before leaving the area. Great Whites (Carcharodon carcharia) are common east of Montauk Point in the summer, attracted by large game fish and the occasional whale carcass. Today, Cape Cod has also become a haunt for Great Whites. The protection of harp, grey and harbor seals in the waters of Cape Cod over the past fifty years has led to an explosion in the population of these marine mammals. These critters are at the top of the Great White's menu so the waters in and around Monomoy Island (the sanctuary for seals) are now the cruising grounds for a number of Great White sharks.

While sharks are not uncommon in the waters of Buzzards Bay, Cape Cod and the Islands, thankfully, shark attacks are very rare. To the best of my knowledge, the only fatal shark attack in the past 100 years in these waters occurred, oddly enough, within 100 yards of shore in Mattapoisett in 1936. According to accounts, the victim was a 16-year-old boy who was swimming in 10 feet of water when he was attacked by what appeared to be a Great White. Witnesses to the tragedy claimed that the shark was 10-12 feet in length and that the color of its sides was much whiter than its back. This was an indication that the shark was a Great White and not a Tiger shark that had also been sighted in Buzzards Bay that year. Unfortunately, the victim in this incident died and the shark was not caught. Since this incident occurred in 1936 when seal populations in an around Buzzards Bay were very low, one might expect that Great Whites may become more common in Buzzards Bay in the future thanks to the geometric increase in seal populations in and around the bay.

~ Chapter 11 ~

Another Circadian Rhythm

We ended 1976 with another year of sailing under our belts and several wins in club racing with the LTYC. Once again, we found that our boat was too small for the burgeoning number of guests and friends we wished to sail with. So, at the end of the season, we were once again in the market for a larger boat. We began out search at the annual Newport In-the–Water boat show. This venue was prefect for perusing the various sailboat options and prices. We were planning to bring Paul and Nancy in with the original three partners, and Carole would be my sailing buddy from then on. In addition, Ed had found a new girlfriend, Pamela, who hailed from Long Island, but would be relocating to Fairhaven to be closer to Ed. We now needed accommodations for seven people, at a minimum. We decided that something in the thirty-three foot range would meet our needs, so the search was on. The Newport show was useful and helped us to narrow down the list to tow boats: the O'Day center cockpit 32 and the Ranger 33.

Throughout October, we spent weekends driving to boat yards and brokerages looking at new and used boats in a caravan of two cars. These excursions would always end at a bar or restaurant where libations would be imbibed as we exhaustively discussed the details of boat brochures and listing sheets. This, as they say, is the best part of buying a boat, looking for the right one. Other than dinner and gas money, it was a low cost exercise. In addition to traveling to view promising candidates, we also voraciously consumed each new Soundings when it appeared on the news stand. At the time, Soundings was the premier print venue for boat listings on the East coast and we circled hundreds of possibilities that fall. We finally settled on a one-year-old Ranger 33 that was loaded with extras and located in Portsmouth NH.

After much debate, we settled once again on the name *Circadian Rhythm* and CR 2 came into being.

Ranger 33, Circadian Rhythm

We chose not to call this vessel *Circadian Rhythm II* as we understood that the C&C 25 would receive a new name, so we stuck with CR. Much to our surprise we soon discovered that Bob Rustle (not to be outdone) had also bought a Ranger 33. The stage was now set. Ed and Bob had grown up in the south end of New Bedford and had been competing since early childhood. Ed was determined to humble Rustle in the sport of sailboat racing. This would unfold later that year at Block Island.

In January, we finalized the purchase of the Ranger 33 and the sale of the C&C 25 which Peter Haines assisted with. Carole, with my inept assistance, was busy during this period making plans for our impending marriage in Roseburg, Oregon her hometown. As the reader might expect, I was excited about marrying Carole, but (to my shame) probably equally excited about the new boat. I asked Ed and Peter to be in our wedding party with my brother Butch as my best man and my sister Deb serving as a maid of honor. The date for the wedding was May 22, 1977 and the plan called for the wedding party and my family to fly to Oregon five days after my arrival there. Carole bought me a new suit (I was still as poor as a church mouse….tell me again why she wanted to marry me?) and she flew out on the eleventh of May. On the 16^h of May, Southern New England experienced a nor'easter of epic proportions that left a six-inch mat of heavy, wet snow through the region. This resulted in power outages as the trees that had sprouted leaves accumulated limb-breaking snow loads felled power lines. I wasn't sure that I would manage to get out of Boston the next morning, but luck was with me and I flew West with no problems.

Carole and Brenda met me in Eugene that afternoon and we drove to Roseburg to get ready for the wedding. Brenda had secured accommodations in town for my family and friends at a local motel. In true Gardner tradition, all of the other details including the honeymoon suite had also been attended to. My family and friends arrived a few days later and we all enjoyed a rousing rehearsal dinner with Ed and Peter providing the entertainment. The wedding went off without a hitch and we all enjoyed a rousing party at the local country club.

The next day Carole and I established a new Gardner family tradition when the entire wedding party loaded into three cars and began a whirlwind tour of southern Oregon. The rationale was that all of my family and friends had never been in the Northwest, so why not show them the sights. Even though Carole and I were now man and wife, she rode with her parents in their car and I drove my parents in their rented car. Our first stop was the Diamond Lake resort located at 5200 feet in the Cascades about 85 miles east of Roseburg. After a mediocre dinner most of the party retired for the night, but some of we more intrepid souls headed for the game room for more beer and some pool. Ed was a decent pool player and challenged a fellow who had won the previous round to a game. As Ed was preparing to make a difficult shot with one leg on the floor and one on the table, another of the players remarked "You play pool like a Portagee". To which Ed responded "that's because I am a Portagee, or at least one-half Portagee". As it turned out, the verbal challenge had come from one who was from San Francisco another hotbed of Portuguese-American culture as is New Bedford. Ed and his counterpart had a lot common and exchanged many stories to that effect.

Our tour ended two days later after staying a night in Bend and lunch at Black Butte resort watching eagles fly over Cascade mountain lakes while enjoying the open fresh air of the high country. Everyone in the party save Carole, her parents, Wendy and me needed to catch planes from Eugene and we were running late as we headed west on Rte 126. Carole insisted that everyone view Clear Lake which is on the route located down a steep grade from the highway. Being in the lead car, she diverted off the highway dutifully followed by the Wendy and the rental car containing the out-of-towners. Upon arrival at the edge of Clear Lake everyone tumbled out of their respective vehicles, cast two-minute admiring glances at the sun-draped environs of Clear Lake and then scampered back into the three cars as we roared off up the steep incline, leaving a trail of dust, and bolting once again on Rte 126 towards Eugene. Fortunately, everyone made their departure flight on time and Carole, John, Brenda and I then boarded a train headed north toward Vancouver, BC. Yes, Carole's parents accompanied us on our honeymoon. My attitude was.....oh, what the hell! As it turned out, Carole came down with a wicked cold in Victoria and I ended up roaming the docks admiring the scores of yachts that had assembled in preparation for the Swiftsure race that weekend. The next day we boarded the steamer Princess Marguerite that provided service between Seattle and Victoria at the time.

Princess Marguerite

This fine old vessel provided traditional service that we sampled, including a very nice dining room with white coat waiters and fine silver flatware. It was a very memorable trip.

We said our goodbyes to Carole's family and flew back to Massachusetts to begin our new life together. My parents had arranged for us to rent a house from one of their neighbors located just down the street from my parents' house on "Poverty Point". The home was owned by Bill and Vivian White, a middle-aged wealthy couple who also owned condos in New Hampshire and South Carolina. The deal was that we would pay a nominal fee for rent and Bill and Vivian would stay upstairs one or two nights when they were transiting north or south to their condos with the change in seasons. We would have the run of the house other than the upstairs bedroom. It was a great deal. In addition, Pam DeFonte, Ed's new flame agreed to rent the cottage at the north end of the property that Bill had originally built for his mother who was now deceased. It was a neat little place, on the water and very private. This was going to be a fun year.

We became established in our new home and with our new boat and began a fun year of sailing and partying with a great group of friends. We sailed each weekend, rain or shine and Edgartown became the destination of choice. The Ranger was considerably faster than the C&C so we could make Edgartown in considerably less time than before. In addition, the

211

Ranger had a gimbaled three-burner stove and oven as well as a reliable
VHF radio. Consequently, we could now call ahead to reserve a mooring
and expect to be there on time to claim it. While all this was occurring,
we could also cook our dinner underway and upon arrival have a piping
hot meal of baked potatoes and meatloaf for all…..this was living.

Upon our first arrival in Edgartown in the Ranger, we hailed Mr.
Prada who was working the town launch with a hardy "Hello Mr. Prada".
To this he responded, "Well, it wouldn't be summer without you clowns!"
Always true to his understated self.

We ended that summer with the first Block Island Challenge Cup
that was a pre agreed on series of two boat match races between the
Rustler and *Circadian Rhythm* around a group of Navy markers in Block
Island Sound on Labor Day weekend. Rustle agreed to meet us at Block
Island since he was keeping his boat in Connecticut (having dumped
Linda) and we would sail up from New Bedford. Ed was aching for this
match up since he was a long-term competitor with Bob Rustle. The
weather that weekend was sublime with moderate airs, warm temperatures
and excellent visibility.

The races were underwhelming as we stomped Bob resoundly that
afternoon even though we agreed to surrender our navigator Peter to
Rustle's crew. Our victory resulted from better sailing and apparently a
faster hull. The former was a foregone conclusion before the race began
as Rustle never took racing very seriously. The latter was a bit of a
surprise, but through the summer of 1978, CR always outpaced the *Rustler*
on all points of sail.

We laid the boat up in late October and settled in for a New England
winter in our new (rented) house on Oxford St. Pam moved into her
cottage at the end of our yard and we socialized frequently with her and
Ed which cemented emotional ties between Carole and Pam. Bill White
was a fanatic about his property and although the main house was
originally built in 1713 (one of the oldest in the area) he had updated and
improved the property without compromising its original structure. The
main house was a center chimney Cape Cod design which meant that the

house was built around a huge center chimney that sported five or six fireplaces to warm each major room of the dwelling. Bill's improvements were substantial like electricity and central heat, but over the three centuries, the basic structure of the house had changed dramatically. The support timbers for the floors had settled the house had sagged. As a result, all of the window frames were far from plum so that the house was very drafty even though it was fitted with storm windows. Each room had doors which we closed to keep the dining room warm when a fire was in the dining room fireplace. The floors were all sloping so that one walked uphill to the center of the living room and then down hill from there to the front hallway. Although the structure had sagged, the house was sound and well decorated. It was a truly unique property.

At least three of the fireplaces in the main house functioned properly and Bill approved of my plan to use wood to help augment the oil burner in the basement to heat the place that winter. Pam's cottage was fitted with a Franklin stove that also was used to augment the central heating system. Faced with these circumstances, Ed and I agreed in early autumn to split the cost of a chord of wood that we planned to store in Bill's garage adjacent to the main house. When the wood arrived, we rented a small chain saw to cut the three-foot maple and oak into manageable sizes and then stacked the semi-cured product in the garage. The old adage is that wood warms you three times. Cutting the three-foot sections represented the first step the next warming step came when we split the one-foot sections into quarters for the fireplace. The final warming step is when one actually burns the wood.

As late fall arrived, when Ed and I returned form work (I was working in Waltham, Ed in New Bedford) we our first stop after greeting our significant others was the garage where we would meet to split kindling and gather split wood to start the evening fire before dinner. Early on, we both realized that beer was the lubricant of choice that greased these efforts, so one night, Ed would bring a six pack and the next night this would be my responsibility. As Ed cut quarters into kindling, I would swig beer then we would trade places and he would swig beer while

I worked. We spent some thirty minutes each evening "getting kindling" (as we told the girls) and each consumed three beers in the process which mellowed out the remainder of the evening.

Winter finally arrived with a vengeance with a major snow storm one weekend in mid-January that dropped 18" of snow on coastal New England. We and our sailing crew had made arrangements to ski at Black Mountain in New Hampshire that Saturday and at first, it appeared that we wouldn't make it. However, we persevered and had a glorious weekend of perfect skiing. The exception was Peter who had nothing but trouble with his older ski equipment and on Saturday after fighting with the skis all day he dumped his entire outfit into a trash can in a final gesture of complete frustration, it was pretty funny. He has never skied again.

We thought that the worst of the winter was over when we arrived back in Fairhaven after our weekend on the slopes. The next weekend Carole, Susie Rustle Goose and I went back to New Hampshire and stayed at Susie's ski club chalet. It was thirty below zero on Saturday morning as Goose and I drive Carole and Susie to Mt. Cranmore in North Conway for their day of skiing. Goose wasn't a skier so I stayed with him and we amused ourselves buying silly things in town and sliding down "mahogany ridge" (the bar). We met the girls that afternoon, had dinner and headed home the next day. Goose and I were commuting to Waltham at the time, I drove a VW squareback and he had a VW bug. The commute to the Boston area was monotonous in the extreme, especially in the winter. So, Goose and I had tried to find ways to amuse each other on this hour and one half (each way) commute. On Monday February 5, 1978 we drove north from Fairhaven on Rte 24 each wearing a beanie with a propeller on top and yellow lensed ski goggles. We were driving in Goose's VW Beetle and as we passed cars, I would stare at the occupants in the other vehicle with my "outfit" hoping to get a response. On occasion, this would occur and Goose and I would get a chuckle out of it.

I was working away at Giner, Inc. when Carole called at around 12:15 to tell me that it had begun snowing in Fairhaven and according to Don Kent (who was the dean of NE weathermen) a severe low pressure area was forming just south of New England and we were in for a whopper of a nor'easter. She said "if you're planning on coming home today, you'd better leave now". As it turned out, truer words were never spoken as the storm quickly intensified dramatically so that by 13:15 when Goose picked me up, it was snowing heavily in Waltham. Added to this, it was quite cold with temperatures in the low twenties. We headed out toward Rte 128 the inner belt around Boston and when we approached in the onramp from Rte 20 in Waltham, we witnessed a seemingly endless sea of bumper to bumper traffic slowly snaking its way along the highway. We got into line and inched our way along in the three lanes of cars headed south. The persistent snow and cold pavement resulted in a thin layer of ice that began to form along the length of route 128. In 1978 the VW beetle was one of the few autos on the road with superior traction by virtue of its rear engine, rear wheel drive. Adding to this superior feature, Goose (who was not one to anticipate events) took the precaution of equipping his car with snow tires. We were in pretty good shape for navigating these troubled waters with the exception of cabin heat. The old VWs heater used the engine cooling fan to drive heat into the cabin from heat exchanger boxes next to the cylinders. As a result, at high rpm, there was plenty of heat in the cabin, but this was not the case here as we inched along at five mph. We began to think that we may very well freeze to death in what may be the only car that could adequately deal with the current climactic conditions.

We managed to successfully negotiate the hill at the junction of Rte 128 and Interstate 95 in Canton. This hill is inclined heading east at about 3% and had long been a bottleneck. The addition of a climbing lane in the 1960s for tractor-trailer trucks helped alleviate some traffic congestion. On this day, thankfully after Goose and I had passed, this hill would cause a big rig to jackknife which would shut down 128 and be the cause of many deaths.

We pressed on south toward New Bedford after reaching Rte 24 and noticed that there were fewer and fewer cars on the road as we drove along at 20 mph. The visibility was down to 100 feet in driving snow and the wind was beginning to build drifts on the road faster than any plows could clears them and there were damned few plows to be seen. We were ending our third hour of this trip that normally took about 60 minutes to complete in normal traffic conditions. The old VW beetle was living up to its billing as an all-weather vehicle as we continued on through Stoughton, Brockton, and West Bridgewater toward Taunton and our last leg of this voyage; south on Rte 140 to New Bedford. The temperature was well below freezing and we were beginning to lose visibility through the windshield as the defroster could not keep up wit the freezing precipitation. We stopped once or twice before reaching Rte 140 to clear the view and remove the ice form the wipers. Thankfully, there are few hills of any note on Rte 24, so there was little chance of a truck blocking the road as was the case on Rte 128.

When we arrive at the off ramp to Rte 140 at dusk and the daylight was a ominous blue grey as the day slowly ended. We were able to slide down to 140 and crawled along at a puttering pace headed toward an uncertain fate as the whiteout and fading daylight obliterated any delineation between the roadway and the gully just beyond the road shoulder. This road had not been plowed for hours and the snow was easily a foot deep with no tire tracks anywhere. We were alone plodding on through wind and snow hoping to stay on the road as we drove along. Added to the abysmal visibility was the persistent icing of the windshield. As the storm continued to strengthen and the evening temperatures continued to drop, we could no longer keep the windshield free of ice. In addition, we occasionally plowed through a deep drift which threw more snow on the windshield causing further deterioration of the icing problem. Finally, in desperation, we improvised a solution. Our silliness from earlier in the day, proved to be our salvation. We both donned the yellow-lensed ski goggles and each stuck his head out the side window watching for the edge of the road as we drove along. I could clearly see the shoulder and whenever Goose got too close I'd yell "left" and he'd steer over a bit to his side of the road, thus avoiding disaster. This went on for about an hour until we finally reached the North End of New Bedford and relative safety. The city streets were in better shape than Rte 140 and we were able to make our away to my house on Oxford St. Goose dropped me off amidst swirling snow and wind and I shouted "I drive tomorrow". He waved and off he went to his house a mile or so away in town. It had taken us four and half hours to make the 65 mile drive.

Little did I realize at that point that I would not drive tomorrow or for the entire next week as the entire eastern half of Massachusetts was closed for a week as the Blizzard of '78 continued its rampage for another 30 hours. During the storm a reading of 980 mb of pressure was recorded making this storm equivalent to a CAT 1 hurricane, hence its nickname, the white hurricane. When it was over, at least 100 people had been killed and 4500 injured. At its height, the storm had been so severe that many people died from exposure within a few feet of safety. As an example, ten-year-old Peter Gosselin, of Uxbridge, Mass. was returning home form his paper route when he became disoriented in the white out conditions. He disappeared in the drifting snow just feet from his home's front door, his frozen corpse was found three weeks later.

On routes 128 and 95 more than 3000 cars and 500 trucks had been abandoned in the drifts that reached fifteen feet in some areas. Many drivers were asphyxiated in their cars from carbon monoxide as they attempted to stay warm in their immobilized vehicles. At least fifty people perished in stranded vehicles or in the process of seeking shelter after abandoning their vehicles.

All of this information was very sobering for Goose and me in light of what we had endured. We thanked our lucky stars for the VW Beetle, the snow tires and the ski goggles.

In Salem, a pilot boat *Can Do* was sunk with all hands attempting to aid Coast Guard rescue boats that had gone out to assist a tanker that had dragged her anchors in the white hurricane and fetched up on a reef outside Salem harbor. This drama was detailed in Michael Tougias's excellent book "Ten Hours 'till Dawn". The crew of four endured unspeakable hardship during their ordeal, but the boat was found after the storm with at least two of the ill-fated crew still aboard. This tragedy was a testament to the tenacity and selflessness of the mariners of Gloucester. This disaster occurred in the lee of Cape Ann in what would normally be considered sheltered waters. That this well-founded, seaworthy vessel came to grief within two miles of shore, it is clear that this was ordinary winter nor'easter. This storm was a killer and made good on that claim of it being a white hurricane. There were several other storm "scares" that winter in which storms built on weekday mornings and threatened to hit in the afternoon. Employers and employees were "gun shy" after the white hurricane and as a result Rte 128 became a parking lot at two or three in the afternoon with cars inching their way along on light snow flurries. Goose and I had learned our lesson after one or two of these and like many other commuters we stopped at a "packie" to get a six pack for the long ride home. One afternoon in one of these 128 parking lot endeavors as we sipped our beer, we pulled up along a BMW and inside a man and women were toasting one another with martinis....with real martini glasses!

Winter finally ended and we looked forward to Pam and Ed's wedding in Long Island in May. It was the "Big Italian Wedding" with a ten-piece band, huge cake, limos, open bar and everlasting parties. Pam and Ed left for their honeymoon and the wedding party retired to Pam's parents house in Wantaugh. Carole took the car back to our motel early, but she suggested that I stay and enjoy the party, wrong suggestion. As the party progressed, it was time to leave and Peter and I were quite intoxicated. Pam's Dad was worried about Peter driving in his state so he suggested that I drive. Unbeknownst to Nick, I was in no better shape than Peter. I got behind the wheel and wove the car for several blocks before our passengers demanded that Peter take over. He acquiesced to the requests and then, in our collective state of impaired consciousness, he and I worked in unison to navigate the vehicle and get all onboard back to our motel in relative safety. It was a great weekend.

We all returned to Fairhaven after the weekend and began the summer with the Ranger launched in late May. We raced her a bit with the full crew, but finally Ed and I became the race fanatics competing in the LTYC Thursday series with Ed at the helm and me trimming sails. We competed in the cruising class so that the chute wasn't required and cleaned up in the first and second Thursday series. We discovered that the Ranger 33 was so tender that a small jib and main were more than sufficient to overpower the competition on most evenings when the sou'wester was blowing at 15-20. On occasion, we would put a reef in the main to keep her on her feet to weather and then shake it out for the inevitable reach or run after turning the weather mark, (usually Bents Ledge or Inez Rock). At the end of that season at the annual LTYC "steakout" the prevailing comment from the other skippers was that when they saw that pale blue Ranger come out with just a couple of handkerchiefs for sails, they knew they were in trouble. We finished first in series one and two.

Two of the more memorable experiences from the summer of 1978 in the Ranger *Circadian* Rhythm were sailing in Edgartown harbor along side Walter Cronkite in his Westsail 42 *Wyntje*. Our crew's collective observation was that "the most trusted man in America" could not be trusted behind the helm of a sailboat. He didn't seem to know what the hell he was doing with that boat.

The most memorable; however, was the July weekend that Ed, his new bride Pam, Carole and I set sail for Nantucket for the long July 4th weekend.

We provisioned the boat and left Fairhaven Marine around 16:30 intending to spend the first night in Vineyard Haven and then push on the next day for Nantucket. The short term forecast was good as we pulled away from the dock on Thursday evening and enjoyed a trouble-free sail including a safe passage through Woods Hole as we dropped the hook in the outer harbor of Vineyard Haven around 19:00 that evening.

Pam had prepared a lovely lasagna and Carole a nice salad with garlic bread that the four of us enjoyed while lazily swinging off our anchor. The alcohol stove and oven worked flawlessly and we began to think we were in heaven. The next morning dawned fresh and clear and after Carole served a bracing breakfast, we hoisted the hook and sails and headed toward Nantucket. The sou'westerly filled in around noon as we approached the channel marks to the south of Horseshoe Shoals. Pam was sitting on the leeward seat sunning while Ed drove the boat and Carole and I sat in the cockpit, Carole reading, me attending to the sails. It was at this point that Pam and Ed had their first marital spat about some foolish thing. I think it had to do with some sunscreen requirements.

Pam became very upset and then she did the unthinkable......she went down below, in a huff. After a few minutes of waiting, Ed asked me to take over, which I did (to Carole's quizzical stare) and then he went below to try to smooth things over. They weren't down there more than five minutes before Pam emerged looking greener than Sean O'Malley on St Patrick's Day in Southie. She sat down in the cockpit as Ed instructed her to stare at the leeward horizon, but by now the damage had been done. We were in a three-foot beam sea as we proceeded to Halfmoon Shoal and the situation would not get much better as we rounded the "R 18" bell and brought the wind more on the starboard bow heading toward Nantucket. The wind would inevitably build further as the afternoon wore on and we would be banging into an increasing head sea as we passed Tuckernuck Shoal and eventually came under the lee of Tuckernuck Island. At that point the seaway would moderate a bit, but that was hours away.

Pam became visibly ill (well,...after all, she was an Ilsley now) and although we ampathized, there was little we could do. We finally entered the channel and expected that Pam's mal der mer would abate with the seaway. Unfortunately, this was not the case as she appeared to be no better in the protected channel than she had out in the Sound. We steamed to our reserved slip in the yacht basin and tied up around 16:30. Pam was beginning to get chilled as the afternoon temperature dropped, so she and Ed went below into the cabin and Ed tried to administer aid in the form of carbonated soft drinks to calm Pam's stomach. This was to no avail and finally Pam demanded that Ed take her to the hospital to stop her stomach from wrenching. They departed, so Carole and I proceeded to prepare dinner for all expecting that Pam would be okay following her visit to the emergency room. About an hour later, the two newly weds returned and Pam appeared to be in better spirits explaining that the doctor at the island hospital had given her a shot of Compazine to settle her stomach.

We proceeded with dinner with Ed enjoying a glass of wine after their vexing trip to the hospital. Pam rested on one of the settees in the main salon when suddenly her jaw began involuntarily wrenched to one side as she screamed in pain. She was yelling at Ed that her face was frozen and she couldn't move her jaw. Ed spurted up his wine and rushed to her side not knowing what the hell to do, Carole and I were aghast and also dumfounded until Carole exclaimed "Take her back to the hospital!" I ran up the dock to find a cab while Ed and Carole escorted Pam to the waiting cabbie. We got the two of them into the cab and off they went. Carole and I stumbled back to the boat, she popped a beer, I grabbed a gin and tonic and we sat down to discuss what had just occurred.

Carole and I ate our dinner worried about Pam and finally around 21:00, Pam and Ed returned to the boat, quite the worse for wear. It was discovered that Pam was allergic to Compazine which had caused the temporary muscle spasms locking her jaw. An antidote made short work of the previous drug alleviating the problem, but Pam was completely wrung out. She made her apologies and turned in for the night. Ed ate some food, had a few beers and then joined Pam in the forepeak.

The next morning, my sister Deb showed up on the *Rustler* having made the journey from Edgartown with Bob, Peter and a few friends. We all spent one day on Nantucket and then Deb claimed that her friends (my sister has an endless list of friends) were also on the island and asked if we could give them a ride to Edgartown the intended destination for us and

Rustler. Deb was sailing with Bob and as CR prepared to leave the yacht basin who should magically appear at the very last moment but Deb's two friends Karl and Rhea. Rhea was a trip, she was Dutch and had absolutely no inhibitions. She was built like the proverbial brick outhouse and had a very outgoing, devil-may-care attitude about life. We were in a box, so we consented to provide transport so long as the passengers found sleeping accommodations elsewhere upon arrival in Edgartown. As it turned out the crew of *Circadian Rhythm* were clean and sober that morning whereas the *Rustler* crew, including Peter Richards, had overdone it and were all hung over. *Rustler* left and hour or so before CR, but Ed and I got the chute up as a southeast wind began to build pushing CR along at ten knots toward Edgartown. We literally flew past *Rustler* as they wallowed under power too hung over to do much sailing. Surprisingly, Pam was feeling fine and suffered no ill effects from the four-foot following sea, (odd thing, that).

We arrived in Edgartown around 15:00 and rafted up with one other New Bedford boat, Kevin Murphy's thirty-six foot Islander sloop called *Irish Rover*. We'd known Kevin for a while, he and his family were quintessential "Southenders" from the Southend of New Bedford. The *Russller* blew in about an hour behind us and all three boats formed a sandwich with *Irish Rover* in the middle. The wind began to build as we served dinner for a gaggle of people from CR's galley. We bedded down under ominous skies and storm warnings from NOAA weather radio. Rhea and Karl managed to find some sleeping space on *Rustler* since they were associated with my sister who was crew on that boat and CR had newlyweds onboard.

The night was fitful as the wind continued to build and gusts would screech through the standing rigging.

The next morning, July 3rd, dawned grey and wet. It was raining in buckets and blowing a good forty knots in the harbor; it was a full blown sou'eas gale. Edgartown harbor is very well protected from all sides and we were situated toward its south end under the lee of Chappaquiddick headland, so there were no waves of consequence. Even so, our raft of boats would swing wildly in unison to meet a gust when it broke over the headland to windward of us and then blew up the harbor. We all ate breakfast on our respective boats and occasionally someone would don foul weather gear and move over to another boat for a consult on the conditions. After checking the weather and considering our schedule it was decided that the ladies would take the bus to Vineyard Haven and then the ferry to New Bedford as it was considered too dangerous for them to sail back to New Bedford the next day (remember those words). Carole and I had a bit of a tiff over all this, but I finally convinced her to take the ferry, she was fuming as we all boarded the launch for the ride to town. The launch ride was rather exciting, because when we arrived at the harbor entrance the SE wind had built a respectable seaway that was coursing in towards town. Seas were breaking over the starboard side of the sturdy diesel launch for the last 200 yards as we traversed the open exposure of the channel. Everyone, with the exception of Rhea, was completely clad in foul weather gear including bib pants and "sou'wester" hats. Between the rain and the spray all were thoroughly drenched by the time we reached the sheltered launch pier. We all tumbled out and began walking into town to get the ladies to the bus.

The general mood in these grey, soaking, chilly conditions was as foul as the water-proof clothes we were wearing. Carole was angry with me, Pam was not happy with Ed and Ed couldn't wait to get his new bride to "safety" so he could begin to party. The singular bright spot in this sea of human gloom was Rhea. Clad in a woolen overcoat with shorts and sneakers, she was soaked to the skin, but as we walked along she continuously picked prim roses from overhanging bushes and sang Dutch songs as she remarked about the beauty of Edgartown. She had few cohorts in her reverie. We finally reached the bus stop and got the girls onboard with soaking Rhea assuring Ed and I that all would be well. The plan was for them to catch the one o'clock boat to New Bedford and we would follow the next day in CR. We waved goodbye as the bus pulled away and splashed its way down the puddle-ridden street towards Vineyard Haven. With that, Ed, Peter, Rustle and I turned around and as we headed back towards downtown, Ed said, "Let's find the nearest bar". Ed loved his new wife, but she had seriously crimped his partying style that July fourth weekend and he was bound to make amends even if he only had 24 hours (remember those words as well).

We landed at the Harborside and began drinking beer while Ed started with gin and tonics. We left there around 16:30 and stumbled over to the Kafe for a bite to eat as the wind continued to build and the heavens pelted down rain. We caught the 18:00 launch back to the boat with the wind still blowing as hard as ever. At the boat raft, the booze continued to be consumed by many (I opted out) and the party was going well on the *Rustler*. Bob's boat was tied directly to the mooring with Kevin in the middle and CR on the outside. I settled into the nav station onboard the relatively tranquil CR and waited patiently for my turn to place a phone call through the New Bedford Marine Operator to talk with Carole at home checking on the girl's well being. With the foul weather, there was a backup of folks wanting to use the marine operator's services to call home and ensure that all was well. As one might imagine, with the crew of goofy people on CR, the New Bedford Marine Operator knew *Circadian Rhythm* very well. We used their services quite often and as a result, we sometimes received preferential treatment as opposed to yachts from other locales. Peter had developed a personal radio relationship with several of the operators who knew him by name. With the advent of the cellular telephone, the marine operator service dried up, but it had been a colorful aspect of yachting in New England for many years. Standing by on the radio waiting for your turn to come was like listening in on a party line.

I finally got through to Carole as the wind and rain blasted against the port next to my head at the nav station. The call was short, but she reported that they had a wild ride on *Schamonshi*, but all were safe and Rhea was staying the night at our house on Oxford St. After a short conversation with many "ovahs" (overs) we both signed off and I headed over to *Rustler* to see how much human damage had occurred. By this time songs were being belted out as Peter's cassette player was blasting away and Ed was completely blotto. I reminded him that we needed to leave in the morning, to which he responded "No problem, I don't have to get up 'till early". It was approaching 22:00 and the Murphys on *Irish Rover* had turned in so I had one last beer and headed back to CR to call it quits. I fell asleep and I think I felt Ed bump down the companionway around midnight. We had Rhea's friend Karl onboard as well, he was asleep around 23:00. Finally, all was quiet save the wind and rain.

At 07:00, Karl was pounding on me to get up, so I opened my eyes, found my hearing aid and took stock of the situation. It appeared that the Murphys were anxious to get going and they were in the middle of the pack, we needed to move our lines over to *Rustler* as *Irish Rover* backed out of the raft to get on her way. I shook Ed awake and the three of us got up on deck to execute the required maneuvers. Ed looked absolutely terrible having had far too much to drink on far too little sleep. He was quite surly at first and couldn't understand why the hell Kevin had to leave at 07:00. But, as we later learned, Kevin was Kevin and he was a bull when it came to what he wanted to do. We had no choice but to comply. Added to the confusion and consternation was the state of the weather. The rain had ended, but the gale persisted, it was still blowing 30 kts in the harbor with higher gusts. We managed to rouse a few souls on *Rustler* who were in the same condition as Ed and by yelling at each other across *Irish Rover* we compiled a plan for extracting *Irish Rover* from the stack. While we tried to execute this plan, Kevin was screaming orders at everyone simultaneously adding to the bedlam and confusion. Finally, he backed away and as our bow line was being passed to Peter on *Rustler*, confusion set in and someone let go of the line. The next thing we knew, CR was adrift blowing towards the lee shore. I had taken the precaution of starting the engine prior to the repositioning (I Anticipated!,...... **Amazing**) so we weren't in desperate straights, but we were underway reconnecting to *Rustler* would be a dicey situation. Ed looked at me in despair and I shouted that we needed to raise the main, since it appeared that we were going home. Fortunately, we had tucked in two reefs two days before, so the main was small as Ed and Karl raised her up in the stiff

226

breeze. Incidentally, Karl had absolutely no sailing experience so he was more of a liability than an asset in this situation.

We literally flew down the harbor on a beam reach motor sailing towards the harbor entrance. When we reached the vicinity of the Edgartown Yacht Club, we hardened up the reefed main made a right hand turn and headed on a close reach up the channel until we fetched the Edgartown lighthouse. We then fell off a bit, heading east toward the "R6" mark. Normally, this stretch of water is fairly flat as the prevailing sou'wes wind blows off the island and waves aren't encountered until one is a mile or so east of the island. In addition, the water is usually clear and is a faint bluish green in color. On this day, the wind was blowing almost on our nose as we struggled to climb the six to seven foot walls of turbid, brownish, green water.

Occasionally these seas would break on our bow sending heavy sheets of spray over our foul-weather gear and us. I was at the helm with Ed and Karl holding on in the cockpit. The reefed main would periodically shutter as I headed her up to avoid a breaker and then refill as we fell off toward our mark. We could see *Irish Rover* a half mile ahead of us as she rounded "R2" and fell off toward Woods Hole. We rounded the same mark ten minutes later and we also eased the main heading for home. We kept the engine running as Ed suggested that we raise our working jib since we were now off the wind. I asked him if he was up to the task as he looked very disheveled and he was beginning to assume a green pallor. I offered to trade places, but he waved me off as he and Karl wrestled the heavy jib up from the cabin and dragged it forward to the bow. The deck was wet with seawater and quite slippery as I yelled to be careful. I wasn't up for any man overboard drills in these conditions.

After what seemed like an eternity, they were finally able to bend on the jib and raise it as I held the sheet to keep it from blowing out ahead of us. The crew struggled back to the cockpit amidst the rolling motion of CR as we now broad reached under main and jib towards our next waypoint. The jib did help to tame the boat motion and also balanced the rig making the weather helm less severe. I killed the engine and Ed rolled his eyes and headed below (**MISTAKE!**) He claimed that he needed to use the head and I watched as he rolled back and forth on the cabin sole trying to extricate himself from his wet bib foul weather pants and jacket. After three or four minutes of heavy weight wrestling with PVC, he was free and then locked himself in the water closet. Above the woosh of the bow wave and occasional scream of the wind, Karl and I could clearly make out the thump, thump, thump sound of Ed pumping the marine head. Finally, after ten minutes the water closet door flung open and with a starboard roll of the boat Ed tumbled out of the head and onto the cabin sole. What a fight! I think he won, though. He pulled himself up from the deck and then reengaged in combat with his PVC foulies; what a truly pitiful sight. Once he was encased in his waterproof clothes he reemerged from the cabin totally exhausted and took a seat on the leeward side of the cockpit clutching a bottle of Sprite and nodding with the motion of the boat. The cloud cover finally broke and the warm July sun appeared and we then began to bake in our PVC foulies until we were far more wet on the inside than the outside.

We caught a break at Woods Hole as the current and wind were with us, so there were no seas in the channel and not much traffic with which to contend. As we headed across Buzzards Bay, the sky cleared completely the wind had veered more to the nor'eas and the air was crisp with seemingly unlimited visibility. Poor Karl was just a lump of humanity having no maritime experience whatsoever, I was chained to the wheel and Ed was in a derisory state. We were now close reaching toward the north side of the bay and Ed consulted the chart periodically, but I don't think it was registering as he guided me closer to West Island than I thought was prudent. As we approached the island, we felt a thud from below, we'd touched a rock. I turned hard to port and fell off headed back the way we came until I got my bearings and then spotted Angelica Point at the end of Sconiticut Neck and headed for that in deeper water. Ed complained that the clear conditions threw off his perception, but whatever it was we had again touched bottom so I was now completely in charge. We sailed up the New Bedford channel and reached C dock at

Fairhaven Marine. Once we were secure, Ed got off the boat and literally dragged himself up the dock to the showers, he'd had it. Fortunately, we hadn't done any damage to the boat and I cleaned her up as best I could.

Carole picked us up after a phone call and we headed back to Oxford St. It was then that the story of the girls' adventure came to light. As Carole began to tell her tale, it was clear that they had a far more harrowing experience trying to get back home the day before than we did. *Schamonshi* was an older car ferry that had a high center of gravity imposed by her high deck house offering limited passenger shelter and virtually no amenities other than a small snack bar and two heads. Carole recounted that the boat was full of passengers (they weren't licensed to carry cars) as they headed out from the relative shelter of Vineyard Haven harbor into the tumult of rain and wind in Nantucket Sound. No sooner had they turned for Woods Hole than the ferry was hit with the full force of wind and waves breaking over the car deck and tossing the passengers to and fro inside the cabin like rag dolls.

All was bedlam with Pam and Rhea shrieking along with most of the other passengers, so Carole left the cabin to get away from the mayhem. She recounted how she sat on the leeward deck outside of the cabin holding onto the deck stanchion for dear life as *Schamonshi* fought her way to Woods Hole in the grey gloom of rain and salt spume. Although it was dangerous on deck, that was apparently far preferable to the insanity and sea sickness inside the cabin. Apparently, there was a great deal of the later and as is well known, once one person succumbs to mal der mer, it quickly becomes an epidemic in a closed, stifling cabin.

Buzzards Bay was a bit easier to take and they landed without any casualties in New Bedford and made their way back home. The next morning, Rhea jumped out of bed and then proceeded to completely clean Carole's house from top to bottom with no prompting or interference. Carole was thrilled since Rhea was extremely thorough and the house was sparkling when she finished. We reunited Karl with Rhea and managed to get them to the bus station on time for their transit back to Amherst. Ed vanished into Pam's cottage and I assume straight to bed, the newlyweds were also reunited. I was just happy to be home in a stationary, clean dwelling with Carole. The weekend had finally ended.

A postscript, it was later reported that the July 4th 1978 weekend had been one of the coolest on record with average temperatures only in the high fifties.

Later that summer we did extensive cruising in the new boat and on one particular weekend, Carole's cousin's Kathy and Richard joined Pam, Ed, Carole and me for a weekend on Buzzards Bay. The first night we stopped at Quissett Harbor which is one of the most picturesque, tranquil spots in the bay. We pulled up a mooring and had a fine dinner and relaxed in the main saloon after cleaning up the galley. We were having an aperitif (I think it was Budweiser) when Richard stood up and moved toward the head. As I described earlier, the head on this boat was about the size of a small telephone booth…..no wait….it was more like half the size of a standard telephone booth. It accommodated a toilet and allowed one to shower utilizing a fitting on the washbasin tap that powered a handheld shower handle which was connected to the tap using a flexible hose. A shower curtain wrapped around the inside of the head so, technically, one could use the toilet and shower simultaneously.

Richard was a large fellow, about six feet tall weighing around 180 lbs and he had very little boating experience. He walked into the head, closed and locked the door as we continued our conversation. After about five minutes our discussion was interrupted by the ..Thumpity, thump, …thump.. thumpity..thump of the marine toilet pump as Richard was busy trying to expel his deposit from the vessel. I had instructed him at length in the operation of the marine head and warned that no foreign objects should be placed in the head and one should flush the device until the flush water ran clear. His pumping went on for a good two minutes, then silence. We all sat there in anticipation of the next act in this play when suddenly the door flung open and Richard fell out sweating profusely. He looked at the assembled group and flatly stated

"I've never worked so hard in my life to take a crap"

Welcome to "yachting" Richard!

Chapter 12

End of the CR saga

The summer of 1978 was the last year that we owned a boat named *Circadian Rhythm*. At the end of that summer, the partnership dissolved and we began our families. All of us, that is, with exception of Peter and Carole's sister Wendy. Peter remained single for the next 18 years finally settling down with Susan in Jericho, VT. Wendy married Phil in 1983 and they now split their time between Oregon and Arizona. Carole and I had two wonderful children, Julie and Bryan and Ed and Pam have Teddy and Andrew. In the true spirit of partnership, Teddy and Andrew were born within a few days of Julie and Bryan. Julie is one year older than Teddy, but both were born in November while Andrew and Bryan are the same age. Ed and I continued to sail together on other people's boats after the Ranger was sold. So, it was seem that we were both timing our marital responsibilities with the sailing season.

Considering my past and continuing to reside on the shores of Buzzards Bay, one can imagine that my sailing and boating experiences didn't end with the sale of the last *Circadian Rhythm* and this was the case. There was a long string of boats thereafter and my family purchased a house on Fort St. in Fairhaven. Fort Street runs parallel to the New Bedford harbor and our house was on this waterfront. It was a dream come-true for me, since our house (number 32) had been built in 1935 by none other than Chester A. Hathaway the founder of the Hathaway, Braley Machine Company and the inventor of the reel winch. The reel winch revolutionized commercial fishing in the 1920s allowing beam trawlers to quickly retrieve and deploy their otter trawl nets. This was accomplished by winding the steel cable that is connected to the net hardware onto a steel drum using an electric motor to spin the drum. Mr. Hathaway realized that the old method of hoisting nets with lines was dangerous and slow and envisioned a new, efficient method for accomplishing this task using commonplace materials. His vision revolutionized the industry and paved the way for the modern stern dragger. He never filed a patent for his invention.

Mr. Hathaway built the house at 32 Fort St at the height of the Great Depression, 1935. He used many of his boatyard workers to construct the house when activities were slow at the machine company. Materials were cheap at the time, so the house was very study and somewhat overbuilt. The most salient feature was the front portico which was built to resemble the bow of a boat complete with bow sprit. This boat bow was supported by two wooden Navy anchors, each standing eight feet tall. It was very impressive and I often dreamed of owning that house when I was a youngster riding my bicycle two and from the public beach at Fort Phoenix at the end of Fort St. Now here I was, 15 years later, the owner, made possible by my marrying a girl from Oregon, you can't make this stuff up. Carole's incredibly generous parents made the purchase possible my gifting us the mortgage down payment.

The house had an outbuilding and ready access to the water. I immediately sunk a mooring just off the beach behind the house and Ed and I borrowed a Rhodes 19 from a friend for the first summer at Fort St.

What followed was many a great summer with a long line of boats including a 22 foot power boat (yes a stink pot) and a J-24. The outbuilding (originally called the quahog club when Mr. Hathaway owned it) was eventually converted to a man-cave complete with NFL satellite TV and refrigerator full of beer and outside decks for sunning. This may be the subject of yet another "boring' narrative.

We were situated right next to Fairhaven Marine which was initially a blessing, but later become a curse as the yard expanded. In the earlier days, on warm summer evenings we would walk down to the boat yard and view the yachts and chat with the owners and transients. These became known as "dock walks". Fairhaven Marine was a stopover for many notables including the late Christopher Reeve who purchased an older Swan 36 and kept her at the yard for a couple of summers. We would often see him as we walked down J dock stopping to chat with Capt. Sven Joffs (pronounced Jarl) the professional skipper of a series of yachts that bore the name *Pleione*. The smallest of these was 57 feet, but around 1991, *Pleione's* owner Arthur Santry commissioned the building of a new seventy-three foot sloop and Sven was her skipper. The new *Pleione* was beautiful, sporting a flush deck, cobalt-blue hull and the latest communication and navigational equipment. By this time Mr. Santry was becoming a bit too long in the tooth to do any serious racing, but his sons were still game and gave Sven a run for his money. Sven was approaching his septuagenarian mile mark, so he was less than enthusiastic about "der owner's" sons wanting to push *Plieone* for all she was worth. He was particularly sensitive about *Plieone* dogging the New York Yacht Club up to Maine on off years during their annual cruise. Sven did not like the cold weather that was common along the Maine coast in the summer. I found this to be quite comical considering that Sven was from Finland and had braved Baltic winters. In addition, Sven had served on the four-masted barque *Pamir* of the Flying "P" line and was interred with her in New Zealand at the outset of WW II. Sven later became a US citizen and a professional sailing captain commanding many of the more successful sailing yachts in the 1950s-70s including many of Sumner Long's *Ondine*(s). By the time we met him in the 1980s, Sven was working full time for Mr. Santry. He was friends with Charlie Mitchell and after Charlie bought the house on Fort St. Sven would bunk there in the early spring when the contemporary Plieone was stored in the Fairhaven Marine shed. Sven would work on the boat all day and then meet Charlie for a bite of dinner before retiring for the night at 26 Fort St. Often Sven would assist Charlie on *Jaguar* when a salvage or towing job cropped up during Sven's tenure at Charlie's house. It was a convenient relationship for both, they enjoyed one another's company and my family came to know Sven from Sunday dinners at Charlie's house. Sven was the quintessential reticent Scandinavian and seldom spoke unless addressed directly. When my daughter Julie was five years old, we were invited to join Charlie, his then girlfriend Janine and Sven for a Sunday dinner in mid-May. Carole had donned Julie in a pretty pink dress and the weather was beautiful that afternoon with bright sunshine, blossoms and light, warm breezes. Julie was quite precocious and was fascinated with Sven who was very quiet and walked slowly about the house puffing on his pipe clad in the traditional khaki clothing of a mariner. Having finished dinner, Sven and I wandered from the dining room into the sunroom which faced west overlooking the harbor. Julie dogged us into the sunroom and when there was a lull in our conversation (happened often) Julie walked right up to Sven and in a loud authoritative tone of voice said,

"So Captain Spen, just what do you think you're doing?"

Sven was flabbergasted, as a life long bachelor, he had very little to do with women or children and now here he was button-holed by a bleach blonde three-foot female who was demanding an answer to an impossible question. As Julie finished her inquisition Sven fumbled with his pipe and nearly dropped it trying to come to grips with this demanding little female. I was equally flabbergasted, but before I could intervene and defuse the situation, Sven looked at Julie and exclaimed,

"Vell......I really doun't know"

That appeared to satisfy Julie who smiled and quickly retreated to the kitchen; crisis averted.

Now that we knew Sven, we made a point of stopping by *Plieone* during our dock walks on J dock when she was in the water to say hi. One of my favorite times was when the actor Christopher Reeves was on his boat close to *Plieone* when we stopped to chat with Sven. You could see the look of envy on Reeves face as my sister-in-law Wendy and I were invited onboard this magnificent 73 foot yacht and given the cook's tour. It was rich.

There were many more sailing and boating adventures after we moved on from the *Circadian Rhythms*, too many to recount in this initial book. As we moved on to bigger boats and blue water sailing, the

Circadian Rhythm crews still had a warm spot in their hearts for these early days of sailing; great times with great people.

About the author

Scott Morris has been writing technical articles, proposals and patents for more than 25 years and this is his first "stab" at a narrative. As the book describes, Scott was born and raised in Fairhaven and after sixty years of New England winters and subjecting his Oregonian wife to 32 years of the same, they elected to head west where the climate is far more forgiving. Scott continues to sail on junkets to New England, when wintering in Texas and on lakes in Oregon. That's one of his buddies (Jack) on deck.

Made in the USA
Monee, IL
27 March 2023

30606551R00133